IMAGE ANALYSIS AND PROCESSING

IMAGE ANALYSIS AND PROCESSING

Edited by

V. Cantoni

Pavia University
Pavia, Italy

S. Levialdi

Rome University
Rome, Italy

and

G. Musso

ELSAG
Genoa, Italy

PLENUM PRESS • NEW YORK AND LONDON

Library of Congress Cataloging in Publication Data

International Conference on Image Analysis and Processing (3rd: 1985: Rapallo, Italy)
  Image analysis and processing.

  "Proceedings of the Third International Conference on Image Analysis and Process-
ing, held September 30–October 2, 1985, in Rapallo, Italy"—T.p. verso.
  Includes bibliographies and index.
  1. Image processing—Congresses. I. Cantoni, V. II. Levialdi, S. III. Musso, G. IV.
Title.
TA1632.I552   1985   621.36′7   86-22668

ISBN-13: 978-1-4612-9312-5   e-ISBN-13:978-1-4613-2239-9
DOI:10.1007/978-1-4613-2239-9

Proceedings of the Third International Conference on Image Analysis and
Processing, held September 30–October 2, 1985, in Rapallo, Italy

© 1986 Plenum Press, New York
Softcover reprint of the hardcover 1st editon 1986
A Division of Plenum Publishing Corporation
233 Spring Street, New York, N.Y. 10013

PREFACE

For the third time the Italian Group on Pattern Recognition has organized an International Conference on Image Analysis and Processing (IAP) gathering together the most active groups working in this area in our country. The first International Conference IAP was held in Pavia (1980) and the second one in Selva di Fasano (1982).

A selected set of distinguished speakers has been invited to talk about their personal experience and views on industrial applications (H Freeman), the critical analysis of medical image processing (D Rutovitz), the advances of robot vision languages (M Silva) and the availability of AI technology for improving the performance of PR and IP programs (J M Chassery).

Four different areas have been covered by the papers submitted and refereed) to the conference first and to a scientific committee next, namely IP Techniques, Multiprocessor Architectures, Robot Vision and IP Applications. A final paper giving the results of a census of the Italian groups is provided showing, with some detail, typical research lines as pursued in working groups both at the University and Industry. About 39 groups are presently active in 12 different places of the peninsula.

We are pleased to announce the 4th International Conference on IAP which will be held on September 25-28, 1987 at Palermo, (Sicily); let us all meet there!

V. Cantoni
Pavia University

S. Levialdi
Rome University

G. Musso
Elsag SpA Genoa

CONTENTS

IMAGE PROCESSING - APPLICATIONS

INVITED LECTURES

SURVEY OF

IMAGE PROCESSING APPLICATIONS IN INDUSTRY

Herbert Freeman

Rutgers University

New Brunswick, New Jersey

INTRODUCTION

Although computers have been used to process images for more than 25 years, it is only recently that we are able to find any significant number of image processing applications appearing in industry. The reason for this is the strict economic test that any image processing application must pass before industry is willing to accept it: there must be a clear, demonstrable economic benefit over alternative methods. The benefit may be direct, such as a reduction in production costs, or it may be indirect, such as a less hazardous or physically less strenuous work environment. Until recently not many industrial applications of image processing were able to pass such economic scrutiny.

The severe requirement for economic viability has also been the reason why virtually all of the pace-setting developments in image processing have originated outside of industry. They have occurred in (1) the military (e.g., aerial reconnaissance), (2) the sciences (e.g,, high-energy physics, astronomy, chemistry), (3) non-military governmental areas (e.g, remote sensing, cartography, environmental protection), (4) medicine (e.g., radiography, tomography, cytology, and cytogenetics), and (5) commerce (e.g., character recognition, picture transmission, image recording, and television). In all of these -- except for the commercial applications -- economic viability just did not play an overriding role, and in the commercial area, the potential economic benefits were so obvious that applications there were pursued without hesitation from the very beginning.

During the last few years the steady lowering of the cost of image sensing and storage, together with the continuing reduction in computing costs, has finally brought a number of industrial image processing applications into the range of economic viability. We shall review here the current state of industrial image processing and attempt to give some indications where future developments in this field are likely to lead us.

IMAGE PROCESSING IN INDUSTRY

Industrial applications of image processing can be broadly classified into two groups - those where computer image processing is a substitute for human vision, and those where it is a replacement for other picture processing methods. The former is commonly referred to as *machine vision* or *computer vision*, and involves tasks that were previously performed (or at least could have been performed) by a human. The latter is found primarily in the graphics arts field and in the processing of photographic films, where computer image processing is increasingly being introduced as a replacement for traditional manual and optical methods.

Machine vision in turn can be divided into four categories: (1) robot vision, (2) inspection, (3) line-drawing conversion, and (4) object modeling, of which the first two are of especial importance. In each of these categories the primary motivation is improvement in productivity or the assumption of a task that for humans is either too hazardous, overly strenuous, or undesirable in some other way. A classification of machine vision is shown in Table 1.

There are some significant differences between the image processing applications typically found in industry and those found in other fields. Foremost among the differences is that -- for reasons of economy -- industrial applications tend to involve only a modest amount of computer processing. (Complex processing tasks require an expensive computer or consume too much time on a low-cost computer). The images tend to be of good quality, relatively free of noise, since the camera location and illumination can be carefully controlled. For some applications, the illumination may even be structured (i.e., patterned) to simplify the image interpretation task. To hold the computation requirements down, only moderate resolution (256 or 512 square) is normally used [11,31,33,36].

COMPUTER VISION FOR MATERIALS HANDLING

One particularly important application for computer vision is in the area of materials handling. Typically, the problem here involves three specific operations: (1) to identify an object from among a limited set of known objects, (2) to determine the object's position in two- or three-dimensional space, and (3) to determine the object's orientation [3,7, 8,15]. The object may be on a moving conveyor, on a stationary platform, or freely placed in a bin. The last-named is the most difficult case because the object can assume virtually any position and orientation, and may, in fact, be partially overlapped by other objects.

Although materials handling normally requires object identification, position determination, and orientation determination, there are instances where only position and orientation determination (or perhaps even only one of these) may be required, thereby simplifying the task [6]. Clearly, if all objects on a conveyor belt are assumed to be identical, object identification is not required. Also, if the objects are always positioned or oriented in a fixed manner, position determination or orientation determination will not be required. Some degree of simplification is achieved in the case where an object is placed on a flat horizontal surface, away from other objects. The object then assumes a *stable position*, of which there are usually only a small number for any object. In contrast, when an object is placed in a bin with many other similar (or different) objects, the object can usually appear in any position and orientation, and there will be no a priori limitation on the possible views that the object may present to the image sensor. This is one of the reasons why the bin-picking problem is still largely an unsolved machine vision problem [20].

Generally machine vision systems work well if certain simplifying constraints can be embedded. One system that has been successfully applied is the General Motors' CONSIGHT system [17]. A line source of light illuminates a conveyor belt at an angle. The image sensor is directly above

Table 1. A Classification of Machine Vision

1. Robot Vision
    a. Materials Handling
        (i) Identification
        (ii) Position and orientation determination
    b. Process Control
    c. Assembly
    d. Motion Control
        (i) Navigation and path control
        (ii) Collision avoidance

2. Inspection and Quality Control
    a. Go/No-go inspection
    b. Quantitative visual inspection

3. Line-Drawing Conversion
    a. Engineering drawing conversion
    b. Map conversion
    c. Free-hand sketch conversion

4. Object Modeling
    a. Image templates
    b. 3D modeling

the place where the projected line of light normally impinges on the belt. When an object passes under the light, the line of light is distorted, with the line deflected toward the left by an amount that is proportional to the height of the object above the belt. The image sensed by the camera thus contains both shape information as well as height information about the object in view. The system has been successfully applied in materials handling applications, where unknown objects are identified and their position and orientation are determined.

Most materials handling systems have been designed for handling rigid parts. One notable exception is the WIRESIGHT system which was designed for locating and identifying flexible wire leads on an electrical component [35]. The system uses sideways illumination to obtain images that contain both object and and object-shadow information. The use of shadows makes it possible to extract the precise location and shape of the wireleads.

APPLICATIONS IN PROCESS CONTROL

Machine vision applications for process control distinguish them- selves from those in materials handling in that they tend to operate con- tinuously and are usually used as sensors in a feedback control loop. They tend to be highly specialized and the vision involved is really more in the nature of optical sensing, with relatively little image interpretation or pattern recognition involved. In most applications the image processing must be very fast (much faster than for materials handling) to be compati- ble with the dynamics of the controlled process [23].

Compared with traditional automation, machine vision may be able to cope with greater variability in the process and provide higher precision at reduced cost. Some successful industrial applications are in vision- guided spray painting [11], in seam welding [24], in automatic gauge reading [2], in material cutting in the presence of defects (e.g., cutting of glass and lumber) [9], and in decorating chocolate pieces [10].

A vision system that has been successfully applied to tracking seams in automotive arc welding is the SEAMSIGHT system [24]. This system, like CONSIGHT, uses an angled-line light source and a vertical camera. A special parallel/pipelined processor is used for tracking a stored reference image in a continuously changing live image. A fast processor is employed, capable of performing 5.5×10^6 pixel-level correlations in 45 milliseconds.

APPLICATIONS IN MOTION CONTROL

Motion control applications of machine vision fall into two categories: path control and collision avoidance. For path control (i.e., "navigation"), a path for motion of an articulated arm or a vehicle is selected and the vision system's task is to guide the arm or vehicle along the path by recognizing "landmarks". Depending on the complexity of the path and the generality with which the path is specified, this can be a most challenging problem [11,19]. Problems of vehicle navigation are still mainly in the research stage; though, some simple industrial applications are expected to be not far off.

Collision avoidance differs from path control in that the path is already established and the problem is to ascertain that there will be no collision with another (unexpected and unknown) object. (Collision avoidance must almost always also be considered in path control; though, the reverse need, of course, not be true.) The pattern recognition aspects of collision avoidance are simpler than those of path control. Also, collision avoidance can be simplified by setting a high acceptance threshold (such as surrounding an object with a rectangular-box rejection area). It is an application where the current state of image processing is in many instances sufficiently advanced to permit economical implementation [22].

Machine vision systems for applications involving motion control must be able to process images at relatively high speed [19,23,24]. In addition to being able to interpret individual images, such a system usually must also be able to extract features over sequences of images, such as frame-to-frame changes, or to be able to track the movement of objects in images from one to a another under changing aspects [19]. Note that in image motion applications, the objects may be in motion, the image sensor(s) may be in motion, a light source (possibly patterned) may be in motion, or some combination of any or all of these.

INSPECTION AND QUALITY CONTROL

The machine vision application category that in the near future is likely to have the greatest economic impact is that of inspection or quality control [30]. Potentially. the advantages of machine vision for inspection are (1) higher precision, (2) greater uniformity, (3) no degradation due to tedium of task, and (3) no required operator training. The range of possible application varies widely, from simple go/no-go tests to complex dimension-checking tasks. Typically in inspection or quality control, there exists a "standard" against which other objects are to be visually compared. The key word here is "comparison". The comparison may involve the entire image, a portion of an image (possibly magnified), or some extracted image features.

High spatial resolution is likely to be required in machine vision inspection applications. This will place a burden on the processing unit; though, there may be ways for avoiding this in particular instances. If the required resolution exceeds 1k per line (or 1k lines), the use of a frame buffer becomes impractical and line-scan processing may be called for. In recent years some excellent moderate-cost , line-scanning equipment has become available, permitting line resolutions in excess of 2k.

One of the most complex machine-vision inspection systems that have been installed was designed for the inspection of jet-engine turbine blades [28]. It uses patterned light in an elaborate scheme for detecting surface flaws. Both visible and infrared light are used to correct for reflectivity differences due to illumination aspect angle. Surface-defect-caused phase variations can then be extracted. The system has 15 axes of variability to provide the necessary set of aspect angles for full blade inspection.

Some other successful industrial applications of note are the inspection of textiles [1], of automobile tires [4], of semiconductor chips [5], of lumber [9], of printed-circuit boards [14], of lamp filaments [25], of LSI photomasks [26], and of hot steel slabs [34]. Experiments have been conducted with machine vision inspection systems that are able to learn and develop their own decision criteria from examples of acceptable and non-acceptable parts [27].

ASSEMBLY

The assembly of parts is traditionally a highly manual operation, except in those industries where the volume of production is so high as to justify the use of costly and inflexible automatic-assembly machinery. Robots offer the possibility of bringing automation also to small- and moderate-volume assembly. If complex jigs and fixtures are to be avoided, robotic assembly almost certainly implies the extensive use of machine vision for handling the parts and for guiding the joining of parts (e.g., attaching a nut to a bolt) and for controlling any required assembly tools (e.g, electric screw driver or wrench). In a sense, the use of vision in assembly involves all the factors present in materials handling as well as in motion control and inspection. It is one of the most complex of the potential applications of machine vision, and for this reason is still largely confined to the research laboratory [8,23,33,36].

Some demonstration systems have been built for the assembly of electric motors, small electrical components (e.g., relays), and small mechanical assemblies (e.g., automobile water pumps) [6,11,15,16,35].

For assembly applications, it is not uncommon to find the use of multiple cameras, one fixed and one movable, with the latter providing a "close-up" vision capability . There is currently also much interest in merging tactile-sensor information with vision-derived information; the tactile information is to provide the close-up data that is beyond the resolution capability of most vision systems and yet is essential for effective parts joining [3,6,7].

LINE-DRAWING CONVERSION

Another area of machine vision in which there is currently much interest is that of line-drawing conversion. Basically it is the problem of digitizing engineering drawings, architectural drawings, cartographic maps, and even free-hand sketches and transferring the data they contain from paper into a digital data base. The application is of great importance in engineering because it will give electronic access to the large quantities of existing engineering drawings, permitting their editing, checking, and merging with new design data. Similarly, in the field of cartography, efforts have long been under way to place all geographic and thematic map information into digital data bases, to facilitate updating and permit made-to-order map production. In both applications, the processes require high-resolution line scanning, recognition of application-specific symbolism, and high-level recognition of context-dependent patterns based on drawing syntax and semantics. In most instances, even the best of automatic line-drawing conversion cannot be expected to be error-free, and interactive editing is nearly always required [12].

A variation on the above is the conversion of free-hand sketches to syntactically correct application drawings, primarily in engineering and architecture. Such conversion would have to be subject to possible interactive editing to correct minor errors that may be introduced by the process [13].

OBJECT MODELING

For identification of an unknown object it is necessary to have models of known objects against which the unknown can be compared. For high-level identification, we shall need high-level models. The models may be simply one or more sample images of the objects, they may be feature vectors that describe the objects in some transformed domain, or they may be full 3D descriptions of the objects. Obtaining object models can be difficult; however, image processing offers a possible approach. One simply obtains a set of images of each known object in a manner similar to the way the image sensor views the unknown objects. The collection of images then can represent the model data. If an object can be identified by its two-dimensional silhouette when in a stable position, one view for each stable position may be all that is required for modeling. In contrast, an object that may be in a bin, resting against other objects, can assume virtually any position; for such an object a complete 3D object description may be required. One way of obtaining such a model is by taking a large number of photographs of the object, at least one from every characteristically distinct vantage point, and then assembling the data from these photographs into a complete surface description of the object. Patterned light can be helpful here in simplifying the image interpretation and image assembly tasks required to obtain such a model [29,37].

Computer-aided tomography, an image processing procedure that lies outside the domain of machine vision, has been successfully employed to model skeletal structures and from these create custom-designed prosthetic implant devices [32]. The approach has potential application also in a number of other industrial modeling applications.

SUMMARY

At present most industrial applications tend to be very simple. Typically, only binary silhouette images are extracted and processed for identification and for position and orientation determination. Of systems actually installed, very few make use of greytone imagery, and virtually none attempt to extract true 3D information. The limitations at present are primarily the cost/speed ratio of required processing. Significant further progress must await the arrival of high-speed processing chips that

6

will permit faster processing by a factor of 100 or more. Such chips are expected to become available within the next few years.

Image processing appears to be on the threshold of finally gaining acceptance in industry. Technical developments have advanced to a point where a number of industrial tasks can be effectively handled by commercially available image processing systems. The cost/benefit ratio has dropped to where it no longer poses the formidable economic barrier that it was in the past. There is every reason to believe that the next few years will bring the same kind of rapid expansion to industrial image processing that occurred in the field of computer graphics in the late 1970's.

ACKNOWLEDGMENT

The writer wishes gratefully to acknowledge the support of the National Science Foundation, Computer Engineering Program, under grant ECS84-07900.

BIBLIOGRAPHY

1. F. Ade, N. Lins, and M. Unser, Comparison of various filter sets for defect detection in textiles, *Proc. 7th Intl. Conf. Pattern Recogn.*, 428-431, Montreal, (1984).
2. M.L. Baird, Gagesight: a computer vision system for automatic inspection of instrument gages, *IEEE Comp. Soc. Conf. Record of Workshop on Indust. Applic. of Machine Vision*, 108-111, (1982).
3. R.C. Bolles and R.A. Cain, Recognising and locating partially visible objects: the local-feature-focus method, *Robotics Research*, 1:3, (1982).
4. M. Borghesi, V. Cantoni, and M. Diani, An industrial application of texture analysis, *Proc. 7th Intl. Conf. Pattern Recogn.*, 420-423, Montreal (1984).
5. R. Brauner and D. Epstein, Automated chip (die) inspection, *IEEE Comp. Soc. Conf. Record of Workshop on Indust. Applic. of Machine Vision*, 43-50, (1982).
6. W. Brune and K. Bitter, S.A.M. Opto-electronic picture sensor in a flexible manufacturing assembly system, in *Robot Vision*, 325-337, A. Pugh, ed., Springer-Verlag, Berlin 1983.
7. B. Carlisle, S. Roth, J. Gleason, and D. McGhie, The PUMA/VS-100 robot vision system, in Robot Vision, 313-322, A. Pugh, ed., Springer-Verlag, Berlin (1983).
8. R.T. Chin, Machine vision for discrete part handling in industry: a survey, *IEEE Comp. Soc. Conf. Record of Workshop on Indust. Applic. of Machine Vision* (1982).
9. R.W. Connors, C.W. McMillin, and R. Vasquez-Espinosa, A prototype software system for locating and identifying surface defects in wood, *Proc. 7th Intl. Conf. Pattern Recogn.*, 416-419, Montreal (1984).
10. A.J. Cronshaw, Decoration of chocolates using robot vision, *IEEE Comp. Soc. Conf. Record of Workshop on Indust. Applic. of Machine Vision*, 224-231, (1982).
11. G.G. Dodd and L. Rossol, *Computer Vision and Sensor-Based Robots*, *Plenum Press*, New York, (1979).
12. M. Ejiri, S. Kakumoto, T. Miyatake, S. Shimada, and H. Matsushima, Automatic recognition of design drawings and maps, *Proc. 7th Intl. Conf. Pattern Recogn.*, Montreal, 1296-1305, (1984).
13. M. Furuta, N. Kase, and S., Emori, Segmentation and recognition of symbols for handwritten piping & instrument diagram, *Proc. 7th Intl. Conf. Pattern Recogn.*, Montreal, (1984).

14. Y. Hara, N. Akiyama, and K. Karasaki, Automatic inspection system for printed circuit boards, *IEEE Comp. Soc. Conf. Record of Workshop on Indust. Applic. of Machine Vision*, 62-72, (1982).

15. P.F. Hewkin and H-J. Fuchs, OMS-vision system, in *Robot Vision*, 305-312, A. Pugh, ed., Springer-Verlag, Berlin (1983).

16. J-P. Hermann, Pattern recognition in the factory: an example,,in *Robot Vision*, 267-275, A. Pugh, ed., Springer-Verlag, Berlin (1983).

17. S.W. Holland, L. Rossol, and M.R. Ward, CONSIGHT-1: a vision-controlled robot system for transferring parts from belt conveyors, in *Computer Vision and Sensor-Based Robots*, G.G. Dodd and L. Rossol, eds., Plenum Press, New York (1979).

18. T. Inari, K. Takashima, M. Tanaka, N. Nakano, M. Katagiri, and H. Ohya, Visual sensing system for automatic control of reclaimer in raw material yard, *IEEE Comp. Soc. Conf. Record of Workshop on Indust. Applic. of Machine Vision*, 217-223, (1982).

19. R.C. Jain, Segmentation of frame sequences obtained by a moving observer, *IEEE Trans. PAMI*, 6:5, 624-629, (1984)

20. R.B. Kelley, J.R. Birk, H.A. S. Martens, and R. Tella, A robot system which acquires cylindrical workpieces from bins, in *Robot Vision*, 226-244, A. Pugh, ed., Springer-Verlag, Berlin 1983.

21. M. Kohno, H. Horino, and M. Isobe, Intelligent assembly robot, in *Robot Vision*, 201-208, A. Pugh, ed., Springer-Verlag, Berlin (1983).

22. J.Y.S. Luh and J.A. Klaasen, A three-dimensional vision by off-shelf system with multi-cameras, *IEEE Trans. PAMI*, 7:1, 35-45, (1985).

23. A. Makhlin and G.E. Tinsdale, Westinghouse grey scale vision system for real-time control and inspection, in *Robot Vision*, 346-354, A. Pugh, ed., Springer-Verlag, Berlin (1983).

24. I. Masaki, SEAMSIGHT: a parallel/pipelined vision system for seam tracking, *Proc. 7th Intl. Conf. Pattern Recogn.*, 424-427, Montreal, (1984).

25. J.L. Mundy and R.E. Joynson, Automatic visual inspection using syntactic methods, *Proc. IEEE Comp. Soc. Conf. on Pattern Recogn. and Image Proc.*, 144-147, Troy, NY, (1977).

26. K. Okamoto, K. Nakahata, S. Aiuchi, M. Nomoto, Y. Hara, and T. Hamada, An Automatic visual inspection system for LSI photomasks, *Proc. 7th Intl. Conf. Pattern Recogn.*, 1361-1364, Montreal, (1984).

27. W.A. Perkins, A learning system that is useful for industrial inspection tasks, *IEEE Comp. Soc. Conf. Record of Workshop on Indust. Applic. of Machine Vision*, 160-167, (1982).

28. G.B. Porter and J.L. Mundy, A model driven visual inspection module, *1st Workshop on Robotics Research*, M.I.T. Press, Cambridge, MA, (1985).

29. M. Potmesil, Generating models of solid objects by matching 3D surface segments, *Proc. 8th Int'l. Joint Conf. Artif. Intell.*, 1089-1093, Karlsruhe, FRG, August (1983).

30. T. Pryor, Optical inspection and machine vision, *IEEE Comp. Soc. Conf. Record of Workshop on Indust. Applic. of Machine Vision*, 3-20, (1982).

31. A. Pugh, ed., *Robot Vision*, Springer-Verlag, Berlin 1983.

32. M.L. Rhodes, Image processing tied to CAD/CAM produces customized prostheses, *Information Display*, 1:8, 18-21, (1985).

33. C.A. Rosen and G.J. Gleason, Evaluating vision system performance, in *Robot Vision*, 97-103, A. Pugh, ed., Springer-Verlag, Berlin (1983).

34. B.R. Suresh, R.A. Fundakowski, T.S. Levitt, J.E. Overland, T.L. Beckering, and T.M. Wittenburg, The automated surface inspection system of hot steel slabs, *IEEE Comp. Soc. Conf. Record of Workshop on Indust. Applic. of Machine Vision*, 112-118, (1982).

35. S. Tsuji et al, WIRESIGHT: robot vision for determining 3D geometry of flexible wires from shadow information, *Proc. 7th Intl. Conf. Pattern Recogn.*, 1358-1360, Montreal, (1984).

36. P. Villers, Present industrial use of vision sensors for robot guidance, in *Robot Vision*, 157-168, A. Pugh, ed., Springer-Verlag, Berlin (1983).

37. P.M. Will and K.S. Pennington, Grid coding: a preprocessing technique for robot and machine vision, *Artificial Intelligence*, 2:3/4, 319-329 (1971).

ROBOT PROGRAMMING AND ROBOT VISION

M. Silva and A. Roy

Departamentos de Automática y Electrónica
E.T.S.I.I. de la Universidad de Zaragoza
Ciudad Universitaria
50009 Zaragoza

1. INTRODUCTION

Robotic advanced systems integrates many sophisticated sensory devices. Among others we can consider vision, touch, force, proximetry,... The main emphasis of this paper is on the programming of a robot system including essentially vision.

The programming subsystem of industrial robots is the interface which permits access to its functional capabilities. This paper gives a brief survey of robot programming languages and of industrial robot vision systems.

Because of the range of levels of complexity in the tasks of an industrial robot and periphery (which can include a vision system), as well as the technical/economic compromise between the expressive capacity and the cost of the computer and control system, the number of types of realizations becomes very important. It is no exageration to say that the current situation resembles the biblical mention to the Tower of Babel. In any case, it is only fair to note that the tendency is towards the promotion of the most advanced systems because:

1) They give a greater expressive capacity, which increases production flexibility thanks to the greater ease of programming or reprogramming tasks.
2) They include functions which allow a greater adaptation of the robot to its environments, which reduces the engineering costs of automation (prepositioners, precision feeders, etc.). This adaptation is achieved by incorporating complex perception functions into the robot control system. These include tactile perception, proximetry, force sensing, artificial vision, etc. According to the Robot Institute of America (now the Robotics Industry Association) in 1990, 25% of industrial robots will be equipped with vision and 90% of the tasks of industrial inspection will be automated.

Robot programming languages are examined starting from the different basic modes of programming, considering the main specific features of the mode known as **explicit textual programming** (§2). Commercialized vision systems are studied on the basis of the most frequently used concepts and techniques (§3). Finally, in §4, the principal features of "robot vision

11

programming", which has evolved parallel to "robot programming", are discussed.

2. BASIC ROBOT PROGRAMMING MODES

Servocontrolled robots can be programmed in two basic modes:

a) Guiding or Teaching-by-showing
b) Textual programming

In the first case, the operator **moves** the robot's effector along the trajectory he wishes it to repeat. In the second case, the programmer first **writes** a text (program). These two modes are not mutually exclusive, and it is common to find textual programming systems which include teaching-by-showing.

Under the influence of computer graphics and of computer-assisted design (CAD), a new mode of robot programming has appeared in recent years: **graphics programming**. This, essentially, is no more than a valuable technical asset which permits an increase in programming productivity and secureness. This is achieved by using graphic simulators of the robot's behavior in certain environments and, occasionally, geometric inference systems.

2.1. Teaching-by-showing

The movement of the robot's effector can be achieved by:

a) a guiding device (keyboard, joystick, etc.)
b) direct moving, after placing the robot in a "state of total mobility", having compensated all forces (gravity, inertia, etc.).
c) a light replica of the robot (**mannequin**). This technique is used almost exclusively when we wish to memorize a complete trajectory, and not just a finite number of situations (positions and orientations) of the effector.

In this last case, programming can be carried out in **closed loop**, where the operator observes, in real time, the effect of the mannequin's movements on the robot.

The **advantages** of a teaching-by-showing robot programming system are: 1) conceptual simplicity and 2) low cost of the computing system. It's conceptual simplicity means that the operator-programmer only needs basic computer training.

The **limitations** of a teaching-by-showing robot programming system are many and varied. They include:

1) (Partial) immobilization of the production system during programming, which is done on line. This implies a low productivity (and low flexibility) for the system. Furthermore, it is important to note that programming can only begin when the robot, its environments and the prototype parts are available.
2) The lack of program portability to other robots.
3) Robot's low adaptability to changes in its working environment.
4) Reduced precision

Teaching-by-showing's low expressive capability makes it suitable for such conceptually and operatively simple tasks as painting or spot-welding. In order to take advantages of the strong points of gestural programming, many systems propose **extensions** which reduce the extent of the limitations. Thus, very often a large set of **predefined functions** are added to a keyboard, or a combined teaching-by-showing/textual programming, guided by a "menu", is introduced.

2.2. Textual programming

Within textual programming, it is important to distinguish between at least two basic levels. These depend, essentially, on whether we specify **what** must be done (the specification concentrates on the objects or goals; this is called **task level** programming) or **how** it must be done (this is called **procedural** |(M. Silva, 1985)| or **robot level** |(T. Lozano, 1983)| specification).

2.2.1. Procedural programming

A procedural programming system sets out to satisfy the following basic requirements:

1) Specification (geometric-kinematic) of movements (positions, orientations, velocities, precision, continuous path, etc.)
2) Integration of the information from environment sensors (forces, vision, touch, proximetry, etc.)
3) Off-line programming (to increase productivity and flexibility)
4) Easy interaction on production line during program debugging
5) Robot independence (robot portability)

Procedural programming languages usually appear as extensions or variations of widely-used computer programming languages (BASIC, PASCAL,..). They can also be based on machine-tool programming languages (APT, in particular), as is the case with ROBEX and RAPT. Program 1 is representative to capture the programming style with procedural languages.

```
1.        SETI N.PARTS = 0
2.   100  VPICTURE
3.        VLOCATE PART,100
4.        APPRO CAMERA:PART:PICK.UP,50
5.        MOVES CAMERA:PART:PICK.UP
6.        GRASP 25
7.        DEPART 50
8.        APPRO PALLET,50
9.        MOVES PALLET
10.       OPENI
11.       DEPART 100.
12.       SHIFT PALLET BY 5.2,25.4,0
13.       SETI N.PARTS = N.PARTS+1
14.       IF N.PARTS NE 10 THEN 100
15.       STOP
```

PROGRAM 1. Program to palletize 10 blocks using vision (written in VAL)

Programming systems of this level are **real-time** systems in which the adaptation to the robot problem is achieved, essentially, by means of special instructions in order to:

1) define the robot's movements (free motion, guarded moves, and compliant motion) (see for example (T. Lozano, 1983), (M. Silva, 1984)).
2) have access to information from the sensors
3) actuate on equipment peripheral to the robot.

Some more advanced languages provide special **data types** (essentially, they apply to the manipulation of geometric type entities). Rather than considering very specific languages, the great diversity of sensors and other automatic equipments would make it advisable to use general-purpose programming languages, which have been duly completed, and provided with powerful and **extensible** input/output.

Some representative examples of this level of language are: (VAL-II (User's guide to VAL,1984), LM , PROSPRO, AML (Taylor R.H., Summers P.D., Meyer J., 1982)), etc.

A large number of realizations |see, e.g., (S. Bonner, K.G. Shin, 1982), (T. Lozano, 1983), (Gruver et al., 1984), (M. Silva, 1984)| of very varied characteristics belong to the level of explicit languages. Actually, the more advanced systems integrates the concept of **TCP** (**Tool Center Point**), with which the task is described in terms of the (cartesian) displacements and operations of the effector, independently of the robot's actuators.

The presence of a TCP is important since it implies the existence of a system of reference coordinates. **Transform composition** permits the robot to operate in situations with objects determined by external sensors (especially vision). Furthermore, the description of the task in terms of the effectors movements increases program portability.

The presence of an **absolute reference** and the possibility of transform composition allows the robot's **universe** to be expressed in a structured way (Fig. 1). This structure typically takes the form of an arborescence. This gives a **model** of the robot's environment. A path from the tree root to a node gives all the transformations to be composed in order to find the absolute reference situation which labels that node. If a given rigid solid has certain references associated with it, a displacement obliges the programmer to update all of them. To avoid this tedious task, some programming languages (AL, LM, SRL...) have AFFIX/UNFIX instructions, with which the task is carried out automatically.

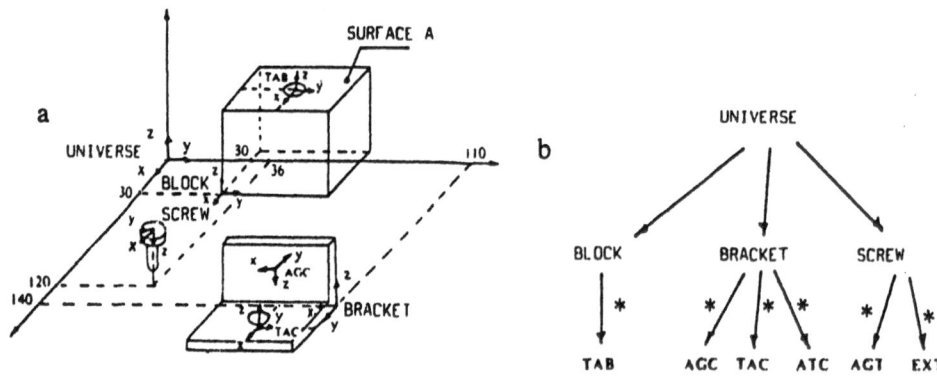

Figure 1. An arborescent model of the robot environment.

The presence of a model of the robot's environment is a non-procedural programming element in an essentially procedural programming. **Task** level programming, the next textual level, inverts the relative importance of declarations and instructions.

2.2.2. Task programming

In principle, procedural programming can express all types of behavior. However, it is necessary to point out the difficulty of programming robots, mainly due to:

1) the difficulty of expressing positions and orientations in 3D
2) the strong interaction of robot movements with sensors
3) the high level of concurrency

For these reasons, it is of interest to move towards task programming.

From a computing point of view, in specifying tasks in languages of this level, what is important is the set of **declarations** (static definitions), rather than **instructions**. The declarations define, more or less completely, the robot's universe (objects, environment and the robot itself) in such a way that movements and operations strategies, which may be based on advanced perception, can be generated automatically.

The importance of defining the objects to be manipulated leads these programming systems to include a **body modeller subsystem.** The complexity and cost of constructing objects models means that this type of programming is interesting only if the modelling work is shared with that of design. Computer assisted design (CAD) and computer assisted manufacturing (CAM) form part of an unique overall process.

The type of programming considered in this section is known in robotics as **task level** programming, since the robot's movements become less important than the **operations** to be carried out and/or the **states** to be reached. Task level programming allows the programmer to ignore the details of manipulation, and there is a corresponding increase in productivity and in program transportability.

Task level programming can be conceived at very different levels of abstraction. At the highest one, **objective level,** as well as a detailed model of the robot's universe, the **initial** and **final** states of the universe need to be defined. The computing system must automatically generate **action plans** (Artificial Intelligence), which will allow the desired transformation of the state of the universe. If the specifications of the task indicate the intermediate operations to be carried out (PLACE, INSERT, TURN, ...) the computing system must automatically generate only a detailed definition. This is called **object level** programming (see Program 2).

```
1. OPERATE nutfeeder WITH car-rer-tab-nut AT fixture nest
2. PLACE bracket IN fixture SUCH THAT bracket bottom
        CONTACTS car-ret-tab-nut-top
        AND bracket hole IS ALIGNED WITH fixture nest
3. PLACE interlock ON bracket SUCH THAT
        interlock hole IS ALIGNED WITH bracket hole
        AND interlock base CONTACTS bracket top
4. DRIVEN IN car-ret-intlk-stud INTO car-ret-tab-nut
        AT interlock hole
        SUCH THAT TORQUE IS EQ 12.0 IN-LOS USING air-driver
        ATTACHING bracket AND interlock
5. NAME bracket interlock car-ret-intlk-stud car-ret-tab-nut
        ASSEMBLY support-bracket
```

PROGRAM 2. A task level specification: Bracket assembly (written in AUTOPASS).

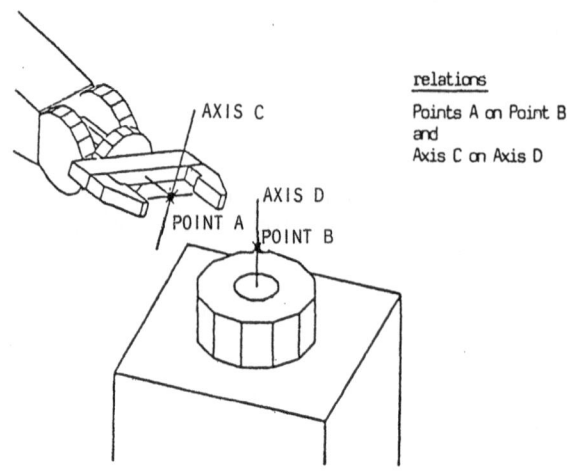

AXIS C
AXIS D
POINT A
POINT B
relations
Points A on Point B
and
Axis C on Axis D

Fig. 2. An example of geometric relations in CATIA

1
2
3
4

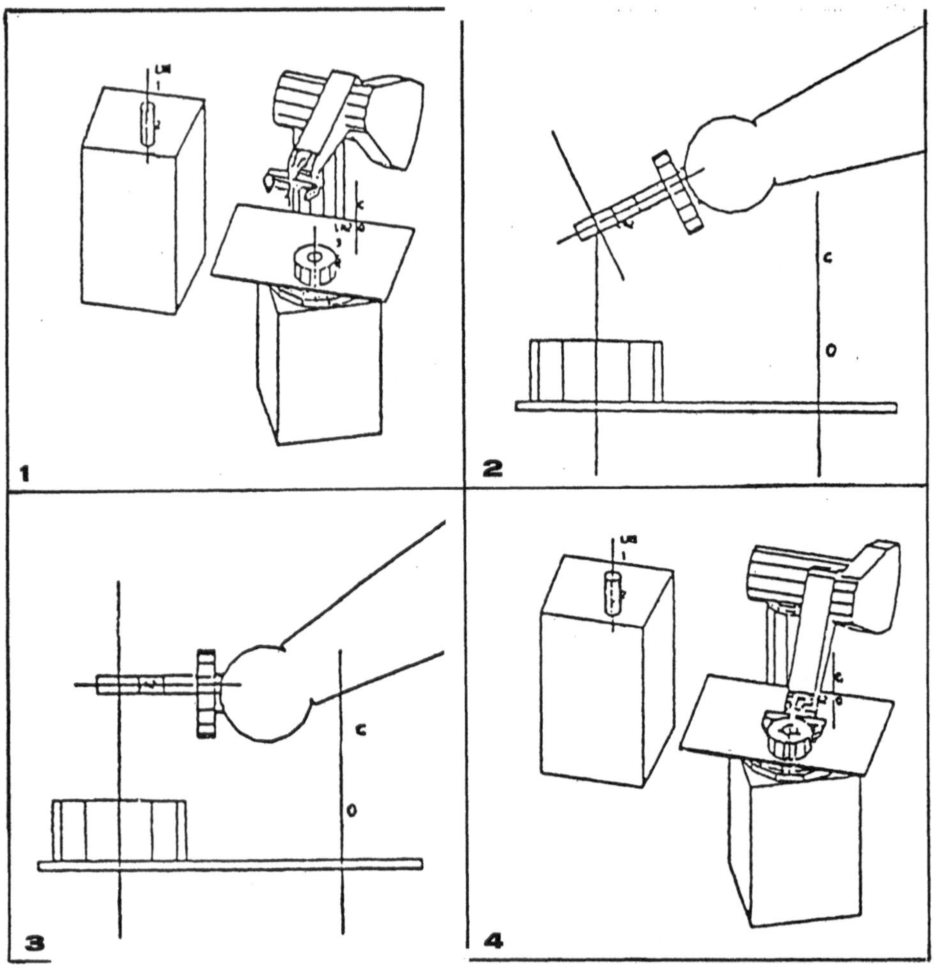

Fig. 3. Different states of the nut grasping (graphic display of CATIA).

Currently, there is **no** operational task level programming system, although work is proceeding on it. The production and dissemination of systems of this level will be a goal in the next decades.

2.2.3. Graphic programming: guiding-graphic and textual-graphic

The cost/performance ratio of computer assisted design (CAD) has dropped considerably in recent years. This has had an immediate influence on robot programming.In its conceptually most simple form,this is shown by the appearance of **graphic simulators** of the robot and the task.

The purpose of graphic simulation is to improve off-line programming productivity and correctness. Basically, the simulator's function is to make a pseudo-robot act on a graphic terminal. The simulation can range from presenting a sequence of specifically-designed stills, to kinematically simulating the complete movement by superimposing proximate images.

Graphic programming **alone** is no more than a sophisticated tool for **off-line** guided programming. This is called **guiding-graphic** programming. The pseudo-robot is moved using a keyboard, "mouse", digitalizing tablet, etc. The advantages expected from graphic simulation are:

(1) The definition of the situations (position plus orientations) in which the objects, gripping points, etc. are located.
(2) Collision analysis.

In their simplest form, graphic simulators work on the basis of:

(1) A **geometric model of objects** (available if the design is computer assisted, CAD)
(2) A **geometric-kinematic model of the robot** (this, in principle, could be provided by the manufacturer of the robot or of the simulator, or by an independent services company, etc.)
(3) A **geometric model of the robot's environment** which gives the locations of objects and their relation to the robot. This must be defined by the programmer himself, since it depends on the actual application.

The combination of textual and graphic expressions in defining a task originates very interesting programming systems, since the descriptive power of textual expression is added to the ergonomic advantages of computer-assisted graphic design. Sophisticated graphic simulators work from the above-mentioned models (geometric model of objects, geometric-kinematic model of the robot and geometric model of the environment) and from the textual program written for the application in hand. In this case, the simulation comes from interpretation of the robot's program. Depending on the language used, the geometric model of the environment can be defined, to a greater or lesser extent, in the application program (e.g. structured languages of the type AL, LM or PROSPRO).

Another more advanced graphic-assisted way for defining situations involves the use of a subsystem for calculating **geometric relationships**. Here the situations are defined **symbolically** and not directly **quantitatively**. Fig. 2 shows the learning of the robot's approach movement to grasp a nut. Once points A and B and axes D and G overlap, the nut is grasped by lowering the robot arm vertically and then ordering the hand to close.

Fig. 3 shows the sequence of operations during the graphic programming of the above task with the system CATIA.

In spite of the importance of graphic expression as a means of communication between man and machine, it does have some serious limitations. Firstly, all operations are defined on the basis of **models** (abstractions of reality) and not on reality itself. Here it is also important to note the difficulty of simulating sensor behavior. Secondly, one must not forget the complications involved in manipulating 3D images on a screen. Finally, it must be considered that graphic expression will, in general, never supersede textual expression, since the latter is semantically much richer (i.e. it has greater expressive capacity).

In conclusion, it is worth noting that it is in the cooperation between graphic and textual expression that the benefits of graphic computing in robot programming are most clearly seen. These include not only the program design and development phase, but can even extend to facilitating the choice of the optimal positioning of the robot and its peripherals (i.e. installation design).

3. CONCEPTS AND TECHNIQUES USED IN COMMERCIAL ROBOT VISION SYSTEMS

For approximately one decade there exist companies which build and sale processing systems to handle images for different purposes. Only since early 80's this group of companies has been considered as a distinct industry. This industry has evolved mainly from the research effort made in the late 60's and the 70's, throughout a few university departments and laboratories. Although machine vision has been technically possible for years, it has become practical only very recently, due mainly to the advent of microprocessors (specially 16 bit ones), which have done cost-effective the industrial applications of the advances obtained in image processing research.

Computer vision is a mean of simulating the recognition capability of the human eye/brain system. This definition can be translated to the concept of machine vision as "the automatic interpretation of images to control a manufacturing process" (Tech Tran Corp., 1985).

3.1. Image Processing and Robot Vision

Image processing involves all computer techniques which use images as input data. These techniques can be very different, as their use in different areas suggest. Many scientific fields during the last 25 years have used images for studying natural and artificial phenomena. Medicine, meteorology, space-science among other sciences has been pushing the development of image processing both theoretically and practically.

Which are the diferences between Image Processing (IP) and Robot Vision (RV)? Both involve processing pictures taken from a scene with a computer, but their basic requirements are distincts.

The main requirements for RV to be sucessful on a floor plant might be the following ones

- Reliability of operation
- Simplicity in adjusting and programming
- Very fast image processing (real-time is usually necessary)
- Easy scene illumination
- Low cost

Many times these requirements are diametrically opposed to the results regularly published by research groups working on IP. As an example gray scale image processing offers impressive results in contrast enhancement, noise reduction, picture data compression, etc. but these results are achieved at the expenses of computer size or architecture and processing time. Today such results can not be transported to a factory. RV need most of the time simplification of the IP results. In this sense, actually most of the robot vision systems working on factory floors can be characterized by:

- Moderate spatial resolution (typically 256 x 256)
- 2D processing
- Binary silhouttes used as raw data for object parameter extraction
- Non-overlapping object recognition
- ...

Probably, the single aspect which can characterize better RV is the control of the illumination of the working area. This aspect was initially overlooked, but researchers have found several techniques to simplify greatly the processing of images (structured light, laser beam superposition, etc). (See Fig. 4). The disadvantages of the control of illuminations is its specific matching to the set of scenes for which a special illumination has been designed. The good results obtained with a specific illumination may not be useful at all when changing the working area, the parts to be handled, or any other parameters of the industrial process.

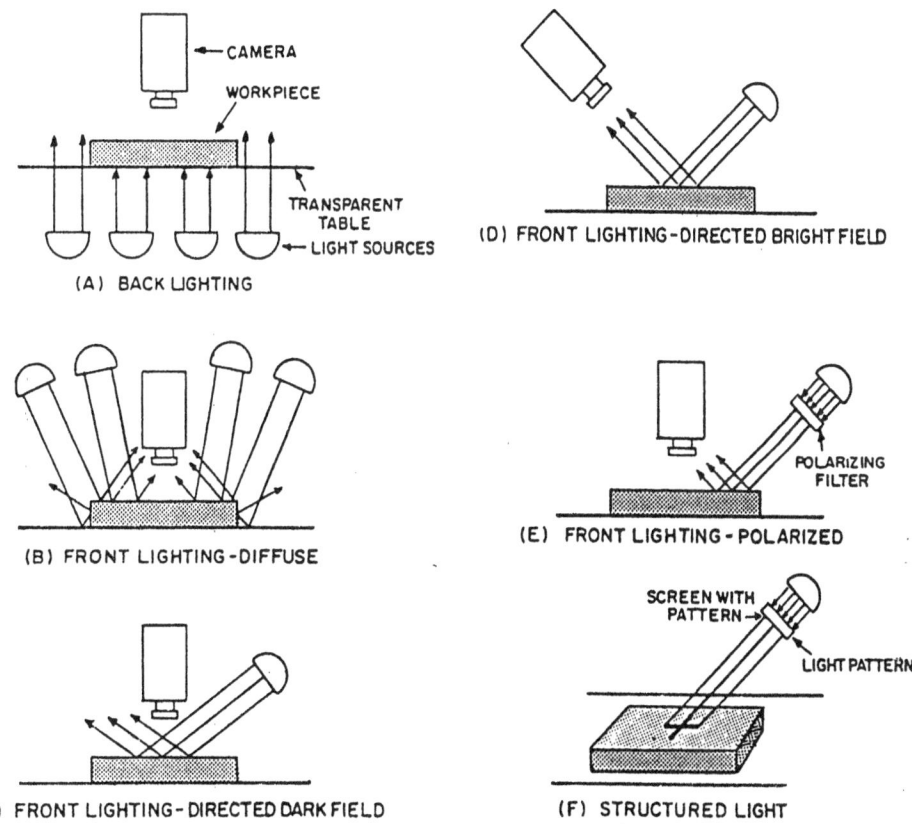

Fig. 4. Illumination techniques (Tech Tran Corp., (1985)

Ideally, a RV system should be capable of taking a picture of a scene, analyzing and interpreting it correctly, in order to output realiably the right control command to a robot or process control equipment, all these functions being performed in real time. Such a system must be also cost-effective.

3.2. Techniques of RV

Three basic processes need to be present in a RV system:

- Image capture
- Image analysis
- Image interpretation

The conjunction of these three processes make a clear distinction between IP and RV.

RV systems incorporating the above functions can be used for two main purposes: to produce some inmediate decision during a production process, or to build a data base about a set of parts, in order to develop a formal model to describe objects expected to be recognized in the future. As a general goal RV system intends to reduce indetermination and ambiguity of industrial scenes.

3.2.1.- Image capture

The usual imaging devices currently employed are TV cameras. Two kind of TV cameras exist depending on the light sensor device: vidicon or solid state devices. Vidicon cameras are being slowly discarded for the reason of its sensitivity to the industrial environment working conditions, but its low price make them attractive in some applications.

Solid state cameras look as the best for state-of-the-art RV systems. There are two solid state camera types, depending on the employed sensor. Both are silicon chips, but one is a charge-coupled-device (CCD) technology chip, and the other charge-injected-device (CID) technology chip. The difference between CCD and CID sensors depends basically in how the voltages of the individual array cell are extracted. CCD generates the voltage signal a row of cells at a time, but CID can read individual cell voltage in a random access manner.

The resolution of industrial cameras is very variable depending of application. Typical matrix cameras have 256 x 256 detector cells, but other resolutions are popular, such as 128 x 128, 64 x 64, 512 x 512, 384 x 491. In linear arrays resolutions of 4096 elements are attainable, being standard resolutions between 256 and 1024 elements. Cameras with linear sensor obviously need linear relative movement (for example, if pieces are on a conveyor) to acquire the picture.

At the time of digitizing the image, very recent advances in integration have allowed to dispose of "flash" converters which can digitize a picture to 8 bits, or even 9 bits, at the full speed of the video signal coming from the TV camera. However, these great grey level resolutions implies a large amount of data, which suppose increasing processing time. In order to avoid long processing time RV systems do not normally reach more than 6 bits (64 gray levels), being 1 bit systems the most commonly employed. This fact has classified RV systems in **binary** and **gray** scale systems.

Usually after digitizing, RV systems preprocess the picture to prepare it for the analyzing process. This preprocessing usually incorporates techniques as:

- Contrast enhancement   - Gap filling
- Edge extraction   - Curve smoothing
- Thresholding   - Run length encoding
- Thinning

These techniques are very well described in the literature |(Ballard D.H., Brown C.M., 1982); (Castleman K.R., 1979); (Paulidis T., 1982)|. The use of these techniques depends mainly on the following processes used by the system, which depend mostly of the application involved.

3.2.2. Image analysis

This step consist in analyzing the picture by measuring properties (features) of the objects on the scene to describe either the objects or the scene in a compact manner. The features extracted may belong to the image, to one object, or to a part of one object.

Important features which RV commercial system usually extract are position and orientation of objects, distance of the object from the system camera, object global or local parameters, object shape description, etc.

Image analysis usually is approached by RV systems analyzing geometric properties of the image by segmentation. Image segmentation consists in detecting lines between regions on the scene. The lines extracted are boundaries corresponding theoretically to the border of objects, shadows, object shape details, etc. If the scene background is uniform, regions extracted on the scene must correspond to the object presence. This is the most used hypothesis in RV commercial systems, which provide with means to adjust the thresholds to emphasize objects. At this stage of the process, most of commercial RV systems have binarized the picture. Usually, actual RV systems work well with non-overlapping objects, obtaining individual line pictures for every object on the scene. After object isolation, feature extraction for every object takes place. Depending of object complexity more features need to be extracted to proceed correctly with interpretation.

Area, perimeter, centroid, circunscribing rectangle, moments of inertia, axis of minimum moment, number of holes, curvatures of certain lines, are the most common features extracted. A specific set of measured features describes one object on the scene (region on the picture).

Some RV systems structurate the extracted features in a hierarchical way, giving not only feature values but also relationship between the features in a tree-like structure.

The segmentation step is the most critical one of the RV process. Usually the user must adjust his scenes to the segmentation process controlling illumination, adjusting thresholds interactively, and introducing his own software into the system.

3.2.3. Image interpretation

Some conclusion must be reached at the end of the visual process. For example a part is or is not present, identification of one object among some candidates, agreement of disagreement of the measured parameter of an object with some preadjusted limits, recognition of an object, its position and orientation, to control a manipulator which is going to grasp it, etc. RV system proceeds to identify objects on the scene with different methods. The two most frequently found are feature weighting and template matching. The first method consists in the evaluation of a scalar by adding the feature values weighted by some preadjusted constants. The closest value to a given one, extracted in the training of the system, identifies the object. The second method consists in generating internally a mask or template at the training time, then superpose the mask to the object image, and "fastly" calculate the fitness between mask and image. The image which best fit to the corresponding mask identifies the object. This kind of interpretation is mostly used in inspection task to output a "pass" or "reject" decision.

3.3. Performance characteristics of commercial RV systems

Due to the ample differences found among RV systems it is difficult to compare their performances. We have choose a few characteristic to give some idea of the possibilities which the industry actually offers. Resolutions, grey level discrimination, processing speed and reliability are the most frequently employed characteristic to show the capabilities of RV systems. The first two are absolute and objetive characteristic, the last two are actually application dependent, and manufacturer estimations are somewhat optimistic. Two important characteristic usually not found in commercial RV systems are 3D processing and recognition of partially occluded objects.

Table 1 shows a sample of different systems with their main characteristics. The table does not show reliability in the sense of **percentage** of correct decisions, because that characteristic depends very much of the object variability, scene conditions (e.g. illumination), amount of training performed on the system, and other factors. It is generally accepted that an 95% rate is good enough in many tasks of quality control and inspection.

Processing speed is another characteristic which is "ill" defined. Sometimes, the bits that the processor CPU process at a time is the claimed speed. More interesting is the speed at which a decision is taken by the RV system in a given application. Manufacturers do not generally deliver data of this speed. However, some method for comparing RV systems performance has been described and proposed (Rosen C.A., Gleason G.J., 1983). There are very few comments from the customers of RV systems. In (Walter W.W., 1984) the experience of an user with an advanced RV system in solving the bin picking task is shown. Among the most important conclusions are the limitation to identify only spherical and cylindrical parts, 9 seconds approximate time of part acquisition, and software settings are not easy to adjust, requiring some operator training.

There are permanent software and hardware improvements which increase the performance of RV systems. Detailed information can be found in (Pugh A. Ed., 1983); (Tech Tran Corp., 1985) and (3rd. Conference on Applied Machine Vision, 1984) which give an up-to-date panorama of actual commercial RV Systems.

Special consideration deserves the real time terminology applied to RV systems (RVS). Real-time in manufacturing environments might be understood as the maximum time that the manufacturing process allows to the RVS to take a decision before the next move of the robot is performed, in order that the robot can execute any control command issued by the RVS. Another interpretation can be derived of the fact that any robot operation trys to substitute to a human operator. But, which is the performance of a human operator? Some measure of this performance can be extrapolated from results shown in (Ballard D.H., Brown C.H., 1985) taken from (Treisman A.M., 1983). Fig. 5 shows results which can justify that man needs between 0,5 to more than 2 seconds to react when he is using his visual system to recognize features. Why do not take for real-time operation when RVS outputs a decision before 2 seconds?. In many industrial application it seems that such reaction times are fast enough to be better than economical. In (Walter W.W., 1983) a RVS system was tested and the time employed to recognize one object was approximately 3 seconds, taking the robot 6 seconds to acquire the object (the testing task was bin-picking

Table 1

MANUFACT.	MODEL	VIDICON	SOLID STATE	CAMERA #	TYPE	BITS	SPEED	B/N	COLOUR	GREY LEVELS	PIXELS	CHARACTERISTICS	APPLICATIONS
VICOM	VICOM	x		1	68000	16	---	x	x	256	256 x 256	Real time image processing Array processor)x) convolution and point processor, Assembler, Fortran and Pascal	Analysis an Inspection
KONTRON	IPS 1	x		1	Z80	8	13 sec.	x		256	512 x 256	Basic and Fortran programming	Microscopy and Inspection
KONTRON	IPS II	x		1	Z80	8	6'5 sec.	x		256	512 x 256	Basic and Fortran programming	Microscopy and Inspection
DIG. DESIGN	VISIONIX		Fotodiodos	1	68000	16	10 sec.	x		256	256 x 256	Real time, Forth and Pascal programming	Moving objects inspection, Measurement
CONTROL	INTERVISION IM 2000		x	64	8086	16		x		64	320 x 484	Location identification, alphanumeric or symbolic matching, Forth programming	Inspection
AUTOMATION	INTERVISION IM 1000		x	4	8086	16		x		64	128 x 128	Location identification, alphanumeric or symbol matching, Forth programming	Inspection
AUTOMATION	CAN-1000 VISION SYSTEM		CCD	4	8086	16		x		80	128 x 128	Real-time	Inspection, Robotics
GS BEAM POSITIONNING COMPONENTS	gn/EYE CONFIGURATION TWO	x		1		16		x		20			Part positioning in inspection Robotics
ICOS N.V.	ICOS 2000 SYSTEM	x	x	2	68000	16		x		256	2000 x 2000	Gray-level histograms, area and perimeter counts, centers of gravity, etc., gray-scale processing, region and contour pro	Inspection
FOXVILLE	DIGI/CAM IMAGIN SYSTEM	x	x	1			45 sec.	x		4	128 x 256	Image processor, feature extractor and matching	Inspection
OFS	OFS SCAN SYSTEM MODEL 100	x		1		8		x					Pattern recognition, inspection Robotics
MICRON TECHNOLOGY, INC	MICRON EYE		x	1	6502	8		x			256 x 256	Programming in Basic	Microscopy and Inspection
FAIRCHILD	SYSTEM WITH CAMERA CCD 3000		CCD	1	F9445	16	10 sec.	x			256 x 256	Global parameters	Robotics
TS PRODUCTS	INSPECTOR	x		1				x					
OFS	i-bot 1		CCD	1	8086	16	3 sec.	x		256	256 x 240	Real-time image processing	Inspection, Medicine
LI.ACOM	CMO 02	x		1	8 x 305	8		x	x	256	256 x 256	Real-time image processing	Inspection, Medicine
LI.ACOM	OAO 02	x		1	8 x 305 + Z80	8		x	x	256	512 x 512	Real-time image processing	Inspection, Medicine
LI.ACOM	HMD	x		1	8 x 305	8		x	x	256	1024 x 1024	Real-time convolution and arithmetic/logical combinations of images (array processor) Fortran and Basic programming	Medicine, Cartography, Inspection
ARDIN	ALY 5000D	x		1	8086	16	7 sec.	x	x		2048 x 2048	Gray-scale enhancement, correlation detection, spectrum analysis, pattern analysis	Inspection
OLBI COMP	CS-5	x		1				x	x		512 x 512		Microscopy, Medicine Inspection
EIKONIX			x	1		8	17 sec.	x		256	1024 x 1024		

cylinders). The total operation was considered generally slow for many industrial applications.

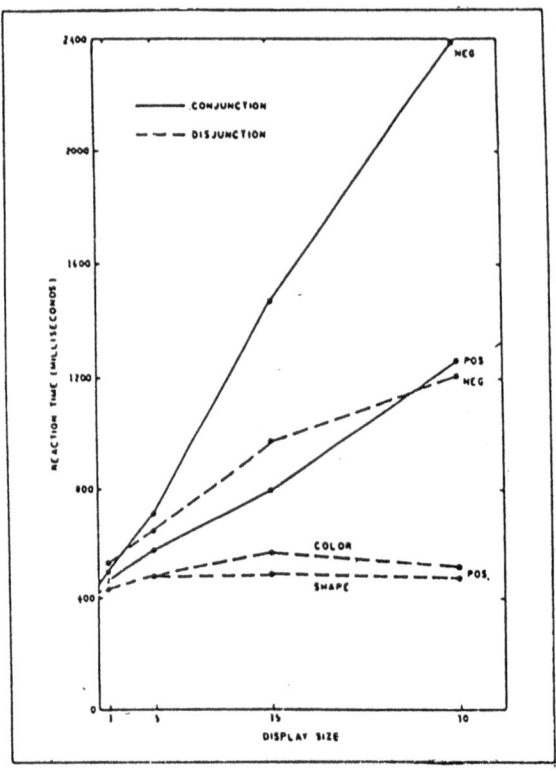

Fig. 5. In recognizing a single feature such as "red" or the letter "T" a subjects reaction time is constant if the feature is in the display (POS). If it is absent or, more importantly if the stimulus is a conjuction (i.e. red T depicted by a solid line) the response time increases linearly with the size of the display.

To reach the above mentioned processing speed there are two alternatives. The first one deals with increasing the power of the computer, which can be enhanced in two ways thru the computer architecture (for example see in this book papers on PAPIA machine) and/or device technology improvement (device speed is approximately doubled every two years) . The new computer architecture solution is not fully mature and several years have to pass to be transportable to factory floors. The second one is to design VLSI chips incorporating much of the software in ROM, PLA or other integrated technology Such a system has been built (Visiomat), and its manufacturer claims a real-time processing operation.

4. ROBOT VISION PROGRAMMING

We will restrict this discussion of the programming of industrial vision systems to those used basically in robotic applications (manipulations, inspections). A more general outline of textual languages for image processing can be found in (S. Levialdi, 1983).

Analyzing commercialized robot vision systems we find that the majority are programmed by the "teaching-by-showing" method, using **fixed** algorithms for analysis and interpretation. In general these systems are produced by the robot manufacturers themselves (ASEA, UNIMATION,...) who consider vision systems as an elaborate peripheral of the manipulator.

The basic mode of operation of these systems is extraordinarily simple. It consists of the following fundamental steps:

(1) **Calibration** of the camera's coordinate system, which is usually done by ordering the robot's TCP to adopt a given position and orientation. Usually it is defined in relation with some feature of an object captured by the camera.

(2) Interactive **training** of the system with the working objects. During this phase the operator locates each object in different positions and orientations and the system elaborates a model of each one.

(3) **Integration** of the vision and the manipulation system. In particular the manipulator is shown the positions and orientations it must adopt to grasp objects.

Once the learning phase is over, the vision is controlled by the robot program, with certain special instructions appearing in its text. In VAL these are: VPICTURE (acquisiton of an image), VLOCATE (process the image and extract the object's position and orientation), etc. If we consider Program 1 again, it is clear that it permits the object "PART" to be moved from an initial position (determined by the vision system) to the situation named "PALLET". Instruction no. 3 means: localize the object "PART" in the last image acquired and if "PART" does not appear, execute the instruction labelled with 100 (which can be a wait loop).

The programming of the first vision systems is, therefore, conceptually analogous to that of the simplest robot programming systems - teaching-by-showing-. To remove the limitations imposed by **teaching-by-showing, textual** programming is developed for robot vision systems.

Explicit textual programming is used, basically, in order to codify different pre-processing, analysis and recognition algorithms. The ideal is to achieve flexibility, reliability, easy use and computational efficiency.

Because universal artificial vision systems are utopical, different systems would be needed for different applications. Here it is worth noting the frequent dichotomy between:

(1) "in situ" vision systems, and
(2) development systems for vision applications.

The purpose of the latter is to facilitate the production of software which configurate the former for a given class of application. That is, the above distinction is analogous to that in the world of microprocessors between (1) a particular system, and (2) a microprocessor developing system. Application development systems usually have an important software environment which includes:

(1) General-purpose operating systems
(2) High-level programming languages (PASCAL, ...). Also for reasons of computational efficiency, they can include medium-level languages (e.g. C) and even assemblers.

(3) Subroutine library containing subroutines for image processing: representation, enhancement, geometrical transformation, analysis, interpretation, etc.
(4) Application packages.

Explicit textual programming languages of vision system must: (1) be able to manipulate images with different grey levels, (2) lead to the elaboration of programs with structured control, and (3) be equipped with geometric data types (points, straight lines, circumferences, etc.) in order to facilitate model construction.

The wide range of potential users of a vision system leads to the use of **multi-level** programming systems |see AML(R. Taylor, P.D. Summers, J.M. Meyer, 1982) or LIVIA (Cividini C., Gini M., Gini G., 1983), for example|. We generally find three basic levels:

(1) **User** (plant operator) who needs very basic training, adapted to the class of problems he deals with. Here operation is based on the use of **"menus"** and/or **softkeys.** The operator hardly knows any of the algorithms used in the phases of image processing.

(2) **Application,** in which are defined the different particularizations caracterizing "user machines". The application consists of a set of software packages used in the class of operation at hand (arc-welding, assembly, etc.)

(3) **System,** in which the levels of application are constituted from the basic software (operating system, special data types, procedure library, etc.). Programming at this level is only for the expert in vision and computing. At this level what is manipulated is, basically, the **vision machine** (camera control, basic preprocessing algorithms, analysis and interpretation). It is vital to have direct access to the information which defines an image, in order to apply new treatment algorithms to it.

AML/V (Lavin M.A.,Lieberman L.I., 1982) is a collection of vision subroutines which is added to AML. The subroutines of AML/V belong to three groups:

a) Camera control and image acquisition
b) Binary region analysis (e.g. FINDREGION selects a region by means of a filter)
c) Image arithmetic (e.g. BIXOR makes the OR-exclusive of two images, pixel by pixel).

AML/V has two limitations: (1) it only works with binary images, and (2) the only visual data type it has is the **image.** The existence in AML of a type-constructor called **"aggregate"** eliminates this second difficulty.

Following the analogy between robot programming languages and vision system programming languages, explicit textual systems not only increase the expressive capacity for operations but also allow the **off-line** definition of object models based on their geometry (models of 2D projections, 3D geometric models from CAD).

Finally, in speaking of task-level textual programming, instead of considering the vision system alone, we consider the integration of vision and manipulator. In any case, it is important to note that at this level models must be 3D (and volumetric) in order to predict projections, deduce "grasping configurations", etc. Here we can mention the experimental systems ACRONYM(SRI) and RVL/V (Matsushita et alt.,1984). Let us consider the second as it is more specifically robotic.

RVL/V is a model-based 3D experimental system of which only two characteristics interest us here:

(1) The hierarchy of visual data and processing
(2) An elaborate hand-eye control including two approaches: hierarchical and rule-based.

In the hierarchy of visual data we find the levels **pixel, feature, object** and **scene.** The hierarchical hand-eye control is based on the presence of an **object-level loop** and a **feature-level loop** (see Program 3). The second loop has a shorter cycle time. It executes until the feature is lost. In this case the control system executes the object-level loop until object localization. Later, control is returned to the feature level. The basic idea of rule-based control is not to numerically calculate transforms for defining hand movements, but to apply an action rule depending on the difference between the actual state and the goal state. The visual feedback program (Program 4) is repeated until the difference is null.

```
O-LOOP
  (FIND 'OBJECT)
  (MEASURE 'OBJECT 'FRAME)
  (MOVEHAND 'OBJECT)
  (SETQ 'OBJCT.FEATURE
    (EXTRACT FEATURE 'OBJECT))
F-LOOP
  (COND
   ((FIND 'OBJECT.FEATURE)
    (MEASURE 'OBJECT.FEATURE 'FRAME)
    (MOVEHAND 'OBJECT)
F-LOOP-END
      (GO F-LOOP))
O-LOOP-END
      (T(GO O-LOOP)))
```

PROGRAM 3. Hierarchical Control Program in RVL/V

Rule-based control is similar to our own behavior, reducing the effect of measurement errors and camera-manipulator calibration errors.

RVL/V is under development and is mainly implemented on LISP.

Visual feedback program:
```
(WHILE
  (SETQ  dif
    (WATCH object_1 object_2 goal_statement))
  (RULEMOVE  dif  rule_base))
```

Rule-base:
```
RULEBASE:  IF state = E1  THEN use H1   (rule 1)
           IF state = E2  THEN use H2   (rule 2)
```

PROGRAM 4. Basic ideas of RVL/V rule-based control

5. CONCLUSIONS

This paper has presented a brief survey of robot programming *languages*, emphasizing the layering of the programming modes in teaching-by-showing and textual (explicit and task levels). Furthermore, it has been analyzed graphic programming, which will be a very important tool in the near future.

The programming modes of visual robot systems follow a parallel way to the manipulator programming. After the appearing of the teaching-by-showing mode, there exist today comercialized system with explicit textual programming. The task level is an artificial intelligence level, where manipulation and sensing aspects strongly interact. These aspects are closely related to the work developed in CAD stages (by reusing the same models).

Concepts and techniques of commercial visual systems for robots has been reviewed, noting the difficulties of comparing its performance characteristics, specially when real-time operation is claimed.

The future of robot system is on task-level programming including sensor integration. Sensor integration means that a robot will incorporate high level sensing capabilities like vision, touch, proximetry, force, hearing, ... By using task-level programming the robot system will be "conscious" on what it is doing. Then, robot programming will be easier, leading to flexibility and portability. As a consequence safeness will be achieved, because the robot will be able to handle unespected events.

Many efforts need still to be made to reach a robot programming environment, integrating high level perception and artificial intelligence techniques, to fit user's needs.

Bibliography

Ballard, D.H., & Brown, C.M., (1982): "Computer Vision", Prentice Hall, Englewood Cliffs, N.J., USA.

Ballard, D.H., & Brown, C.H., (1985): "Vision", Byte, April, pp 245-261.

Bonner, S, K.G. Shin, (1982): "A comparative study of Robot Lnaguages". Computer, December, pp 82-96.

Castleman, K.R., (1979): "Digital Image Processing", Prentice Hall Int., Englewood Cliffs, N.J., USA.

Cividini, G., Gini G., Gini M., Villa G., (1983): "A user oriented language for image processing and object recognition (LIVIA)", Proc. of the Automation of Industrial Processes. Torino 14-16 December, pp 239-244.

Duff, M., Levialdi S., (1981): "Languages and Architectures for Image Processing", Academic Press. London.

Gruver, et al., (1984): "Industrial Robot Programming Languages: A comparative evaluation". IEEE Trans. on SMC, 14,4,July, pp 565-570.

Lavin, M.A., Lieberman L.I. (1982): "AML/V An Industrial Machine Vision Programming System". Int. J. of Robotics Research 1, 3, pp 42-56.

Levialdi S., (1983): "Languages for image processing". In "Fundamentals in Computer Vision" (Ed. by Faugueras O.D.). Cambridge University Press, pp.459-478.

Liegeois A., Dombre E., Borrel P., (1982): "Developement d'un systeme de CAO et de simulation de robots manipulateurs", Premières journées ARA, Poitiers, Septembre.

Lozano Pérez T., (1983): "Robot Programming". Proceedings of the IEEE, July, vol 71, 7, pp 821-841.

Matsushita T., Sato T., Hirai S., (1984): "Robot Vision Language RVL/V: An integration scheme of visual processing and manipulator control".

Paulidis T., (1982): "Algorithms for graphics and image processing", Springer Verlag.

Pugh, A. Ed, (1983): "Robot Vision", IFS Publication & Springer Verlag.

Rosen, C.A., & Gleason, G.J., (1983): "Evaluating Vision System Performance", in Robot Vision, A. Pugh, Ed. IFS Publication & Springer Verlag.

Silva M., (1984): "Lenguajes de programación para robots industriales". In "Inteligencia Artificial y Robótica Industrial", (Ed. by Silva M., Roy A.). Publicaciones de la Universidad de Zaragoza. pp 11-80.

Smith B., Peterson C.V. (1984): "An Integrated Robot Vision System for Industrial Use". Proceedings Third Conference on Applied Machine Vision, , SME, Feb 27-March 1, Schaumburg (Chicago), Il, USA.

Taylor R.H., Summers P.D., Meyer J.M., (1983): "AML: A Manufacturing Language". Int. J. of Robotics Research 1,3, pp 19-41.

Tech Tran Corp., (1985), "Machine Vision Systems: A Summary and Forecast", Illinois, USA.

Third Conference on Applied Machine Vision, (1984), Society of Manufacturing Engineers, Feb. 27-March 1, Schaumburg (Chicago), Il, USA.

Treisman,A.M., (1983): "The Role of Attention in Object Perception", in O.J. Braddick and A.C. Sleigh, Physical and Biological Processing of Images, Berlin, Springer- Verlag.

User's guide to VAL, (1980),(1984): "A robot Programming and Control System". Unimation Inc. (1980), Adept Technology Incorporation (1984).

Visiomat, Robotronics, Matra Automation, Rue J.P. Timbaud B.P. 66, 78390 Bois d'Arcy, France.

Walter, W.W., (1984): "Applying Robotic Vision for Assembly and Fabrication", in 3rd Annual Applied Machine Vision, Schaumburg (Chicago), Il, USA.

EXPERT SYSTEMS AND IMAGE PROCESSING

Jean Marc Chassery

Reconnaissance des Formes et Microscopie Quantative
Laboratoire TIM3 — IMAG
BP n°68 - 38402 Saint Martin D'Heres Cedex - France

INTRODUCTION

Since 1960's Computer Image Analysis has resolved a lot of problems, from data acquisition to image interpretation.

The constant evolution of the set of solutions which are actually proposed in that domain is due to different factors :
- the necessity to develop new research axes according to the growing diversity of applications ;
- the evolution of computers toward dedicated machines ;
- the development of softwares for information processing, specially in signal processing, image representation, image featuring and pattern recognition ;
- the integration of perceptual models ;
- the integration of 3D featuring from 2D imagery based on geometrical considerations as well as shading, texture and shape featuring.

All these developments have been performed in close relationship with different scientific domains such as signal analysis, applied mathematics, and computer science. Image analysis was born from several preoccupations common to predefined orientations. We are actually in presence of a multiform discipline including image processing, image understanding and pattern recognition.

Many research activities have been developed which incorporate solutions to problems of image representation such as encoding, enhancement and restoration. Numerous results have been obtained for image analysis according to segmentation methods and feature extraction. The interpretation level was essentially considered as a data analysis problem, giving rise to the elaboration of classification methods.

Nevertheless, in parallel, we observed the elaboration of sophisticated interpretation methods, working at a semantic level, invoking Artificial Intelligence techniques. Such methods were initially applied to the recognition of polyhedral objects and later to the analysis of objects represented by means of generalized cylinders[2,3] . It was already an Artificial formulation of the representation problem.

It is thus essentially in the domain of interpretation and understanding that, in the middle of 70's, could be remarked the integration of Artificial Intelligence in a new science dedicated to scene analysis and namely referred as "image understanding".

Moreover it has been frequently pointed out, that the initial conception of image analysis, described by the successive phases of acquisition, preprocessing, segmentation and featuring was not a sufficient scheme to give access to the diagnostic phase. The essential reason concerns the fatal errors arising from the segmentation step.

In opposition with such linear scheme, and with the purpose to conceive powerful recognition machines[4] , two approaches appear conceivable and reflect the human recognition process :

- the first approach is oriented toward the modelisation of the human perceptual system. Such model, involving the understanding of the human neural processing, should explain the functions of visual recognition and human interpretation. Such research actually mainly concerns the modelisation of neural nets activity and behaviour [5,6] . It concerns also their simulation by means of cellular automata. The use of associative memories allows to model the contextual influence at a specified representation level. Numerous hardware development are associated to this approach, essentially based on parallel architectures

-the second approach is oriented toward the symbolic representation of concepts. Symbolic and relationnal processings are conducted to derive meaningful tasks of image interpretation.

Such an approach has to satisfy a set of constraints which are presented by NAGAO [7] . In particular, it has to define the integration mechanisms of ponctual, local and global functions operating on the image as well as the control modules enabling the evolution of the level representation from the low level (image as a set of picture elements) to the high level (image as a scene interpretation), and conversely.

Processing level-Bottom up - Top down - Feedback[8]

The classical scheme of image analysis is associated to a bottom up strategy. Such bottom up strategy starts from a spatial or spectral representation of the image. After successive steps of detection grouping and featuring, parameters are extracted from the image and the objects are classified. Such a processing method is criticized because of its deterministic aspect. The description phase, including the segmentation and featuring, comunicates according to one unique way with the interpretation phase. it is then not possible, at that final stage, to be aware of to handle eventual segmentation errors[9].

In opposition with such an approach, different processing strategies have been developped : top-down and feed-back.

In the case of a top-down strategy, the analysis starts with a set of standard models and proceeds according to possible matches detected between objects and models. Top-down approach is always combined with a bottom up feature extraction process in order to characterize the image components of interest. Primary example of these methods are region growing and split and marge segmentation algorithms.

Finally a control strategy of interest is designed under the term of feedback.

Feedback processing allows to handle the eventual errors occurring during image analysis. It offers the integration of local or global interpretation to adapt the analysis.

Checking can thus be performed at every stage of the process evolution and an eventual feedback to a previous stage may be decided to conduct the analysis once again in a different contextual frame. NAGAO illustrated the feedback process for the face analysis[7] and MONTANARI for the contour following by dynamic programmation[10,11].

All these methods support the qualification of pre-determined for the reason that the evolution of the analysis does not allow the integration of the informative content of the image. Such consideration conducts to orient image analysis toward Artificial Intelligence with the notion of production systems.

The following remarks should be made with respect to human beings visual interpretation abilities :

- an important perceptive power linked to the capacity of focalization on the object of interest in a big image,

- an important understanding power linked to the possession of adequate strategies based on deductive as well as relational reasoning.

It is well known that man is involved in a learning process as soon as he explores an image. He tries to associate what he is seeing with what he has learned. There exist classical situations for which without any learning or information, human being has some difficulty to give an interpretation.

The human intelligence, when implied in a scene analysis task is able to cope not only with the visual items coming from the scene under interest but also with various contextual informations presenting any relationship with that scene. Once again there exist situations for which two observations can give rise to different interpretations.

These remarks, imply two notions which are essential to the conception of an intelligent image analysis system :

- the notion of knowledge
- the notion of control and strategy

These notions constitute the basic elements of the conception of a production system in Artificial Intelligence.

The data section involves the available a priori knowledge as well as the knowledge about facts that could be deduced by explication of the production rules. Definition of analyzing strategies allows the adaptation to a particular situation by means of a judicious choice of data (knowledge), rules of production, order and type of activation.

Knowledge level [12]

In vision the term of knowledge is fundamental and as it will be described, the knowledge is not only related to the model that we try to put in correspondance with some image features.

Such a concept is rapidly insufficient when we consider invariance problems such as illumination, orientation, positionning ... Difficulties are also encountered in 3D analysis for which the 2D representations suppress all considerations of depth if we do not use a stereo-vision method.

A vision's system can be describe as a set of processing in close relationship ; each process is attached to a progressive transformation of the information in reference to perceptual, functionnal and semantic models.

These models integrate more particularly the knowledges which are specific to the different processing since the image acquisition until the symbolic and semantic description of the image without missing the segmentation and identification of the attributes which compose the scene.

Knowledge may be associated to different levels [12] :

- physical knowledge : this is the knowledge about the environment of the image acquisition. We have geometrical consideration, spectral and cinematics characteristics.

- perceptual knowledge : this is a knowledge used to elaborate processing on the entities which compose the image. It is associated to the concepts of neighbouring, similarity, smoothness, contrast. This knowledge is related to the evolution of the representation's level of the scene. The low level consists of the pixel entities and by grouping techniques we arrive to local or global entities as frontier elements and contour for example. This type of knowledge is essentially used in segmentation to obtain a symbolic representation of the image in accordance with the human visual system[13].

- semantic knowledge : in order to recognize objects it is necessary to have information about them. These informations characterize the relations between perceptual knowledges and characterize the rules of organisation. The semantic knowledge is specific of the scene. They are acquired by the decription of the scene and the rules of organisation must be sufficient to manipulate perceptual knowledge according to the final interpretation of the scene. If we want to obtain an intelligent system, it is necessary that such a level of semantic knowledge be the most complete. Moreover we have to consider that these knowledges are in constant evolution during the analysis of the image. It is from such source of knowledge that the system will be able to identify objects in the set of picture elements. For example, from the concept "house", with consideration of semantic knowledge, we must be able to access to the perceptual knowledge and next to identify the elements which are eventually recognized as an house.

Really it is complex and the elaboration of such procedure need to take into account different notions :
- the notion of information level
- the notion of rule of production
- the notion of control and strategy.

In image understanding to obtain the interpretation of a scene it is necessary to consider hierarchical levels. At each level we can elaborate appropriate procedures in relation with the type of knowledge they have to use and to provide. At a same level these procedures can be actived in a parallel manner, all the knowledge being accumulated in a common data base called the blackboard. The information acquired in the blackboard are analyzed and useful ones are retained to increase the data section.

The notion of level of information is associated to the terms of low level process, middle level process, high level process[14].

A low level process is characterized by the ponctual primitives on which it will operate. This type of process is related to physical knowledge and their activation give a representation of the image in terms of entities. For example filtering, edge detectors are low level process for which the entity is associated to notion of texture, frontiers.

A middle level process is characterized by tehnics of primitive grouping to obtain global entities.

These process use perceptual knowledge such as information of similarity (example of approximation by facet model) or information of continuity (example of contour following).

At the middle level we have to take into account the problem of ambiguity : there are many possibilities in labeling or grouping

A solution to this problem can be found in the use of relaxation[15].

The main task of the high level process is to perform a match between the object model and the information extracted from the image. Such a process is related to semantical knowledge of the concept being present in the image.

The notion of rule of production may be interpreted as a type of process to be activied at some given moment.

The choice of such a process is oriented by a strategy derived according to a set of hypothesis obtained by applying production rules on the set of knowledge. Next, using a control process, hypothesis may be confirmed and thus constitute a new knowledge element. A simple procedure constitute a rule of production, as for example the contour following which associates the term of contour to pixels characterized by the term of frontier points. In segmentation we can mention production rules associated to region growing or relaxation.

The notion of control level can be characterized by different factors :
- constraints or compatibilities (example for relaxation),
- context formulated from the semantic knowledges,
- convergence criterium in the case of an iterative process,
- Tolerance-error in the case of approximation,
- similarity in matching problems including the notion of prototype.

Strategies

The definition of the strategy is useful to developp a smart analysis method which can escape a huge amount of computation at the image level. According to the strategy, featuring should be performed only when needed during the activation of dedicated processes.

To do that the deviation of top down process allows to focus the processing upon regions of great interest.

The choice of a strategy must combine the image complexity with the complexity of processing.

The image complexity can be described by means of a structural scheme. Semantic as well as descriptive knowledge are organized within such scheme according to "is-a" and "part-whole" relations [16,17].

"Is-a" relations are generally associated to different representation modes for an object. Such a relation associates to the object some knowledge (numerical, descriptive or semantic).

"Part-whole" relations are used in top-down or bottom-up process. Such a relation leads to the composition or the decomposition of entities at different hierarchical levels.

Major problems encountered when defining a particular strategy are the proper selection of production rules and the derivation of control tools, based upon contextual information, in order to reduce possible ambiguities.

After the previous descriptions of the evolution of Image Analysis toward the Image Understanding approach, we shall specify the system expert introduction.

Characteristics of the Expert Systems [18,19]

- The notion of expert system has been conceived to reach the high level of performance characterizing the human expert in some involved specified tasks. Such a conception is in close relationship with the activities in image understanding.

- The expert system structure is adapted to manipulate knowledges qualified as declarative ones, and given in a highly symbolic form. Particular problems thus arise when trying to transduce these in a numerical form.

-To resolve a problem with combinatory orientation, the expert system uses heuristics to make a modular approach to the solution. The notion of heuristic may be associated to the concept of strategy in image analysis.

Nevertheless due to the numerical aspect of the image taken at the first level of representation it is evident that the classical expert system notion is limited to the semantic level during the interpretation. The system must be completed by numerical modules able to provide a quantitative knowledge.

Expert systems and Images. Realisations [20]

In the various domains of application their exist at the present time 2 classifications of expert systems : classification by problems, classification by activities.

In case of classification by problem we find the class of interpretation systems which are oriented toward a better understanding of an initial set of data. We have examples in signal analysis and in pattern recognition. Others examples of such class which belong to that first classification are predictive systems, diagnosis systems, design systems, monitoring and control system.

In case of classification by domain it is essentially in the medical domain that we encounter the famous expert system MYCIN. Other domains developed expert system for example in computer configuration with the system R1 and the system DENDRAL in chemical domain. In cancerology we realised an expert system based on the observation of microscopic slides. Such a system can be connected to an image analysis system to integrate image quantification and image understanding of the analyzed specimen.

If we consider again the first classification, one of the problem to be solved by Image Analysis Expert System is the problem of image segmentation.
The concept of expert system appears well adapted to solve this last problem for two main reasons :
- the combinatorial
- the necessity to develop strategies involving perceptual as well as semantic knowledge about the scene.•

Expert System organisation [18]

As for the presentation of existing expert systems, only a brief discussion will be associated to the expert system organisation. More informations are easily found in the literature.

The basic structure of an expert system is organized around two fundamental modules
- the knowledge base
- the inference engine.

The knowledge base can be structured in two bases :
- the rules which contain the production rules in a procedural form
- the facts which contain the set of deductions performed during the activation of the system.

The inference engine is considered as the cognitive process of the system. One of its main task is to evaluate and activate the production rules.

Expert System - Image Analysis - Segmentation problem

In segmentation the notion of spatial information is essential. Such information is particularly expressive of the topography and topology of the different entities.

A first definition of a segmentation process using a control strategy was given by relaxation. It is a computational scheme for low and middle level processes in image understanding. Limitations of relaxation can be described from two viewpoints :

- Poor descriptive ability :
relaxation uses only labels and compatibility coefficients. This is not sufficient do describe knowledge about complex scenes. The knowledge organization is not represented sufficiently.

- Uniform processing over the entire scene :
relaxation does not involve any possible focus of attention, nor any global contextual considerations.

Nevertheless, relaxation have been successfully used for a wide variety of applications.

The use of expert systems have been introduced to test the feasibility of image understanding. It was essentially in domain of image segmentation that many efforts have been realized.

One of the more complete realisation concerns the system SIGMA of Matsuyama which consists of three experts : Geometric Reasoning Expert, Model Selection Expert and Low Level Vision Expert [21].

The Geometric Reasoning Expert represents the central reasoning module. It controls the evolution of the analysis by combining bottom up and top down processes. The top down orientation is used to detect new objects while the bottom up orientation is used to establish relations between objects.

This expert module creates an Iconic Database in which evidences are accumulated for the interpretation phase.

It communicates directly with the Model Selection Expert. The Model Selection Expert uses the contextual information given by the Geometric Reasoning Expert. By reasoning about the different models and selecting the most promising it search for the object.

The Low Level Vision Expert uses the selected models from the Model Selection Expert. It works on the picture and define adequate image processing operators by taking into account the knowledge about picture processing methods.

An important work is currently performed to identify the characteristics (effectiveness, cost of computation) of the elementary processes used for image segmentation and featuring [22].

Illustration in Cell Image Analysis [23]

Similar considerations have lead us to elaborate an expert system for cytologic image segmentation. We describe the knowledge organization and the analyzing process and strategy in terms of the works of Matsuyama.

The knowledge base involves the following items :

- The image is composed by 4 regions :
    . background
    . cytoplasm
    . nucleus
    . red cells.
- The nucleus region and the background region are roughly homogeneous. The nucleus contains low level values and the background contains high level values.
- The nucleus region is included into a cytoplasmic region to compose a cell (also named leukocytes).
- The red cells and leukocytes satisfy a convexity predicate.

The first analysis of the image is initialized by a Model Selection Expert. Taking into account the predicate of uniformity on background and nucleus, it decides the activation of a thresholding method based on histogram analysis. It asks the low level vision expert to extract two thresholds and to perform an initial segmentation.

Two regions are thus defined from the support image X

X_1 = background and X_2 = nucleus

Next by considering the region $Y = X \setminus X_1$, defined as the complementary of the background, the geometric reasoning expert examines each one of the connected components included into Y and select the only one including nucleus points. It asks next the Model Selection Expert to verify the convexity predicate. If the convexity predicate is satisfied, then the object is defined as a correctly segmented leukocyte. Such situation is generally encountered in the case of well contrasted isolated cells.

On the countrary the Geometric Reasoning Expert decides the activation of an iterative process based on a region growing method. Starting from a connected component designed as nucleus (already detected during the initial phase) :

- The Model Selection Expert selects a color reference by examination of the newly aggregated pixels since the previous iteration step.

It asks to the Low level Vision expert to detect the connected blobs associated to that new color reference, and to aggregate them by tacking into account considerations of connectivity :

- the Low Level Vision Expert performs color computation and activate the labeling procedures ;

- the Geometric Reasoning Expert controls the evolution of the shape by using a convexity criterion. More precisely it studies the variation of the difference value between the area of the proposed object and the area of its convex hull.

It controls the convergence of the iterative process. Moreover it performs further analysis of the proposed object and it formulates a message of correct or incorrect segmentation.

It is important to notice that we have elaborated a strategy allowing the adaptation of the computational complexity to the complexity of the image organisation and allowing a control of the proposed result.

CONCLUSION

In conclusion, at present there exists two approaches in Image Analysis oriented toward Artificial Intelligence.
The first one concerns the integration of image analysis features in Expert System to solve some specific problem supported by image information.
The second one concerns the integration of Expert Systems to perform different tasks in Image Understanding such as segmentation and interpretation.

The elaboration of an intelligent image understanding system has to integrate a mutual cooperation between the two approaches. As mentionned by Shapiro [4] about the future orientations of vision systems many efforts have to be done on the use of knowledge, particularly in surface representations.

REFERENCES

1. M. Brady, Computational Approaches to Image Understanding, ACM, Computing surveys, 14, 1, pp 3-73, 1982.
2. D. A. Huffmann, Impossible objects on nonsense sentences, Machine Intelligence, 6, pp 295-323, 1978.
3. M. B. Clowes, on seeing things, Artificial Intelligence, 2, 1, pp 79-116, 1971.
4. L. G. Shapiro, Computer Vision Systems. Post Present and Future. Pictorial Data Analysis, Haralick ed. Nato Asi Series 1983.
5. J. P. Crettez, Modélisation des voies visuelles primaires : première étape de la perception des formes. Thèse d'Etat, Paris VI, 1984.
6. F. Fogelman, Contributions à une théorie du calcul sur réseaux. Thèse d'Etat, Grenoble, 1985.
7. M. Nagao, Strategies for Human-like Image Understanding Systems, Proceedings of Cognitiva 85, pp 26-32, CESTA, Paris.
8. M. Nagao, Control Strategies in Pattern Analysis, Pattern Recognition, vol 17, n°1, pp 45-56, 1984.
9. L. C. Shapiro, R. Haralick, Structural descriptions and inexact matching, IEEE Trans Pami, 3, 1981.
10. U. Montanari, On the optimal detection of curves in noisy pictures. Comm. ACM., 14, n°15, pp 335-345, 1971.

11. H. Ney, Dynamic programming as a technique for pattern recognition, Proc of 6th ICPR, pp 1119-1125, IEEE Computer Society Press, 1982.

12. T. Matsuyama, Knowledge organization and control structure in Image Understanding Proc of 7th ICPR, pp 1118-1127, IEEE Computer Society Press, 1984.

13. D. Marr, Vision, Freeman ed. San Francisco, 1982.

14. A. Rosenfeld, Image Analysis : problems, progress and prospects, Pattern Recognition, vol 17, n°1, pp 3-12, 1984.

15. L. S. Davis, A. Rosenfeld, Cooperative processes for low level vision : a survey. Artificial Intelligence, vol 17, pp 245-263, 1981.

16. J. K. Tsotsos, Knowledge of the visual process : content, form and use. Proc of 6th ICPR, pp 654-669, IEEE Computer Society Press, 1982.

17. R. J. Brachman, What IS-A is and isn't : an analysis of taxonomic links in semantic networks. IEEE Computer, vol 16, n°10, pp 30-36, 1983.

18. H. Farreny, Les Systèmes Experts principes et exemples. Cepadues ed. Toulouse, France, 1985.

19. A. Bonnet, L'Intelligence Artificielle : promesses et réalités, Interéditions, Paris, 1984.

20. F. Hayes-Roth, D.A. Waterman, D.B. Lenat, Building Expert System. Addison Wesley, 1983.

21. T. Matsuyama, V. Hwang, Sigma : A framework for Image Understanding. Integration of Bottom-up and Top-down Analyses. Proc. of IJCAI, pp 908-915. 1985.

22. A. M. Nozif, M.D. Levine, Low level image segmentation : an expert system. IEEE Trans PAMI, vol 6, pp 555-577, 1984.

23. J. M. Chassery, C. Garbay, An iterative segmentation method based on a contextual color and shape criterion. IEEE Trans PAMI, vol 6, ppp 794-800, 1984.

MULTIPROCESSOR ARCHITECTURES HARDWARE AND SOFTWARE

A SYSTOLIC ARCHITECTURE FOR CARTESIAN – TO – POLAR COORDINATE

MAPPING[1]

C. Braccini, A. Grattarola, A. Maestrini, and T. Vernazza

Department of Communication, Computer and System Sciences
University of Genova
Viale Causa 13, Genova, Italy

ABSTRACT

An optimized parallel architecture is presented for real time image processing. The architecture, suitable for VLSI technology implementation, performs efficient cartesian – to – polar coordinate mapping over raster scan images. The goal of the mapping is to exploit the properties of the log – polar computational space to perform classes of space – variant operators, useful in machine vision applications, by means of shift – invariant operators. After a description of the architecture, the optimization methodology is illustrated and a numeric example is presented.

INTRODUCTION

Scale invariant processing[1-3] is needed in image filtering whenever an image containing objects of unknown size must be preprocessed (e.g., for noise cleaning or edge crispening) before the object recognition step is performed by one of the available scale invariant pattern recognition techniques[4-8]. Such a preprocessing is aimed at preserving the shape of the pattern, so that the overall processing is truly scale invariant. The systems characterized by this property, which are a subset of the shift – variant filters, can be implemented in several ways. Among the possible solutions, a very interesting one for its implementation simplicity is considered here. It is based on using classical shift – invariant systems operating in a suitably transformed image domain (sometimes called "computational space"), where the transformed domain is the $(\ln r, \vartheta)$ plane, (r, ϑ) being a polar coordinate system centered on the image . The log – polar domain turns out to be very well suited to low – level scene analysis, also in connection with the behaviour of the peripheral visual system in man[9-12].

In the subsequent sections we introduce a parallel architecture which exploits VLSI technology to obtain images in the new computational plane $(\ln r, \vartheta)$ in real time (or with time delays of no practical importance for TV rate processing). In section two we describe the system in its basic components from both hardware and software viewpoints. In section three the functional scheme of

---

[1] Work supported by the M.P.I. of Italy.

each processor is sketched. In section four we discuss the structure optimization problem and define some possible indexes of merit and the most important design variables to be considered. In section five we give an example of a possible optimum structure. Finally, in section six, we mention briefly some further applications besides the simple coordinate transformation.

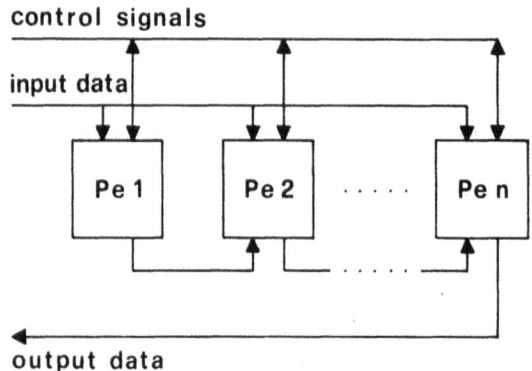

Fig. 1 : Basic interconnection network among the processors.

SYSTEM ARCHITECTURE AND ALGORITHMS

Our parallel system can be viewed as a SIMD one[13,14], because all the processors execute the same procedures on different data, i.e. on different image regions. Therefore, the time required by the slowest processor represents the time that the whole system needs to execute the transformation of the source image. The input data are fed to the processors through a q − bit bus whose speed is the upper bound of the system throughput, where q is the grey level quantization (i.e. each pixel can assume one of 2^q different values). Referring to the possible applications of our system, we suppose to receive data at a normal TV raster scan rate (64 μs/line). Every processor is given a dedicated logic in order to store only data belonging to the image region it has to process. The output bus is organized as a daisy − chain structure, i.e. all the processors are linked sequentially. Each processor, at the proper time, puts its data into the pixel stream coming from the previous one (see Figure 1). A different choice could be an output bus common to all the processors: hovewer, this solution gives some problems because of the high fan − out that every processor should sustain. It is worth noticing that no alignment network is needed, due to the absence of communications among processors and of a central memory. It follows that the system architecture is greatly simplified and easily implementable[15].

Each processor processes an image region whose boundaries are defined by two arcs and two radius segments,

$$R_1 \leqslant r \leqslant R_2$$
$$\vartheta_1 \leqslant \vartheta \leqslant \vartheta_2 \tag{1}$$

where

$$x^2 + y^2 = r^2$$
$$y / x = tg(\vartheta)$$

See Figure 2 where the first quadrant only is displayed for simplicity. Obviously it must be: $R \leqslant N/2$ if N is the image linear size.

In this way each processor is defined by two pairs of values (R_1, R_2) and $(\vartheta_1, \vartheta_2)$: changing these values produces a different total number of processors and a different throughput of the system.

The choice made here to partition the source image, besides being simple and clear, presents the great advantage to simplify the output of the processed image by rows (constant radius) or by columns (constant angle). This structured output is of basic importance whenever we need a fast access to memory. Besides, by properly varying these radius – and – angle pairs, we can evenly distribute the input data sequence among the processors. In this way each processor gets a constant and bounded maximum number of pixels every row being scanned, so that all the pixels coming from a row can be processed before next row pixels are available on the input bus, and the time required for processing is constant for all the processors.

The algorithm that implements the coordinate transformation on each processor is extremely simple: once the image region to be processed is defined, by the pairs (R_1, R_2) and $(\vartheta_1, \vartheta_2)$, each processor stores the pixels of the (x,y) grid belonging to its region. Afterwards, it scans all the pairs (r, ϑ) which satisfy Eq. (1), keeping the radius or the angle value fixed. For each couple (r, ϑ) whose ordinate $y = r \sin(\vartheta)$ equals the row presently stored, it computes also the abscissa $x = r \cos(\vartheta)$ and then stores the pixel whose coordinates are (x,y) in the output memory, at the address (r, ϑ).

In this way a minimum distance interpolation is performed. For more sophisticated interpolation, such as the bilinear one, some more operations would be needed, but the kernel of the algorithm would not change: obviously the time bounds would become more critical[16,17,18].

For each processor, the time constraints are determined by the number of operations to be performed while each row of the input image is scanned. This number linearly depends (1) on the number of the $(\ln r, \vartheta)$ plane pixels whose grey level can be computed when the data of input row i are available. Let $\pi(i)$ be this number. (2) on the number $(R_2 - R_1 + 1)$ of radius samples or $(\vartheta_2 - \vartheta_1 + 1)$ of angle samples of the image region to be processed, depending on whether the pairs (r, ϑ) are scanned keeping the angle or the radius fixed. The scanning procedure is chosen according to an efficiency criterion, so that the resulting number of scanning steps will be $\min(R_2 - R_1 + 1, \vartheta_2 - \vartheta_1 + 1)$. Let n be this number.

Therefore, if $\mu(i)$ and $\alpha(i)$ are the number of multiplications and additions to be performed for input row i, we can write

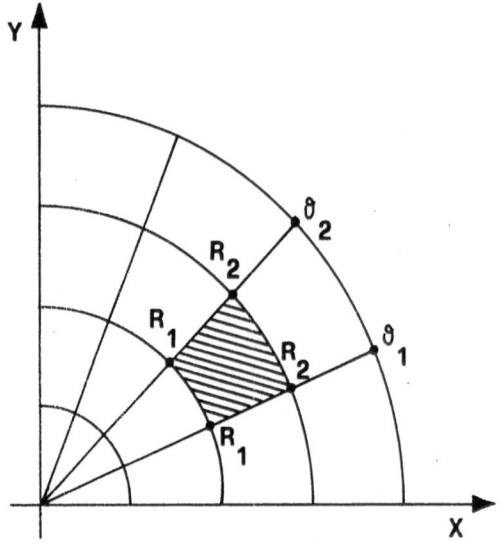

Fig. 2 – Parameters of the image region processed by a single processor.

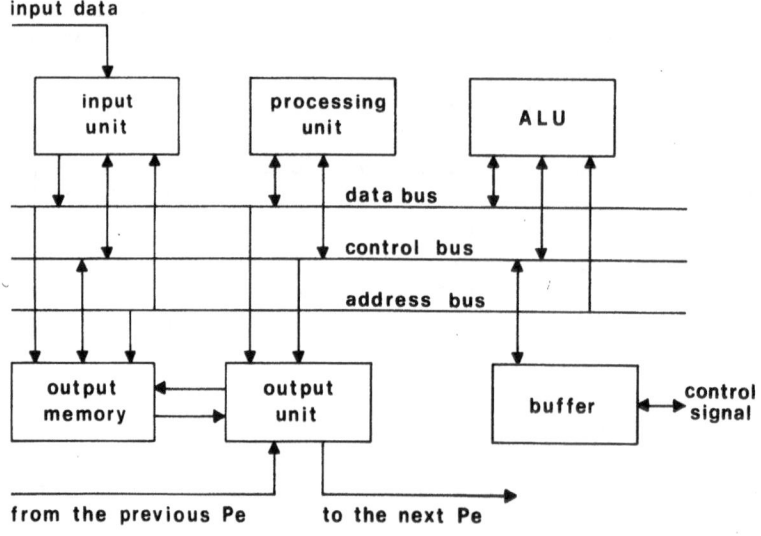

Fig. 3 – Simple block scheme of the processor.

$$\begin{vmatrix} \mu(i) \\ \alpha(i) \end{vmatrix} = \begin{vmatrix} O_1 & O_2 \\ O_3 & O_4 \end{vmatrix} \begin{vmatrix} \pi(i) \\ n \end{vmatrix}$$

Hence, each processor must be able to perform m multiplications and a additions in the time one row is scanned, being

$$m = \max \ \mu(i) \qquad 0 \leqslant i \leqslant N - 1$$
$$a = \max \ \alpha(i) \qquad 0 \leqslant i \leqslant N - 1$$

It follows that

$$\begin{vmatrix} m \\ a \end{vmatrix} = \begin{vmatrix} O_1 & O_2 \\ O_3 & O_4 \end{vmatrix} \begin{vmatrix} p \\ n \end{vmatrix} = O(p,n)$$

where $\quad p = \max_{1 \leqslant i \leqslant N-1} \pi(i)$

Sometimes, an additive constant may be added due to the specific algorithm implementation (see Sec. 5).

INTERNAL PROCESSORS ARCHITECTURE

From the functional viewpoint, each processor can be viewed as a four block system: see Figure 3.

The first block corresponds to the input unit endowed with a double management memory: it can be read with random access (RAM) and written in a list (F.I.F.O.) fashion. A controller, asyncronous with respect to the central unit (second block), stores sequentially the input pixels for every row, getting started by a proper syncronism. When storing ends, the central unit (a finite state machine with a microprogrammed memory for more flexibility[19]) executes the allocation algorithm, exploiting a dedicated arithmetic unit (third block). The arithmetic unit greatly affects the system throughput: depending on the degree of parallelism used to implement it, different operators $O(p,n)$ are obtained and consequently different processing speeds. Pixels of the $(\ln r, \vartheta)$ plane are stored in a memory unit which we can logically place in the output unit (fourth block). This latter, like the input unit, is able to send data out leaving the central unit free to process new pixels. Like input memory, output memory too can be managed in two ways: it can be written onto with random access by the central unit and can be read from sequentially (F.I.F.O. policy) during the output step. Output unit also needs a multiplexer in order to mix its data with the data coming from the previous processor (see again Figure 1) through some synchronization registers.

OPTIMIZATION OF THE STRUCTURE

Here we propose an optimization methodology suitable not only for this particular application, but also for more sophisticated types of image processing based on the proposed architecture. In fact the special characteristic of our parallel architecture, i.e. the absence of an interprocessor network, prevents us from exploiting some useful systematic methodologies, which can be found in the literature[20-23], to reach an optimum implementation of our algorithms.

First of all, the optimization methodology is described in the case of cartesian – to – polar coordinate mapping, then its most general form is derived.

The parameters affecting our system from a design viewpoint are:

- the total number of processors of the system;
- the system throughput, i.e. the coordinate transformation speed that should ideally equal the speed of every single processor (in order to avoid idle processors);
- the output memory size, which can be very critical when a large image region has to be processed by a single processor;
- the transformation accuracy, i.e. the number of bits used to define a data word or an address word and the interpolation function.

The problem of optimizing this system can be seen as a constrained minimization problem. We must minimize the total number of processors with three constraints, obtaining: (1) a certain minimum transformation speed, (2) an output memory size compatible with the available area on the chip (depending on the present integration techniques, VLSI), and (3) a reasonable global error (depending on the specific application).

Among the various error sources affecting the transformation from cartesian to polar coordinates[24], the most important ones are the quantization of the trigonometric functions and the different sampling law of the two grids[25-28]. In fact, while the linear coordinates (x,y,r) depend only on image size (their maximum value is $N/2$), the angular coordinate (ϑ) accuracy depends on the number of bits used to store the sin and cos functions. It has been shown[24] that 8 bits are enough to have a maximum error in address computation less than the one implicitly made during polar resampling.

As for data, accuracy is strictly tied to the number of grey levels used to represent the source image, unless interpolation techniques different from the nearest neighbour (where no operation on the data is required) are used.

As for the other two bonds, we define a function that suitably weights the system throughput and the memory size. This function must be kept constant while minimizing the number of processors.

The time needed to process the source image depends on the pair (m,a) through a function $F(m,a)$ that expresses the level of parallelism used to perform different instructions and then, through the operator O, depends on the pair (p,n). Consequently, once we fix the maximum time T within which to perform the coordinate transformation, we must minimize the total number of processors in such a way that the possible values of (p,n) satisfy the following expression:

$$F(m,a) = T \qquad (2)$$

If $F(m,a) < T$ is true, we have different processing times among the processors, therefore some of them can be idle and their throughput could be improved.

As for output memory, if we want to have enough chip area to integrate it, it is necessary to satisfy the following bond:

$$(R_2 - R_1 + 1)(\vartheta_2 - \vartheta_1 + 1) \leqslant M \qquad (3)$$

where M is a constant depending on the number q of bits of data words (2^q are the grey levels) and on the technology used for integration. Moreover, it has been shown[24] that all the other memory blocks of the processor are size irrelevant with respect to the output memory. The solution chosen minimizes the total number of processors taking into account only bond (2): the output memory is implemented externally in a separate chip. In fact, while it is easy to implement a RAM memory chip large enough for our needs (for example 2Kbytes if $q = 8$) in the present technology, several problems raise if we try to integrate a memory of this size together with all the logic we need for our processor. If we wanted to take into account bond (3) as well, we would be forced to design very small storage processors.

The optimization technique we propose allows us to minimize the number of processors that can satisfy the time constraints imposed by the desired image processing algorithms. It is mainly fitted for algorithms requiring essentially a sequence of additions and multiplications, and therefore also for algorithms operating in the computational space (ln r, ϑ), to perform scale–invariant processing by means of simple shift–invariant filtering. The optimization methodology is based on the following steps:

– from the input data rate and the number of operations to be performed on each pixel, compute the maximum number of multiplications and additions in any row of the scanned image, i.e. the vector

$$\left| \begin{matrix} m \\ \\ a \end{matrix} \right| = O\,(p,n)$$

– depending on the possible overlapping of the sequence of operations in the desired algorithms, compute the maximum time needed in any row to process the input data, i.e.:

$$T = F\,(m,a)$$

– minimize the number of processors with the constraint:

$$T \leqslant N\,t_p$$

where t_p is the input data rate (μs/pixel) and N is the input image linear dimension. For example, for a row of 512 pixels and an input data rate of 8 Msample/sec, the value of such a constraint is 64 microsec.

NUMERIC EXAMPLE

We refer to a source image whose linear size is $N = 512$ pixels. Each pixel is quantized in 256 gray levels ($q = 8$). Using a minimum distance interpolation function, from the algorithm implementation it is easy to show that the O operator is defined by :

$$\begin{aligned} m &= 2p + n \\ a &= p + 2 \end{aligned}$$

In fact, for each pixel of the (ln r, ϑ) plane whose grey level is computed, two multiplications must be performed:

$$\begin{aligned} x &= r\,\cos(\vartheta) \\ y &= r\,\sin(\vartheta) \end{aligned}$$

Moreover, one addition for each pixel is necessary to transform the computed absolute ascissa x into the actual address in the input memory, being such address the distance from the first stored pixel of row y.

The maximum level of parallelism consists in performing all the operations at the same time, so that the time necessary to perform the maximum number of multiplications and additions F(m,a) is proportional to p, that is to the maximum number of pixels whose grey level is computed for each row. For example, if each pixel is processed in 1 μs and the scanning time is 64 μs/line, bond (2) becomes F(m,a) = 64 μs and the maximum number of pixels that can be processed for each line is therefore p = 64.

In the case of operations performed sequentially, if t_m and t_a are the times needed to perform a multiplication and an addition respectively, we can derive the following:

$$F(m,a) = m\, t_m + a\, t_a = (2p + n)t_m + (p + 2)t_a$$

If we suppose to perform a multiplication or three additions in 1 μs and that the scanning time is again 64 μs/line, it follows that

$$F(m,a) = [\, 2p + n + (p + 2)/3\,]\ \mu s$$

and bond (2) becomes

$$[\, 2p + n + (p + 2)/3\,] = 64$$

from which it is possible to derive p for each n. Refer to tables 1 and 2: in both cases we used the solution with external output memory. However, if we want to satisfy bond (3) and have just one chip per processor, the value of 1k is a practical choice for M (q = 8). It follows then that the total number of processors is about twice the numbers reported in tables 1 and 2.

CONCLUSIONS

It is a fact that the processing algorithm we propose is nothing but an image resampling. However, in our case it is impossible to apply already developed systematic procedures for image resampling, like the one described in Warpenburg[22], because we must compute a non-uniform resampling, i.e. a resampling whose spatial spacing varies in the original image, getting more sparse and scattered as it moves farther from the center. Still the proposed architecture operates in a SIMD fashion[22], and exhibits the following advantage. Differently from Warpenburg[22], we do not need any inter-processor transfer, so that no interconnection network is needed and the resulting structure is very simple and easy to implement. This is even more true when recalling that communication between chips is expensive[23]: therefore architectures like the one described here, in which communication is localized, are convenient. The locality of communications of the proposed architecture represents the "wavefront" or "systolic" type of computation[23]. Using the terminology of Seitz[23], we could describe our system as a homogeneous machine, in which each node (i.e. each processor) has only two channels of communication: an input bus, shared by all the nodes, and an output bus directed to the following processor. Here applies the model of computational arrays[23].

Finally it is important to note that our system can be used also for more sophisticated processing, like scale invariant filtering[2,3], provided that only multiplications and additions are required. Then it can be easily optimized by the proposed procedure, once the O operator is derived from the algorithm that performs the desired processing.

TABLE 1 –

Source image partitioning among the processors (first quadrant only) with constraint of maximum parallelism.

Processor	R_1	R_2	ϑ_1	ϑ_2
1	1	255	52	90
2	1	255	28	51
3	140	255	0	27
4	71	138	0	27
5	34	70	0	27
6	16	33	0	27
7	8	15	0	27
8	1	7	13	27
9	1	7	1	12
10	1	7	0	1

TABLE 2

Source image partitioning among the processors (first quadrant only) in the case of sequential computation.

Processor	R_1	R_2	ϑ_1	ϑ_2
1	1	255	77	90
2	1	255	65	77
3	1	255	54	65
4	1	255	44	53
5	1	255	36	44
6	1	255	27	35
7	1	255	20	27
8	161	255	0	20
9	133	160	0	20
10	110	132	0	20
11	90	109	0	20
12	72	89	0	20
13	56	71	0	20
14	44	55	0	20
15	33	43	0	20
16	24	32	0	20
17	17	23	0	20
18	12	16	0	20
19	8	11	0	20
20	5	7	0	20
21	1	4	13	20
22	1	4	6	12
23	1	4	0	5

REFERENCES

1. D.Casasent, D.Psaltis, New optical transforms for pattern recognition, *Proc. IEEE*, 65:77 (1977).

2. C.Braccini, G.Gambardella, Linear shift variant filtering for form invariant processing of linearly scaled signals, *Signal Processing*, 4:209 (1982).

3. C.Braccini, A.Grattarola, Scale invariant image filtering with point and line simmetry, *in*: "Digital Image Analysis", S.Levialdi, ed., Pitman, London (1984).

4. C.Braccini, G.Gambardella, Signal detection and estimation techniques based on linear shift variant filtering and short space frequency variant spectral analysis, *Proc. of the Italy–USA workshop on Digital Signal Processing*, Portovenere, 164 (1981).

5. D.Casasent, D.Psaltis, Position,rotation and scale invariant optical correlation, *Applied Optics*, 15:1795 (1976).

6. C.Braccini, G.Gambardella, A.Grattarola, The form invariant 2D filtering and its application to pattern recognition, *in*: "Signal Processing II: Theories and Applications", Proc. of EUSIPCO 1983, North–Holland, Amsterdam, 207 (1983).

7. D.Casasent, D.Psaltis, Deformation invariant, space variant optical pattern recognition, *in*: "Progress in Optics, vol.XVI," E. Wolf ed., North Holland (1978).

8. A. Rosenfeld, Image pattern recognition, *Proc.IEEE*, 69:596 (1981).

9. C.Weiman, G.Chaikin, Logarithmic spiral grids for image processing and display, *Comp. Graphics and Image Processing*, 11:197 (1979).

10. P.S. Schenker, Toward the robot eye: isomorphic image recognition for machine vision, *SPIE vol.283, 3–D Machine Perception*, 30 (1981).

11. P.S. Schenker, K.M. Wong, E.G. Cande, Fast adaptive algorithms for low–level scene analysis: applications of polar–exponential grid representation to high–speed, scale and rotation invariant target segmentation, *SPIE vol. 28, Techniques and Applications of Image Understanding*, 47 (1987).

12. C. Braccini, G. Gambardella, A. Grattarola, The use of Computational spaces for 3–D object recognition, *Proc. of the Int. Conf. on Digital Signal Processing*, Florence, 759 (1984).

13. A.Rosenfeld, Parallel image processing using cellular arrays, *IEEE Comp. Mag.*, 16:14 (1984).

14. V.Zakharov, Parallelism and array processing, *IEEE Trans. on Comp.*, 33:45 (1984).

15. C.Mead, L.Conway, Introduction to VLSI systems, Addison Wesley, Reading, chapter 8 (1980).

16. W.K.Pratt, "Digital image processing", Wiley, New York (1978).

17. C.Braccini, G.Gambardella, A.Grattarola, Digital image processing by means of generalized scale invariant filters, *in*: "Issues in Acoustic Signal/Image Processing and Recognition," C.H. Chen Ed., NATO ASI series vol. F1, Springer–Verlag, Berlin (1983).

18. C.Braccini, G.Marino, Fast geometrical manipulations of digital images, *Comp. Graphics and Image Processing*, 13:127 (1980).

19. A.K.Agrawala, Foundations of microprogramming, Academic Press, New York (1976).

20. D.I.Moldovan, On the design of algorithms for VLSI systolic arrays, *Proc. IEEE*, 71:113 (1983).

21. G.J.Lie, B.H.Wah, The design of optimal systolic arrays, *IEEE Trans. on Comp.*, 34:66 (1985).

22. M.R.Warpenburg, L.J.Siegel, SIMD image resampling, *IEEE Trans. on Comp.*, 10:934 (1982).

23. C.L.Seitz, Concurrent VLSI architectures, *IEEE Trans. on Comp.*, 33:1247 (1984).

24. C.Braccini, A.Grattarola, A.Maestrini, T.Vernazza, Study of a parallel architecture for cartesian–to–polar coordinate mapping oriented to VLSI implementation (in Italian), *DIST Technical report*, University of Genoa (1984).

25. R.C.Gonzalez, P.Wintz, "Digital image processing", Prentice–Hall, Englewood Cliffs, chapter 9 (1977).

26. G.M.Robbins, T.S.Huang, Inverse filtering for linear shift variant imaging systems, *Proc. IEEE*, 60:862 (1972).

27. A.V.Oppenheim, R.W.Schafer, "Digital signal processing" Prentice–Hall, Englewood Cliffs, chapter 9 (1975).

28. L.R.Rabiner, B.Gold, "Theory and application of digital signal processing", Prentice–Hall, Englewood Cliffs, chapter 5 (1975).

MODULAR ARCHITECTURE FOR A FAST 2D CONVOLVER

L.Borghesi, E.Giuliano, G.Musso
F.Cabiati, and P.Ottonello

Elettronica S.Giorgio ELSAG S.p.A. - Genova
Dipartimento di Fisica - Università di Genova

ABSTRACT

Convolution, one of the most widely used functions in early vision processing, is, at the same time, highly demanding in terms of computing power. This paper describes a dedicated coprocessor able to perform 1D and 2D convolutions; the latter case is applicable only if the convolving bidimensional filter is separable. Details concerning the main building blocks are given together with experimental results showing the overall performances of the system.

INTRODUCTION

Image processing and feature extraction generally represent the first stages in an artificial vision process, in which some level of understanding of a real scene is obtained from information present in one or several bidimensional scene images. These processing procedures, belonging to the early vision area,[1] usually are intensive in terms of computations to be done on large rates of acquired data. On the other hand, feature extraction procedures cannot be oversimplified without losing great part of the information present in the image or getting detection accuracies too poor, and generally not sufficient, for building up a consistent image description.

As described by D.Marr and H.Hildreth,[2] the Difference-of-Gaussian filter plays a central role in early stages of biological and artificial vision system, particularly in edge extraction processes.[2,3] The basic idea of the Difference-of-Gaussian filter is closely related to the following formulas :[4]

$$\nabla^2[G(x,y) * I(x,y)] = [\nabla^2 G(x,y)] * I(x,y) \qquad (1)$$

where :

$G(x,y) = K \cdot \exp -(4 \cdot (x^2 + y^2)/w^2)$ represents the filter impulse response

∇^2 represents the Laplacian operator ;

* means bidimensional spatial convolution.

In the computational model described by (1), the Gaussian filter perform a smoothing process on the image, and the Laplacian operator, due to its second order derivative content, transforms smoothed brightness edges into zero-crossing points in the transformed image. Moreover, taking into account the separability properties of ($\nabla^2 G$) operator ($\nabla^2 G$ is a sum of bidimensional functions obtained by the product of unidimensional functions in x and y),[5] this model is suitable for fast implementation: indeed each 2D separable convolution may be executed by means of a couple of cascaded 1D convolutions :

$$\left[g_1(x) \cdot g_2(y) \right] * I(x,y) = g_2(y) * \left[g_1(x) * I(x,y) \right] =$$
$$g_1(x) * \left[g_2(y) * I(x,y) \right] \qquad (2)$$

In doing computations as described in (2), in the discrete case, the number of multiplications required for computing a transformed pixel is 2N instead of N^2, where N is the size of the square discrete convolution matrix.

Just to give an example of one possible use of edges in the field of Robot Vision, we can mention the Generalized Hough Transform method, applied to 2D shape recognition independent of translation, rotation and scaling factor.[6] The recognition process is based on a matching procedure between all edges detected in the image and shape prototypes described in terms of their visible boundaries. Performances of such a recognizer strongly depend on the accuracy in estimating edge location and orientation by a spatial operator, which as a consequence, must be generally defined using large convolution masks. In addition to edge extraction procedures, shortly discussed before, we have to note the general importance of performing fast convolution in the broad field of image processing; each time we can define or approximate a convolution mask with a separable matrix, we can implement this convolution in a fast way.

This paper presents the implementation of a fast 1D-2D convolver, realized on a programmable special purpose hardware which uses separability properties for 2D convolutions. The size of the convolution matrix, its coefficients and the order of x and y partial convolutions are settled, as parameters, by the user program. This hardware has been designed and implemented with a modular structure, capable of being implemented using custom VLSI technologies.

GENERAL DESCRIPTION

This coprocessor operates in connection with a host computer to which it appears as a DMA controlled peripheral calculating convolutions on images (512x512 pixels, 256 grey levels). In fact, as far as the computer is concerned, the convolver, in its normal mode of operation, receives the original image, performs convolution on all the video buffer and returns it back to the host computer.

The general architecture of the coprocessor is sketched in Fig. 1, evidencing the three main blocks :

- Video Memory (V.M.) ;
- Control & Interface ;
- Arithmetic Unit (A.U.) .

Being the coprocessor structure highly modular, the overall performance depends on the number of elementary modules present inside the V.M. and A.U. sections. The convolver in its minimal configuration is equipped with 256 Kbytes of RAM and with an arithmetic module implemented around a core of eight multiplier circuits.

Operations, after the image transfer from the computer to the V.M., proceed as follows :

1) the coefficients (up to 32, 8 bits wide) and additional information concerning the desired convolution are sequencially transferred from the computer into 8 bit registers inside the A.U.;

2) the convolution is initiated by a "GO" command from the keyboard or by program: data are picked up in sequence from the V.M. and processed according to the discrete convolution algorithm as addition of suitable products between elements of the image and filter coefficients. Calculations are made without any approximation by 8x8 multipliers and 20 bit adders ;

3) the results may be stored as 8 bit words in the same memory from which input data flow toward the A.U. or in a different memory module when available. In the first case neither item of information is lost nor does overlap of image occur because a result is available when the corresponding pixel in the original image is no longer required for the calculation. The 8 bits are selected among the 20 bits of each result by means of a final approximating circuit.

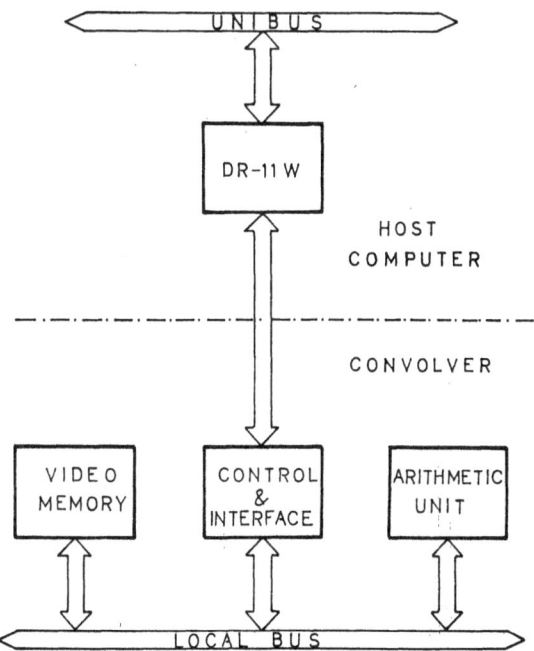

Fig. 1. Block diagram of the convolver.

When a greater precision is requested, a second operating mode can be selected allowing each result to be immediately transferred (as a 16 bit word) to the computer with no local storage. The overall processing time, once the image is stored in the V.M., is linearly dependent on the size of the filter and on the hardware configuration of the coprocessor. In its minimum configuration, the coprocessor can perform 1D convolution of a 512x 512 pixels image with an 8 coefficient filter in 35 msec. This figure direct· ly derives from the processing power of the arithmetic module, which reaches 128 MOPS (Million Operations Per Second).

IMPLEMENTATION DETAILS

The Arithmetic Unit

The A.U. is a FIR digital filter operating with constant coefficients on data words flowing from the V.M. at the main clock rate of 8 MHz. In Fig. 2 the canonical FIR architecture is shown; it is worth noting that the addition of all the different product terms may be obtained in two different ways both with certain drawbacks. In fact a tree structure of two term adders, which could be a first solution, is intrinsically non modular; on the other hand the alternative solution of cascading several adders is slower.

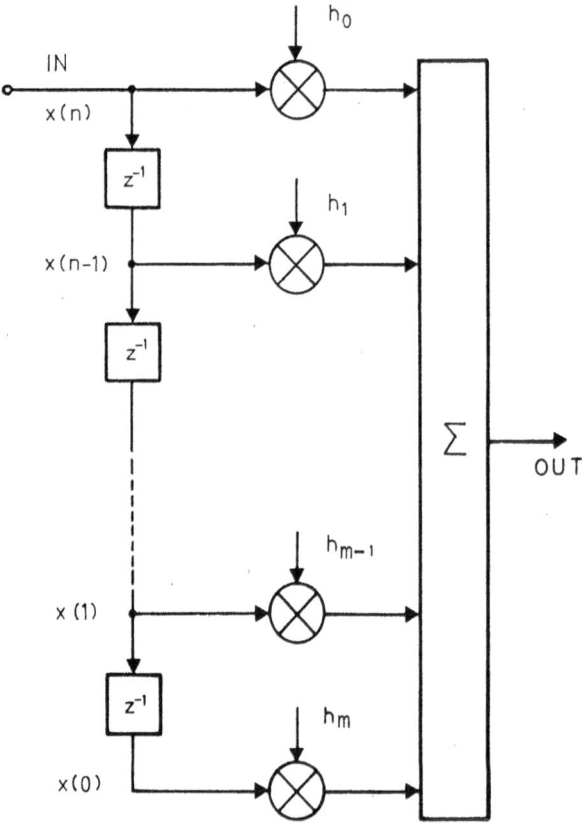

Fig. 2. Canonical FIR filter architecture; the block Σ is actually implemented with several two input adders.

It is easy to obtain a more efficient architecture by starting from the discrete form of the convolution integral :

$$y(n) = \sum_{i=0}^{m} x(n-i) \cdot h(i)$$

by defining, as usual, the delay operator z^{-1} as :

$$z^{-1} \left[x(n) \right] = x(n-1)$$

and, finally, by noting that the filter coefficients $h(i) = h_i$ = constant. The above relation becomes :

$$y(n) = x(n) \cdot h_0 + x(n-1) \cdot h_1 + \ldots + x(n-m) \cdot h_m =$$

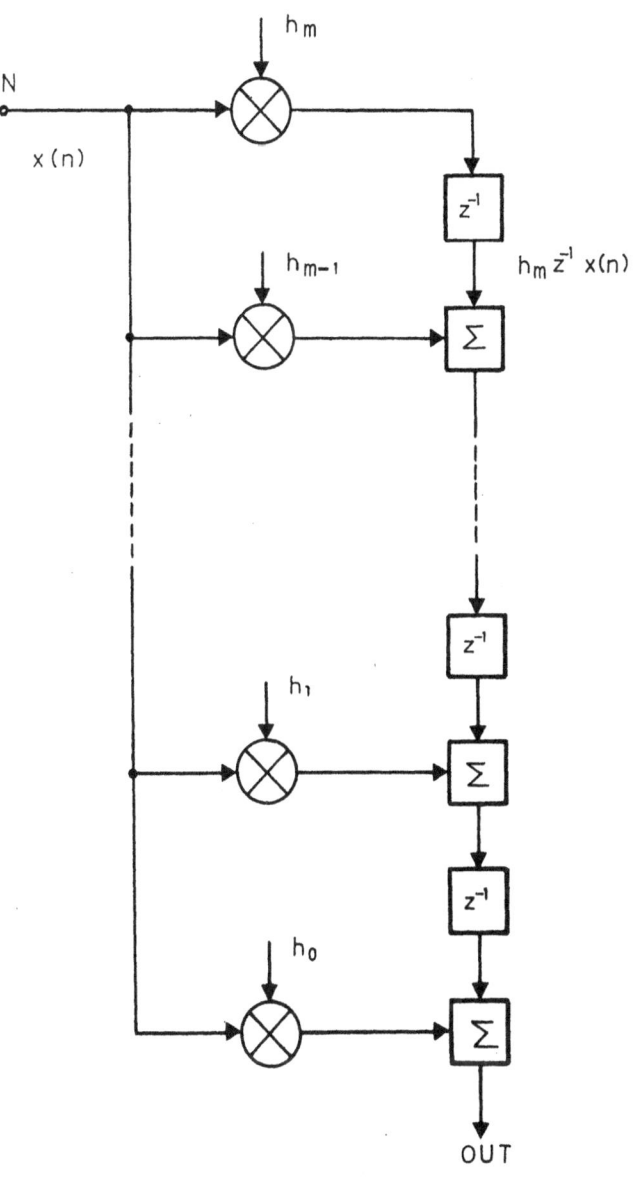

Fig. 3. Modified FIR filter architecture.

$$= x(n) \cdot h_o + z^{-1} x(n) \cdot h_1 + z^{-2} x(n) \cdot h_2 + \ldots + z^{-m} x(n) \cdot h_m =$$

$$= x(n) \cdot h_o + z^{-1} \left[x(n) \cdot h_1 + z^{-1} \left[x(n) \cdot h_2 + \ldots + z^{-1} \left[x(n) \cdot h_m \right] \ldots \right] \right]$$

In Fig. 3 the modified architecture,[7] directly related to the last expression, is shown. The main difference between this architecture and the canonic-

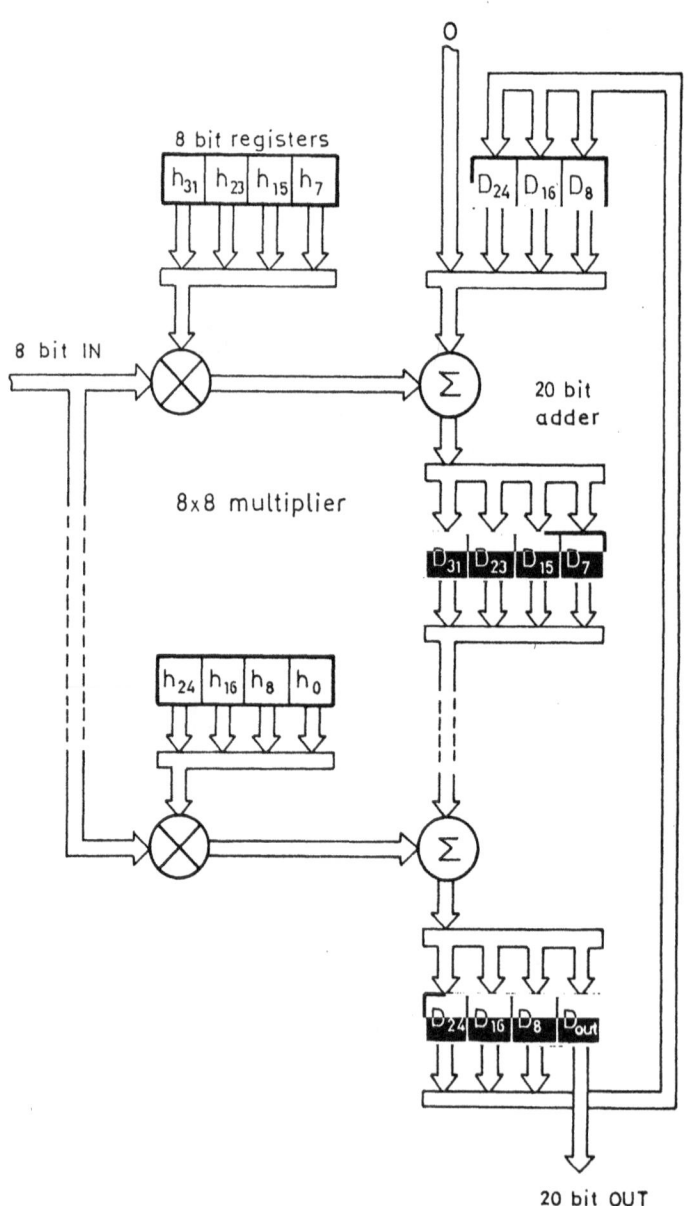

Fig. 4. Schematic diagram of the arithmetic module. Convolutions with a filter size larger than the number of multiplying stages are performed by recirculating partial results inside the module.

al one can be easily understood by noting that each stage both multiplies
and adds its own result to that obtained by the upstream stage during the
previous time clock interval. In this case it would be possible to increase
the filter size by inserting or cascading further stages without any other
change. The arithmetic module of the present convolver implements an improved version of the structure of Fig. 3, with eight multiplier-adder stages.
The main novelty, as is evident from the schematic diagram of Fig. 4, is the
possibility of recirculating intermediate results inside the module. In fact
each pixel in the original image can be convolved with 8, 16, 24 or 32 different coefficients by an hardware based on only 8 stages; this performance
is obviously only possible at cost of a longer processing time. For example
a convolution with a 32 coefficient filter proceeds through 4 steps each
operating with 8 coefficients. The process starts with a programmed number
(O in Fig.4) set by the approximating circuit (see below) at one input of
the first adder and with coefficients h_{31}, h_{30}, ... h_{24} (first column) at
the input of the multipliers. Eight terms are calculated during the first
clock time interval. At the next clock pulse the partial result, stored in
the D_{24} register, is put back at the input of the first adder; the second
step begins and other eight terms calculated with coefficients stored in
the second column are added. The process is repeated recirculating the content of register D_{16} and D_8 ; then the fourth step ends with a final result
(i.e. an addition on 32 terms) available at the register D_{out} .

The input and the output of the adder chain in the module can be used
as cascading input and output when several (up to 4) modules are connected
in order to improve the overall performances. In the first module additions
start again from a programmed number while in the following ones the input
for the first adder is supplied by the output of the upstream module.

The Video Memory Unit

The memory module has a capacity of 256 Kbytes and can be thought of
as formed by four independent groups of 64 Kbytes each (see Fig. 5). In the
present case of processing of bidimensional images and in general when data
must be read or written according to a previously known sequence, efficient
memory arrangements are possible that allow to exchange data at a rate higher then that which the single memory circuit could perform. In this case
the addressing and control logic can direct the exchange of two words between the memory and the A.U. during each, 125 nsec long, time clock interval in spite of the longer access time (about 150 nsec) of the employed
high density static RAMs. The image pixels are cyclically sorted out by the
control logic into the different A, B, C, D groups. More precisely if (i,j)
are the coordinates of a pixel, its value will be stored respectively in
group A, B, C or D according to whether :

$$\left| i + j \right|_{\text{mod. } 4} = 0, \ 1, \ 2, \ 3$$

The same control logic allows the access to the video information row by
row or column by column.

For a more general description of efficient multiple addressing methods,
the intersted reader can see Van Voorhis.[8]

As a final comment on this memory module one should mention that the input rate is compatible with most TV standard; that makes possible a future extension allowing image acquisition directly from a common TV camera.

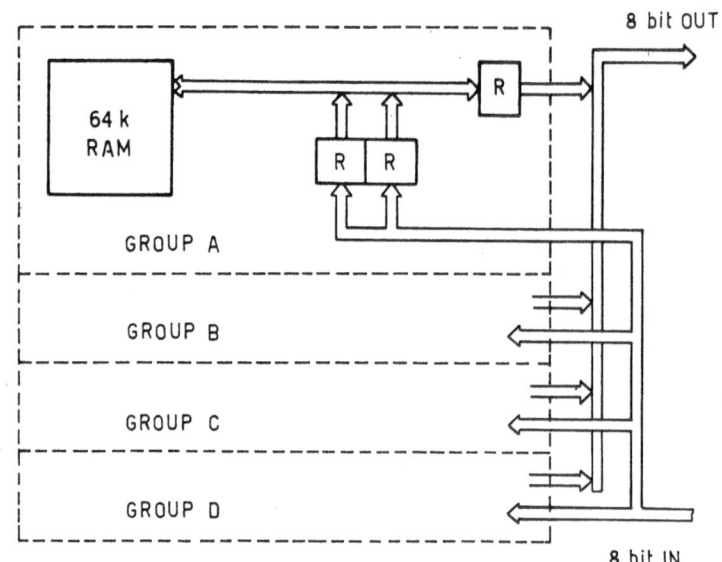

Fig. 5. Block diagram of the memory module.

Control Unit

It is not necessary to give here a detailed description of the control logic circuit because it is strictly dependent on the employed host computer However a note is useful regarding the combinatory circuit which allows the user setting of an 8 bit window anyway inside the 20 bits of every result supplied by the A.U. The user, after selecting the filter coefficients must also decide (sometimes by a cut and try procedure) where the window can be placed for the best use of the available 8 bit format. The approximating circuit, conditioned by the latter information, ensures the rounding of the final result by setting to logic level one the appropriate bit in the word that first arrives at the input of the first adder in the stage chain.
The same circuit also checks up (on each 20 bit result) the most significant bits that are discarded by the window, introducing a saturating logic.

The actually built coprocessor is now working as a peripheral of a DEC VAX 11/780 computer. A software PL1 driver has been developed in order to simplify the exchange protocol between convolver and user program.

As an example, Figs. 6b) and 6c) show results obtained by convolving the original image of Fig. 6a) with a bidimensional filter which is separable and rotationally symmetric. The filter coefficients are samples of $\nabla^2 G(x,y)$ taken over a limited range. The parameter values selected in the two cases are indicated in the corresponding figure captions.

Finally, as far as the CPU time is concerned, there is practically no difference between the CPU time spent for the two convolutions in spite of the different number of coefficients. This is because the processing time, also for convolution with the largest possible filter size, is very short (0.15 sec) compared with the amount of time spent on image transfer from the computer to the video memory (about 2 sec).

a)

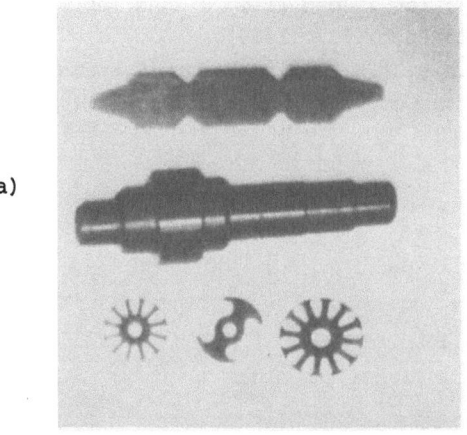

b)

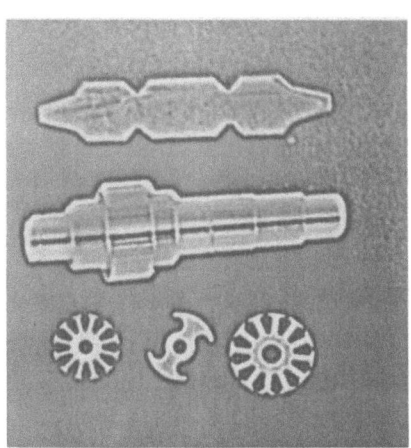

c)

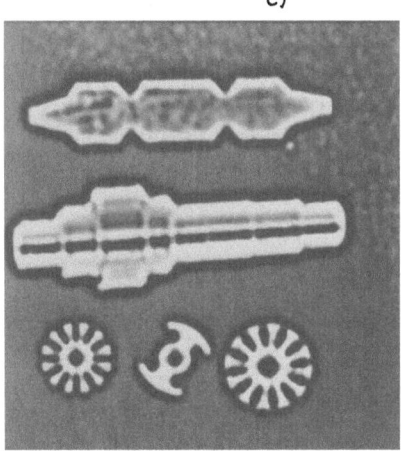

Fig. 6. a) The original image (512x512 pixels, 256 grey levels) to
            be convolved.
        b) Image obtained by convolving the original one with a 16
            coefficient filter; the coefficients are samples of a
            $\nabla^2 G(x,y)$ function having w = 5.19 ;
        c) as in 6b) for a 32 coefficient filter and w = 11.1 .

REFERENCE

1. D.H.Ballard, C.M.Brown,"Computer Vision", Prentice-Hall Inc., Englewood Cliffs, N.J. (1982).

2. D.Marr, H.Hildreth, Theory of Edge Detection, Artificial Intelligence Laboratory of MIT, memo n.518 (1979).

3. W.E.Grimson, Computational Experiments with a Feature Based Stereo Algorithm, Artificial Intelligence Laboratory of MIT, memo n. 762 (1984).

4. H.K.Nishihara, Hidden Information in Early Visual Processing, MIT Artificial Intelligence Laboratory (1982).

5. S.Ullman, Interfacing the One-Dimensional Scanning of an Image with the Application of Two Dimensional Operators, MIT Artificial Intelligence Laboratory, Report 3-60-81 (1981).

6. E.Caianiello, G.Musso, "Cybernetic Systems: Recognition, Learning, Self Organization", John Wiley & Sons Inc., London (1984).

7. TRW VLSI Data Book, 337 (1984).

8. D.C.Van Voorhis, T.H.Morrin, Memory Systems for Image Processing, IEEE trans. on Computers, C27: 113 (1978).

AN APPROACH TO FUNCTIONAL TESTING OF ARRAY PROCESSORS

Lanfranco Liotta and Donatella Sciuto

Dipartimento di Elettronica, Politecnico di Milano
P.za Leonardo da Vinci 32, 20133 Milano, Italy

ABSTRACT

Functional approach to VLSI device testing has been advocated by several authors and various models have been proposed. Aim of this paper is to present functional testing as a methodology to test array of processors. An ordering criterion for instructions is presented, based upon considerations of observability and controllability of instructions independent from the array model adopted. Testing is performed by means of sequences of instructions. Necessary and sufficient conditions are introduced for definition of test sequences leading to optimum error coverage. Finally some criteria aiming to design test procedures are presented.

INTRODUCTION

Image processing systems have been developed in the last twenty years mainly following Unger's suggestion that a two dimensional array of processing elements is a natural computer architecture for image processing and recognition [Ros 83]. Ideally, in this approach, each processor processes one element of the image. Using hardwired communications between neighboring processors, local "low level vision" operations can be performed on the image.

In 1981 a group of Italian universities started a research program for design and construction of a multiprocessor image processing system (PAPIA: Pyramidal Architecture for Parallel Image Analysis): the architecture was defined to be pyramidal (i.e. three dimensional) in order to balance communication time with computation time and to enhance system performances, since the pyramid structure allows processing the same image at different resolution levels. [CFL 85] In 1984 the architecture has been designed and the layout has been made: a prototype of the chip will be built shortly.

Having built the chip the problem of testing it arises. It is then necessary to provide a suitable test methodology, since conventional methods do not appear to be very apt for this particular architecture due to the disproportion between internal complexity and limited number of externally accessible observation and control points.

The work presented in this paper introduces functional testing concepts as a methodology for array processor testing. Several authors have advocated the functional approach to VLSI device testing as the only possible one [T&A 79] for VLSI; we will prove that such approach is feasible, leading to ambiguity not greater than that of any other test procedure designed following different approaches.

The assumption generally made in most papers is that the device model should be derived simply from user-available informations. Basic assumption of correct architecture design is made; since the approach is purely functional, it is obvious that no assumptions on error number or error distribution can be adopted. Therefore, it is not possible to guarantee complete error coverage without any ambiguity (to this purpose, assumptions such as single error or mutual error independence should have to be introduced, but they are not acceptable in a functional approach). Thus, the basic problem of functional testing is detection of errors rather than identification of faults: we will then consider faults as related to operators rather than to the physical structure.

In section 2 the model of the array processor is defined and the error space to be considered in the test action is identified. In section 3 a formal definition of the parameters necessary in design of test procedures with minimum ambiguity and maximum coverage are presented, followed by the definition of the testing criteria used to create the test sequences constituting the entire test procedure. In section 4 the design of the test procedure, based on the nececessary and sufficient conditions identified to obtain maximum coverage and minimum ambiguity with respect to functional test procedures not satisfying such conditions, is presented.

DEFINITION OF THE MODEL

The approach here presented is valid for a class of array processors, characterized by interconnection network topologies, data routing functions and instruction sets available on the single processing elements. We define such class, before introducing the associated error space. Arrays considered are all SIMD machines [H&B 82].

A possible SIMD computer is structured with N_c synchronized PEs, all under the control of a control unit (CU). Each PE_i is essentially an arithmetic logic unit (ALU) with attached working registers and local memory PEM_i, for the storage of distributed data. The CU has its own main memory for the storage of programs which are executed under its control. The function of the CU is to decode all the instructions and determine where the decoded instructions should be executed. Scalar instructions are directly executed inside the CU while vector instructions are broadcast to the PEs for distributed execution in order to achieve spatial parallelism through duplicate arithmetic units, i.e. PEs.

All the PEs perform the same function synchronously in a lock-step manner: vector operands are distributed to PEMs before parallel execution of the operation in the array of PEs. The distributed data are loaded in PEMs via shift-registers acting as input/output channels for every PE_i. Masking schemes are used to control the status of each PE during the execution of a vector instruction. Each PE may be either active or disabled during an instruction cycle; only enabled PEs perform computations. Data exchanges among the PEs are done via inter-PE communication network, controlled by the CU, which performs all necessary data routing and manipulation functions.

The pyramidal architecture (PAPIA) previously mentioned is covered by the model proposed, since the interconnection network and the data routing functions considered are not specific to bidimensional arrays.

Formally a SIMD computer C is characterized as a quintuple:
$$C = \langle N, F, I, M \rangle$$
where

N = number of processing elements (PE) in the system;

F = the set of data routing functions provided by the interconnection network;

I = the set of machine instructions;

M = the set of masking schemes where each mask partitions the set of PEs into two disjoint subsets of enabled PEs and disabled PEs.

An inter-PE communication network can be specified by a set of data routing functions. If we identify the addresses of all the PEs in a SIMD computer by the set $S = \{0, 1, 2, \ldots, N-1\}$ each routing function is a bijection from S to S. When a routing function f F is executed via the interconnection network, PE_i copies the contents of its data routing register R_i into the data routing register $R_{f(i)}$ of the corresponding $PE_{f(i)}$. This data routing operation occurs[1] in all active PEs simultaneously. An inactive processing element PE_i may receive data from another PE_h if a routing function is executed, but it cannot transmit data. To transfer data between PEs which are not directly connected in the network, the data must be passed through intermediate PEs by executing a sequence of routing functions through the interconnection network. [S&S 78]

As regards the internal architecture of the processing elements, each PE_i should be provided with: [Fun 76]

- its own internal random access memory PEM_i;

- a simple serial ALU;

- a data routing register R_i which is connected with all the data routing registers R_h of the other PEs through the interconnection network;

- a masking register G_i (which contains 1 if the PE_i is active and 0 if it is disabled);

- a register S_i used for input/output operations with parallel fast loading.

Instruction Set Definition

In our proposal the machine instruction set is partitioned in four groups according to the different functionalities performed and the different "elements" involved in the execution of each subset of instructions. [H&B 82]

1. **Fast parallel loading.** These instructions allow to load a bit plane into the S registers. While the element PE_i processes data in its own internal memory PEM_i, columns of input data can be loaded and shifted into the left side of the array through the S registers until a bit plane is loaded. The input plane is then stored in the PEM_i. Planes of data are output by moving them from memory elements (PEM_i) to the S registers and then shifting them out, column by column, through the right side.

2. **I/O functions of PE_i.** This group of instructions performs all transfers between S registers and the internal registers of the PE_i.

3. **Data routing functions.** Each PE_i can send data to an interconnected PE_h via data routing functions. Data are stored in the data routing register R_h of the PE_h selected by the function. Masking disables the

sending of data but not the reception.

4. **Parallel instructions.** This group is further divided into three subsets according to functionalities performed by the instructions:

   a. logical and arithmetic instructions;

   b. internal register transfer instructions;

   c. internal memory (PEM_i) access instructions.

Error Space Definition

Our approach based on functional testing implies considering the test problem as detection of **errors** rather than **faults**, i.e. detection of faulty execution of machine instructions. This leads to viewing the error space bounded to the instruction groups introduced previously in the paper.

1. **Fast parallel loading.** The error space in this case is defined by the faults in a shift register [Wil 84], since this is the only element involved in execution of these instructions: fast parallel loading instructions allow moving data planes from the external environment to the I/O shift register S_i of every PE_i and viceversa.

2. **I/O functions of PE_i.** The error space is partitioned in two disjoint sets: errors in the decoding function and errors in data transfer function.

3. **Data routing functions.** We identify three classes of errors:

   a. Errors at function level:
   instead of executing the f_i data routing function (bijection of S to S) the network executes f_i' – this represents a non-applicative relation of S to S (one to many) – or a f_i'' data routing function – which represents a surjection of S to S (many to one) – or a f_k – which represents a bijection of S to S (one to one and onto) following a different law from the one defined.

   b. Storage errors:
   a PE_i does not copy the correct content of R_i register into $R_{f(i)}$ of the selected $PE_{f(i)}$.

   c. Masking errors:
   we identify two types of errors:

      – PE_i disabled does not receive data;

      – PE_i disabled does transmit data.

4. **Parallel instructions.** Here again we identify two types of errors:

   a. We assume that there is only one control unit for all processing elements integrated in one chip. This implies that faults in the decoding and control function results in the same errors for all the PEs integrated in the same chip array, while instructions to be executed are broadcast to all PEs of the array from the Control Unit.

   b. Errors regarding functionalities of the single instructions:

      – data transfer;

      – data manipulation;

      – data storage.

   We assume that this kind of faults leads to different errors in the various PEs, while probability of identical errors in each PE of the array, all executing the same parallel instruction, is almost equal to zero.

Functional testing aims at verifying correct execution of all operators, making visible all possible errors. This can be realized by defining for each operator a test sequence constituted by a set-up sequence which creates the conditions to execute the operator under test and an observation sequence making the results of the operator execution visible at the external environment.

In order to design a proper test sequence we introduce some definitions regarding observability and controllability of instructions which are the parameters enabling the ordering of the instruction set.

We consider a subset $S_c = \{0,1,2,\ldots,N_c-1\}$, constituted by the PEs integrated on a chip, and one data routing function f_i. If we reduce the definition set of f_i to S_c, data routing function f_i determines a new set $S'_c \subset S$ composed by all $PE_{f(s_c)}$. It is in general $S_c \cap S'_c \neq \phi$.

Let (s_c, s'_c) be the couple defined by f_i. If, in a couple (s_c, s'_c), $s'_c \notin S_c$ then we define s_c belonging to the observability frontier for the f_i data routing function: $s_c \in OF_{f_i}$.

If, in a couple (s_c, s'_c), $s_c \notin S'_c$ then s_c belongs to the controllability frontier for a function f_i: $s_c \in CF_{f_i}$.

If we consider the set F of all data routing functions we define as observability frontier for S_c the union of all observability frontiers defined for every data routing function f_i:

$$OF_{S_c} = \bigcup_{f_i}^{F} OF_{f_i}$$

In the same way we define the controllability frontier for S_c as the union of all controllability frontiers defined for each data routing function f_i:

$$CF_{S_c} = \bigcup_{f_i}^{F} CF_{f_i}$$

This leads to the definition of **observable** PEs as $s_c \in OF_{S_c}$: it exists at least one data routing function f_i, whose execution transfers a value outside the S_c set using the external interconnections of the chip.

In the same way we define **controllable** PEs as $s_c \in CF_{S_c}$: it exists at least a data routing function whose execution allows the storage of an external value into S_c set using the external interconnections of the chip.

We identify a relation between the sets F of data routing functions and I of instructions which induces a partition of the instruction set I in two disjoint subsets I_F and I_{NF}. The I_F set is composed of i_k instructions associated with a data routing function: this leads to a surjective application of I_F to F.

It is possible to define observability and controllability frontiers for the instructions $i_k \in I_F$.

Definition 1: An instruction $i_k \in I_F$ associated with a data routing function f_i is provided with **complete frontier observability** if results can be read at the external pins regarding all the functions performed by the instruction i_k for the processing elements $PE_i \in OF_{f_i}$.

Definition 2: An instruction $i_k \in I_F$ associated with a data routing function f_i is provided with **partial frontier observability** if results can be read at the external pins regarding at least one of the functions performed by the instruction i_k for the processing elements $PE_i \in OF_{f_i}$.

Definition 3: An instruction $i_k \in I_F$ associated with a data routing function f_i is provided with **complete frontier controllability** if at external pins the processing elements $PE_i \in CF_{f_i}$ read all input data necessary to execution of the functions performed by instruction i_k.

Definition 4: An instruction $i_k \in I_F$ associated with a data routing function f_i is provided with **partial frontier controllability** if at external pins the processing elements $PE_i \in CF_{f_i}$ read at least one input data necessary to the execution of the functions performed by the instruction i_k.

It is not possible to define frontier observability or frontier controllability either complete or partial for all the instructions i_k belonging to the subset I_{NF}, that is to the instructions which are not associated at least to a data routing function.

DEFINITION OF TESTING CRITERIA

Final aim of this approach is to define a test procedure consisting of test sequences each testing an operator. Criteria here proposed lead to definition of test sequences and to their concatenation in a test procedure in order to maximize error coverage and minimize ambiguity.

Each test sequence $I_i \ldots I_k \ldots I_h$ aiming to testing of instruction I_k can be subdivided into a setup subsequence $I_i \ldots I_{k-1}$ and an observation subsequence $I_{k+1} \ldots I_h$.

We introduce now the concepts of "Controllability Path P_c" and "Observability Path P_o".

A **controllability path** of length 1 is an instruction I_c provided with complete frontier controllability. An **observability path** of length 1 is an instruction I_o provided with complete frontier observability.

The construction of controllability and observability paths of length greater than 1 can be obtained by applying recursively lemma 1 and the composition law defined below.

Composition law. If in the test sequence for an instruction I_k:

$$I_i \ldots I_h I_k I_1 \ldots I_n$$

$I_i \ldots I_h$ (setup subsequence) is a controllability path P_c and $I_1 \ldots I_n$ (observability subsequence) is an observability path P_o, it is then possible to define two new controllability and observability paths P'_c and P'_o where the controllability path P'_c is composed by the subsequence $I_i \ldots I_k$ and the observability path is composed by $I_k \ldots I_n$.

Lemma 1. An instruction I_k is **testable** with minimum ambiguity if the test sequence can be designed as $P_c I_k P_o$ where the controllabilty path P_c and the observability path P_o have been previously built according to the composition law.

Proof. Let path P_c be built according to the composition law: it is constituted by a first instruction with complete frontier controllability followed by instructions already tested. Using the path it is possible to introduce correct input data to the instruction I_h, i.e. the last instruction belonging to the controllability path. Path P_o has been built using the composition law and it is constituted by a last instruction I_n

with complete frontier observability and by previous instructions already tested. Using the path it is possible to observe at the external pins the results of the sequence of instructions from I_1, first instruction of the observability path.

If the output values are different from those expected, the error must be localized at instruction I_k under test.

Theorem 1. Necessary and sufficient condition to design a test procedure with maximum coverage and minimum ambiguity for the whole instruction set is that single test sequences are ordered following the criterion of building the controllability and observability paths with increasing length.

Proof.

a. The condition is necessary.

Assume that the condition is not satisfied for an instruction I_k and that the setup subsequence was constituted by a controllability path P_c followed by another instruction I_n. An ambiguity is then introduced in the test sequence: in case of detection of wrong output values there is the possibility of non correct attribution of the error; the error can be generated either by the instruction under test I_k, or by the instruction I_n belonging to the setup subsequence.

Assume now that the observation subsequence is composed by an observability path P_o preceded by another instruction I_h. Results different from those expected at the observability frontier can lead to masking an error between the instruction I_h and the instruction under test I_k. This introduces higher ambiguity in the test action.

b. The condition is sufficient.

If the condition has been satisfied, no test action involves more than one instruction I_k not tested, otherwise, there would be a design error in the test sequence. If the instruction I_k is completely controllable and observable the associated errors are covered without any ambiguity. Otherwise the introduced ambiguity is not higher than that associated with any test sequence designed in a different way, since in this last case more than one instruction in the sequence might be not tested. In the same way, the coverage is not lower than that given by any different test sequence.

Using the theorem we introduce a first ordering of the instructions following the ordering of increasing lengths of controllability and observability paths. For all paths of equal length we use a second ordering criterion, called instruction cardinality, defined as follows in [A&S 82b]: "Cardinality of an instruction is defined as the number of subsequent accesses to registers". The instruction set is then reordered into subsets identified by common cardinality: $\{i_k\}$ denotes the subset of all instructions with cardinality k.

In [A&S 82a] it was proved that necessary and sufficient condition in order to design a test sequence with maximum coverage and minimum ambiguity is that test concerning subset $\{i_k\}$ be afforded only after completion of test concerning subset $\{i_{k-1}\}$ for any k>1.

DESIGN OF TESTING PROCEDURES

The complete test procedure must include test sequences for all instructions. Instructions are ordered following:

1. increasing length of controllability and observability path;

2. increasing cardinality for instructions belonging to the same class of path length.

An ordering of the instructions into subsets with common class and cardinality is possible. Length classes defined are:

Class 1: **Fast parallel loading.** This class is provided with complete frontier controllability and observability for a subset of the data routing functions.

Class 2: **I/O functions of PEs.** This class is provided with partial frontier observability.

Class 3: **Data routing functions.** This class is provided with partial frontier observability.

Class 4: **Parallel instructions.** The instructions belonging to this class are not observable and controllable at the frontier.

The test sequence is organized in the four steps detailed in the sequel.

Test of class 1 instructions: loading of a bit plane

The test action follows the methodologies of shift registers testing [Wil 84] [M&S 82] to test correct loading and unloading of S registers. After completion of test of class 1 it is possible to obtain frontier controllability and observability of the PE array.

Test of class 2 instructions

Frontier observability of classes 2 and 3 is equal, but instructions belonging to class 2 have cardinality less or equal than those of class 3. Using instructions of class 1, already tested it is now possible to load safely a bit plane and, after completion of transfer operation to internal registers of the PEs (instructions under test), to read result values unloading (instruction of class 1) an output bit plane.

Test of class 3 instructions

Using instructions of class 1 and 2, it is possible to transfer safely external input data into the internal registers of PEs and, after executing data routing functions, to read the output results unloading the bit plane.

Test of class 4 instructions: parallel instructions

Considering the ordering defined by increasing cardinality the first instructions to be tested are those concerning logical comparison among registers. These test sequences aim to identify faults in data transfer, data manipulation, data storage functions and decoding functions.

All functions performed by the logical comparison instructions must be tested first since these instructions will be used for design of test sequences regarding the parallel instructions not directly observable at the frontier.

Test sequences regarding other parallel instructions, aiming to detect faults in data transfer, data manipulation or data storage rather than decoding function will be executed in different time sequences.

First phase: test of the functionalities of data transfer, data manipulation and data storage of parallel instructions.

Anomalous behaviour of one single PE, with respect to the others, may be due to occurence of errors in these functions. After having ordered the parallel instructions in terms of increasing cardinality, every test sequence is composed of the following steps:

1. loading of an input data plane;

2. transfer input data from S-registers into internal registers of each single PE_i;

3. execution of the instruction test sequence: the aim is to verify the functionality of the instruction under test;

4. error detection using the following instructions already tested:

   - data routing functions between the PEs;

   - logical comparison instructions;

5. unloading, to the external environment (instruction of class 1, thus already tested), of a matrix, where each element represents the behaviour of a single PE_i (1 if there is an agreement with the neighbours PEs, 0 otherwise) for the test sequence executed.

Parallel instructions with greatest cardinality concern internal memory access. Test sequences for these instructions are analogous to the ones previously described, but it is necessary to test the internal memory array (PEM_i) of every PE_i. We propose to compact the informations regarding the test of each single memory cell in the PE's internal register (**signature analysis** [SHP 82]) using then data routing functions and logical comparison operations to identify PEs with memory values different from neighbours.

It is possible to take advantage of the parallelism between I/O fast operations and PE's internal computing at two different levels:

1. for a single test sequence, considering more than one input data application, loading the input data plane concerning the next input test data during the processing of the previous data plane;

2. for different test sequences, loading the input data plane concerning the next test sequence during the execution of the previous one.

Second phase: test of decoding and control functions.

Errors generated at this level, given the unicity of the control unit on a single chip, are masked in the first testing phase. To detect decoding and control faults of parallel instructions we propose the following procedure:

1. Fast loading through S registers of a set of bit planes, representing the correct results of m*n test sequences aiming to test control decoding functions of the command interpreter.

2. Execution of m*n test sequences, each regarding a single instruction.

3. After completion of a test sequence the results produced by the PEs (all in agreement) are compared with the correct results previously stored.

4. One PE_i stores the result value of the comparison and is disabled via masking operation.

5. If m*n test sequences have been executed, concerning m*n instructions, every PE_i has stored the result of a single instruction test sequence and the procedure continues in step 6), otherwise step 2) is executed.

6. The bit plane containing the results of the test sequences is unloaded via S-registers.

CONCLUDING REMARKS

The present paper proposes an approach for test procedure generation based upon two ordering criteria: the first criteria concerns the external observability of instructions, the second one uses the concept of instruction cardinality.

It is proved that our approach leads to test procedure generation with ambiguity not greater than that of any other test procedure.

The approach takes advantage of the parallel structure of the device under investigation optimizing the time test and compacting test data. Efforts will be made to develop automatic or semiautomatic tools for test generation.

As a by-product of the test action, a partial localization of faults is obtained.

REFERENCES

[A&S 82a] M.A. Annaratone, M.G. Sami, "An Approach to functional testing of Microprocessors", Proceedings of FTCS 12 (1982)

[A&S 82b] M.A. Annaratone, M.G. Sami, "Software Testing Technique for Universal Building Blocks of Multimicrosystems", Proceedings of NCC (June 1982)

[CFL 85] V. Cantoni, M. Ferretti, S. Levialdi, R. Stefanelli, "PAPIA: Pyramidal Architecture for Parallel Image Analysis", in Proceedings of 7th Sysmposium on Computer Arithmetic, ed. IEEE, Urbana, IL (June 1985)

[Fun 76] L. W. Fung, "MPPC: A massively parallel processing computer", Goddard Space Flight Center Image Systems Section Rep. (Sept. 1976)

[H&B 82] K. Hwang, F.A. Briggs, Computer Architecture and Parallel Processing, ed. McGraw-Hill Book Company

[M&S 82] Yinghua Min, S.Y.H. Su, "Testing Functional Faults in VLSI", in 19th Design Automation Conference, ed. IEEE, 1982

[Ros 83] Rosenfeld A., "Parallel Image Processing using Cellular Arrays", IEEE Computer, vol. 16, n. 1 (1983)

[S&S 78] H.J. Siegel, S.D. Smith, "Study of multistage SIMD interconnection networks", Proc. 5th Annu. Symp. Comput. Architecture (Apr. 1978)

[SHP 82] T. Sridhar, D. S. Ho, T. J. Powell, S. M. Thatte, "Analysis and Simulation of Parallel Signature Analyzers", in IEEE Test Conference, ed. IEEE (1982)

[T&A 79] S.M. Thatte, J.A. Abraham, "Test generation for general microprocessors architectures", Proc. FTCS-9 (1979)

[Wil 84] Williams T.W., "VLSI Testing", in Computer, ed. IEEE (October 1984)

THE PAPIA CONTROL SYSTEM (HARDWARE DESIGN)

O. Catalano[+], G. Gerardi[$+], R. Lombardi[*], and A. Machi[+]

[+] Istituto di Fisica Cosmica ed Applicazioni dell'Informatica del CNR - Palermo
[$] Istituto di Fisica - Università di Palermo
[*] Dip. Informatica e Sistemistica - Università di Pavia

ABSTRACT

Aim of the paper is to present some details of the PAPIA system design and to describe its Control System hardware implementation.
In particular the Control design and operation are described.

INTRODUCTION

PAPIA is a multiprocessor system designed for the analysis of image data. It operates as a powerful specialized co-processor hosted in a multiuser serial computer supporting an high level pictorial environment under VMS or UNIX Operating Systems[1].
PAPIA is based on a parallel CPU composed by 21845 Elementary Processors (P.E.), each devoted to the analysis of a single image element[2].
The Elementary Processors are connected in a polimorphic structure composed by 8 arrays holding a decreasing number of elements (128*128, 64*64, ..., 2*2,1 P.E.).
Under software control the arrays may be logically connected to obtain a pyramid structure of processors operating in a SIMD fashion. They may be also logically connected to provide a MSIMD structure composed by a low resolution pyramid and several flat arrays of processors, each section working as a different parallel CPU. Finally to help big images handling, the array connections may be reconfigured from square to pipe arrangement.
The P.E. contain the circuitry necessary to hold temporary data and to perform on them boolean operations. As they always work in SIMD mode, all circuit elements, related to program storage and to control code and data I/O flow, have not been inserted into the VLSI P.E. chip.
PAPIA Elementary Processors are supposed to operate at a minimum

speed of 1 Mhz, executing boolean operations between the content of each P.E. registers and that of neighbour ones.

Arithmetic operations and image functions on multigray level data have to be performed in a bit-serial way. Bit-serial operation requires from a few to hundred machine instructions per operation, but a good speed-up may be obtained if the routines can take advantage of data bit configuration to control their own flow.

An image memory management Unit called "Active Memory Unit" (AMU), operates image data I/O and formatting. It exchanges fixed size blocks of data between the parallel CPU and its image buffers. Data feeding to the CPU planes is performed asynchronously to its operations via the P.E. I/O registers, in a columnwise bitplane format. One parallel I/O channel for each pyramid section will be provide in the final machine, (only one, corresponding to the base, in the prototype). The AMU design is still in course.

Control functions, scalar code execution and parallel arithmetic management are in charge to the pyramid Control System.

The performance characteristics of several commercially available systems based on serial microprocessors were carefully reviewed, in order to implement the PAPIA Control System prototype. The analysis showed that, at present, on one of the considered systems was able to drive the various multiprocessor pyramid sections at the required speed and to perform at the same time data bit manipulation.

On the other side, an entirely hardwired logic was considered to be not sufficiently flexible to follow system improvement.

Then a combination of two different Units, a microprocessor based and a microcoded one was chosen to implement PAPIA Control System. In the following, the Units are referred to as "GCSP" (Global Control Scalar Processing Unit) the first, and "PCU" (Pyramid Control Unit) the second.

The GCSP is devoted to execute scalar arithmetic and program control functions while the PCU is used to format and issue opcode sequences to the multiprocessor pyramid sections.

The GCSP is implemented by means of standard hardware, so only a few details will be given in the first section of the present paper, while the Pyramid Control Unit is described more extensively in the second one.

1. THE GLOBAL CONTROL AND SCALAR PROCESSING UNIT

The GCSP interfaces the machine host computer with the Pyramid Control Unit. It holds user program and scalar data memory, and runs user programs executing scalar code sections on its serial CPU. Libraries of precompiled subroutines may also be loaded on the GCSP and referenced by the user program[3].

A Real-time Multitask Operating System, called PMOS, runs on the GCSP serial CPU to distribute the serial, parallel and I/O tasks among the various PCUs and AMU. PMOS makes use of message exchange and flag mechanisms to synchronize task execution.

The GCSP communicates with the host computer and the CPU by means of parallel ports and (hardware) FIFO buffers respectively.

A console terminal connected via a serial port is provided for GCSP startup, diagnostics and error logging.

The prototype GCSP is being developed on a Philips PG 2000 series Single Board Computer: It is base on the Motorola 68000 CPU and peripherals and it is interfaced to VME bus.

2. THE PYRAMID CONTROL UNIT

The PCU performs all the hardware functions required to feed the parallel CPU with instructions and control signals. A separate module is dedicated to control each pyramid section.

The heart of each module is a sequencer using several specialized registers and a Writeable Control Store to expand a set of Macro-instructions in executable microcodes for the pyramid section. The Macro-instruction set includes[4].

- operations between scalars and images;
- boolean and arithmetic operations between images;
- image analysis primitives[5].

The allowed data types are short and long integer (8/16 bits) and floating point (32 bits).

2.1. PCU ELEMENTS

Fig.1 shows the functional design of a PCU module.

It contains: a sequencer, a writeable control store, several specialized registers, a clock generator, control circuitry and various I/O ports.

The sequencer is a bit-slice family device, able to perform operations useful to control program flow. It holds a program counter and counter register in addition to a small stack.

The sequencer can generate successive addresses, perform jumps to (and returns from) subroutines unconditionally or controlled by external conditions.

In the first prototype the AMD 2910 sequencer will be utilized, it is able to work with at a 100 nsec clock cycle.

The Writeable Control Store is a fast-access memory bank loaded at power-on and reset, with standard or user supplied microsoftware. The WCS software is a binary encoding of the bus line levels required to operate and control each circuital element in the PCU module itself. It also includes the opcodes for the multiprocessor pyramid section controlled by the PCU module. The WCS is implemented using HMOS fast static memory chips.

The specialized registers constitute buffers that hold user subroutine parameters. They allow operations between scalars and images, direct bitplane and neighbour addressing, loop counting and scalar data I/O with the pyramid section. Seven specialized registers are provided for each PCU module, one is used to mantain PCU configuration and Status values.

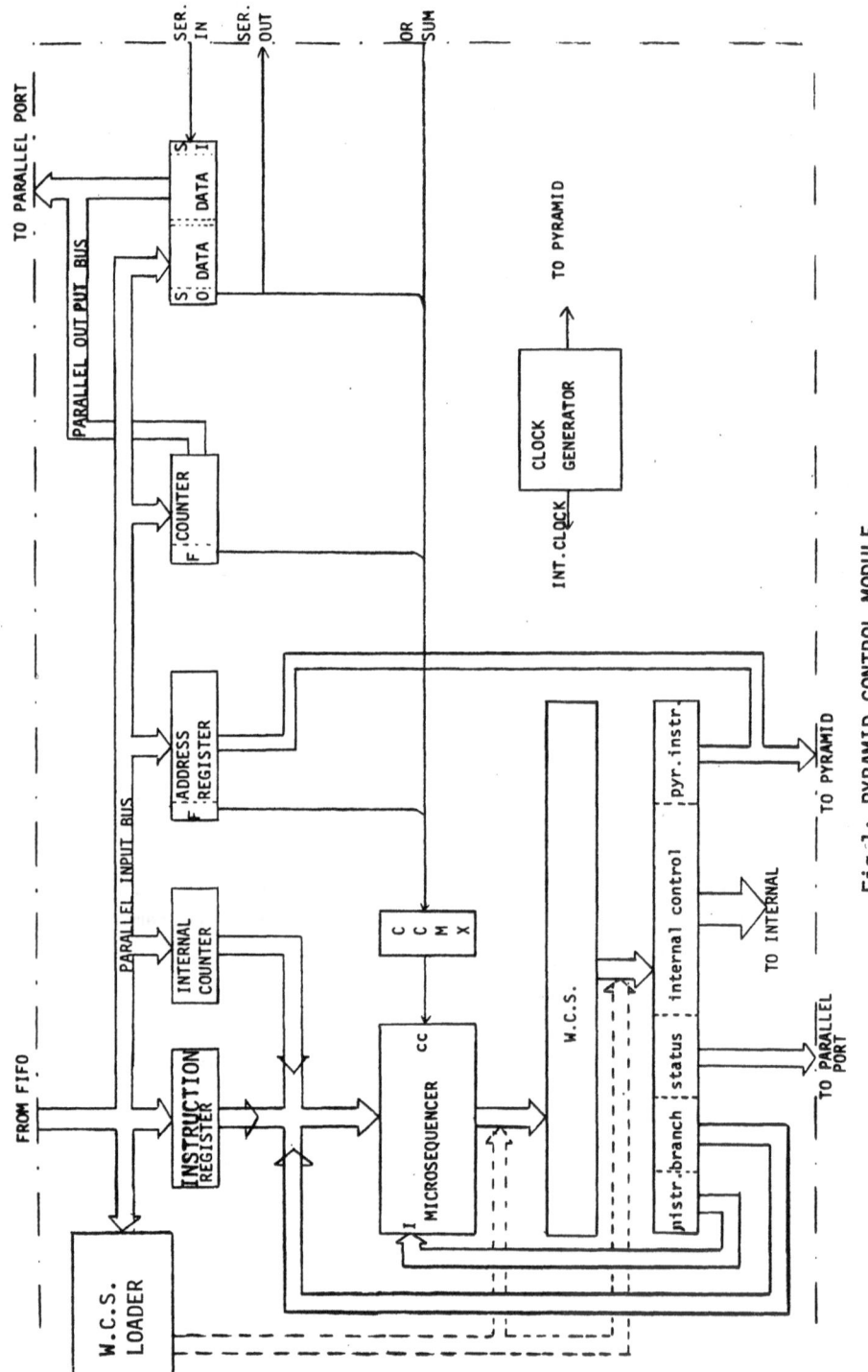

Fig.1: PYRAMID CONTROL MODULE

The module register set includes:
- One 12 bits write-only "Instruction Register": it is used to hold WCS addresses (Macro-codes) coming from the GCSP FIFO buffer;
- one 12 bits write-only "Counter Register": it is used to hold values to be loaded into the sequencer internal counter;
- three 8 bits write-only "Address Registers": they are used to perform direct by-register, bitplane and neighbour addressing;
- one 16 bits read-write "Counter Register": it is used for user program counting purposes;
- one 16/32 bits "Data Register": it is used to hold data that can be accessed in parallel R/W way by the GCSP and in serial R/W way by the pyramid section. Its serial output is also used by the sequencer to control microprogram flow.

A parallel Input Bus conveys instructions and parameter values from GCSP FIFO buffer to the registers. A Parallel Output Bus makes available to the GCSP the content of the "Counter" and "Data" registers. A serial link is used to transfer scalar values between the Data Register and the Pyramid section.

A separate port is devoted to exchange configuration and status values with the GCSP.

2.2. PCU OPERATION

The routines which perform PAPIA arithmetic and image analysis are hidden inside the Writeable Control Store.

The address of each routine entry point into the WCS constitutes its macro-code. The sequencer in the PCU module loads this value from the "Instruction Register" in its program counter. At each clock cycle the program counter is updated, pointing to a new WCS word.

Each WCS word is composed of 64 bits grouped in various fields:
- the "Sequencer Instruction Opcodes" field: provides flow control, directing the sequencer to increment its program counter, or to load a new macro-instruction value from another WCS field (the branch address one), or to perform a three way branch, according to the value of the Condition Code sequencer input,
- the "Condition Code Multiplexing" field: provides selection among the various flags coming from the PCU registers and the pyramid one bit status flag section ("OR SUM"),
- the "P.E. Opcode" field: its value is issued to the controlled pyramid section when all the PCU element are set to the appropriate values and P.E. timing requests are satisfied,
- the "Clock Control" field: it drives a clock generator circuitry encharged to give to the pyramid section the two clocks required with appropriate timings and to generate the PCU module clock,
- the "Register Control" field: it allows register loading/output and increment/decrement,
- the "Status" field: its value is a code for various error conditions and traps. Status field values from each module are grouped in the PCU Status register. Status Register changes are communicated to the GCSP in interrupt mode.

3. CONCLUDING REMARKS

While the chip is already at an advanced implementation stage the Software for the Pyramid Control Units is being built. Hardware PCU design is already and each componing element has been tested. In the near future the overal module will be provide.

REFERENCES

1. Cantoni V., Carrioli L.,Catalano O., Cinque L., Di Gesù V., Ferretti M., Gerardi G., Levialdi S., Lombardi R., Machì A., Stefanelli R. in: "The PAPIA Pyramidal Machine: General Description and Applications" Convegno Nazionale ASTRONET, Roma (1985)

2. Cantoni V., Ferretti M., Levialdi S., Maloberti F., "A Pyramid Project Using Integrated Technology" Integrated Technology for Parallel Image Processing S.Levialdi Ed., Academic Press, New York (1984)

3. Catalano O., Gerardi G., Machì A., "The PAPIA Control System (Software Design)" IFCAI-Int.Rep. 2/85 (1984)

4. Cantoni V., DI Gesù V., Ferretti M., Levialdi S., Machì A., "The PAPIA Software Environment" III Int. Conf. on Image Analysis and Processing, Rapallo, Italy (1985)

5. Cantoni V., Carrioli L., Cinque L., DI Gesù V., Ferretti M., Levialdi S., "Parallel image processing primitives" III Int.Conf.on Image Analysis and processing, Rapallo, Italy (1985)

PARALLEL IMAGE PROCESSING PRIMITIVES

V. Cantoni*, L. Carrioli*, M. Ferretti*,
L. Cinque**, S. Leviali**, and V. Di Gesú***

Pavia University*, Rome University**
I.F.C.A.I./C.N.R. Palermo***

INTRODUCTION

The most common tasks of low level image processing are considered in order to define a set of primitives to be implemented in parallel image processing systems. In particular arithmetic primitives, global features (as grey level statistics), linear transforms and local computations are discussed taking care of the effectiveness of the implementations on array and pyramidal systems. The propagation capability supplied by flat arrays and pyramids is then presented in some extent with the purpose to highlight the performances of this kind of machines in well known low level tasks.

ARITHMETIC PRIMITIVES

The design of arithmetic primitives for parallel image processing has a major influence on the performance of most preprocessing and low level vision tasks. At this stage, input data (image pixels values) are integer numbers, whose range goes from binary values to the 256 or more grey level values typical of robotics and vision. From a numerical point of view, integer arithmetics is quite satisfactory for most applications: local operators generally use small sized, integer constants and there exist some linear transformations (Walsh, Hadamard, Haar ...) which can be implemented accordingly /1/. Still, floating point arithmetics cannot be eliminated: FFT, cosine transform and KLT are well established algorithms which require such a capability. Also, flexibility and generality call for the introduction of floating point arithmetics, to cover the widest possible range of applications a system has to handle.

The set of arithmetic operations in a I.P. system is relatively small, while providing all the necessary features: addition, multiplication, division, absolute value both for integer and floating point numbers, square root, exponentiation (possibly) for float numbers only and lastly format conversion. If this choice can be easily agreed upon, the actual implementation of these operations is open to many alternatives; among the factors which play a role are the range of values associated to image pixels and the architecture of parallel processing systems.

As seen above, pixel values lie in a range of integers typical of the application and vary from 4 to 8/10 bits quantities. It is quite reasonable to offer the high level user of the system an arithmetic system independent of data representation. But an efficient exploitation of the hardware resources calls for a set of primitives which match data and hardware structure as closely as possible. The hardware organization of each P.E. depends heavily on the overall architecture of the system. It is well known that massively parallel systems can be partitioned into two main classes: systems which distribute P.E.s on the image (one P.E. handles a subimage) and systems which distribute the image on the P.E.s (one P.E. is associated to a single pixel). The hardware structure of P.E.s in the first class is typically more powerful and includes some level of word parallelism; on the contrary, P.E.s of the second one are as simple as possible and therefore their data paths are 1 bit wide, which leads to serial arithmetics.

Serial arithmetics is therefore the best candidate to implement arithmetic primitives capable of handling data of variable length; but other hardware features of the P.E.s deserve careful examination. For example, VLSI technology makes feasible the introduction of shift registers in each P.E.; this greatly increases the efficiency of many tasks, by allowing partial results to recirculate in the shift registers, but introduces a non-homogeneity in the design of the primitives. However, if the shift registers are made into variable length, data preserving, sequential accessible local memories, a compromise can be found between homogeneity and efficiency. A possible solution is the design of a basic set of primitives, which handle the smallest type of value (e.g. 8 bit data); these are used to implement the operations for data values multiple of this basic unit.

Also, generality calls for an uniform representation of numbers: two complement format is the best solution for serial arithmetics, both for integers and float numbers, including the exponent.

A second, major feature of arithmetics in I.P. systems stems from the frequent use of small integer constants which are distributed to all P.E.s as operands (e.g. in 3x3 convolution). It is worthwhile to pre-compile in the controller of the system the micro-instructions which make up the whole sequence of operations, instead of using the general primitives (speed up factors of up to 2 can be obtained on the average). So arithmetics is best partitioned into primitives for array-to-array and for constant-to-array operations

One more architectural feature to be considered is the availability in some proposed/realized systems of a look up table mechanism; this might result useful for arithmetics, besides its proven usefulness for other problems. The "distributed arithmetics" approach /2/ deserves a careful analysis to appreciate the tradeoff between increased hardware complexity and improved performance.

So far, parallel processing has shown only indirect impact on the design of arithmetic primitives, which otherwise can be easily coded for serial processing. Some care is required only for format conversions and floating point operations: here data specific actions are required, for example in re-normalization, in the handling of the mantissa, in overflow detection. Since the processing mode is SIMD, these operations must be selectively enabled only in those P.E.s which do require them. This can be obtained by the enabling/disabling feature which is common to P.E.s of these systems.

LOCAL OPERATORS PRIMITIVES

It has been pointed out by several authors that local operations constitute a bottleneck for low level image processing. Nevertheless several families of operators are so oftenly used that they have become a standard: "gradient" operators for edge detection (Sobel, Robert, etc.), smoothing operators (low pass filters) and high pass operators (as Laplacian, sharpening filters, etc.). Therefore a primitive must be devoted to each of the quoted operators to obtain maximum efficiency in these common and frequent tasks.

Both in binary and multilevel imageries more general operators are required, whose frameworks only are defined. In these cases the primitives must implement the frameworks in efficient way.

For binary images the simplest example is the family of boolean near-neighbor functions which implements tasks like contour detection (object edge pixels are characterized by $\cap_G NN$, where G is the set of near-neighbors NN) or isolated pixels detection (1-valued pixels for which $\cap_G \overline{NN} = 1$), etc.

A second family is given by the basic operators of mathematical morphology /3/, namely dilation ($\cup_G X_y$, where Y is the original image, X_y is the structuring element centered in y and G is the subset of 1-valued pixels of Y), erosion ($\{y\}: X_y \subset Y$) and reflection. For each of these operations a primitive has to be built for the structuring element contained in the elementary subarray, and higher level ones to implement the same operation on larger structuring elements by composition of the elementary primitives.

Multilevel local operations are required in matching problems and in the field of linear restoration. In both cases a convolution with suitable mask is required (in the former with a model filter, in the latter with a filter derived from the point spread function). The convolution operation requires a primitive for the elementary 3x3 template and a more general one to operate with larger templates by composition of 3x3 primitives.

Fast inter processor communication is the key factor for effective implementation of all the quoted local primitives. In fact some special connections are devoted in all parallel machines to supply data of near-neighbors. Gating and multiplexing techniques have been used in major array processors (of course gating allows for a very efficient implementation of binary operators).

Also for what concerns tessellation different solutions has been proposed: 4-connectivity (usually with multiplexing technique), 6-connectivity (efficient for particular tasks, e.g. Golay patterns analysis, etc.), 8-connectivity (most suitable for manipulations on the standard template 3x3).

The implementation of convolution primitives by subarray larger then the elementary 3x3 has two general approaches: the cascade of a set of 3x3 suitable masks and the decomposition of the original subarray in a mosaic of 3x3 masks. In the former case two 3x3 convolutions involve a subarray 5x5, three convolutions 7x7, etc.; this is the faster implementation but it cannot be always pursued as the original subarray cannot always be decomposed accordingly (7x7 or 5x5 have 49 or 25 independent weights respectively, instead of the 27 or 18). In the latter case the number of elementary templates is higher and some translation is required: this solution is more general but more time expensive.

SIGNAL PROPAGATION AND RECURSIVE NEAR-NEIGHBOR PRIMITIVES

In parallel machines, such as arrays and pyramids of P.E.s, data must be transferred between non-adjacent P.E.s by means of iterative near-neighbor operations*. In these operations, for each processor transitions are functions of the near-neighbor values (NN).

In recursive operations, the result is also input argument, so that the elementary instructions are effectively repeated until constant values are reached. Then recursive near-neighbor operations supply the capability to propagate signals inside a connected component (until the component is completely covered).

This feature permits very effective operations both in binary and in grey level imageries. In the former case a simple machine instruction permits to perform common tasks such as background/object separation and object extraction (by diffusion of a seed). The recursive near-neighbor functions for these basic tasks are respectively:

$$Y = \bar{X} \cap [\ U_G\ NN_Y\ ] \qquad\qquad Y = X \cap [\ U_G\ NN_Y\ ]$$

where X is the original binary image, Y the partial and resulting image and $U_G NN_Y$ represents the boolean OR operator on the set G of the near-neighbors in Y. In both cases, one seed at least must be included properly in the initial Y image. Combining these operations, very complex problems can be solved, because the near-neighbor iterative facility allows, as has been shown, to use segments (connected components) as atomic data (for some example see /4/).

---

* Often some "ad hoc" hardware is dedicated to speed up this transmission that constitutes a real bottleneck for these powerful systems.

Of course the execution time of a recursive instruction is not well defined: it depends on the number of P.E.s through which the propagation signal must travel. In the most frequent cases, this execution time is close to the maximum radius (referred to seed position) of the convex hull built over the connected component in which the propagation occurs.

Quantitative measures of object's features (useful for recognition purposes), such as elongation respect to a particular axis, can be performed by means of near-neighbor recursive instructions as well. In this case the propagation is not constrained inside a connected component as it has been shown previously, but it is applied along a fixed direction:

$$Y = X \cup NN_y^d$$

where NN_y^d is the near-neighbor value in the opposite direction to the propagation one (see fig. 1). On the border the elongation can be easily computed.

When multilevel propagation is considered, important primitives can be defined either for grey level or for binary image manipulation.

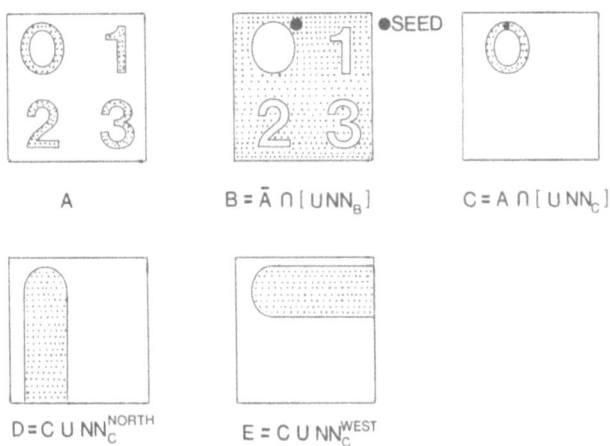

A

$B = \bar{A} \cap [\cup NN_B]$

$C = A \cap [\cup NN_C]$

$D = C \cup NN_C^{NORTH}$

$E = C \cup NN_C^{WEST}$

Fig. 1 : Examples of recursive near-neighbor
and signal propagation primitives

The former case includes tools such as the diffusion operator applied in iterative mode (in /5/ a new fast method is presented which permits contour labeling for recognition purposes based on this operator) and the min/max propagation inside connected components in recursive mode (this is often used for objects labeling).

The latter case is well represented by the distance transform:

$$
Y = \begin{cases}
0 & \text{if } X = 0 \\
\\
\text{MIN } NN_y + 1 & \text{if } X = 1
\end{cases}
$$

this gives an efficient representation of binary segments on which one can easily perform operations like magnification, shrinking, medial axis transform, skeletonization, pruning, etc. For an extensive discussion on these primitives see /6/.

A final comment on the implementation of iterative and recursive near-neighbor operation is needed. Both kinds of operation are data driven and must terminate whenever a stable data configuration is obtained. For this reason a global test is required on the whole array or pyramid of P.E.s. The exclusive OR between past and present state of all processors builds up a general OR-tree that provides a boolean response on the stability of image data configuration. Moreover, global tests on image content can be obtained by coping the content of the status register of each processor into the OR-tree circuitry; this is used especially to terminate iterative operations.

GLOBAL AND STATISTICS PRIMITIVES

A common approach to object recognition is the decision theoretic one (see /7/). This approach is characterized by the representation of objects by means of a vector of features. These features are usually global characteristics computed on segments (or sometimes on the whole image) based on the grey level statistics or on the pixels distribution of the object silhouette.

The most popular descriptor set of the second case is the complete moment set (CSM_n) of order n (usually n=5-6) (see /8/). A moment can be defined as:

$$
M_{pqr} = \iint\limits_{\text{segment}} x^p \, y^q \, f(x,y)^r \, dx \, dy
$$

Usually r=0 and p+q is the order of the moment. The CSM_n is composed of all the moments with $p+q \leqslant n$ and is used for recognition purposes in normalized mode: scaling is obtained by having $M_{00} = 1$, translation with $M_{10} = M_{01} = 0$ and rotation with $M_n = 0$. Moreover luminance effects can be normalized (respect to luminance bias and contrast M_{001} and M_{002} must equal suitable values).

Grey level statistics are often needed both for segmentation (by thresholding) and for texture analysis. Two main primitives can be suggested for these purposes: one for histogram and the second for co-occurrence matrix computation.

The implementation of the quoted primitives is widely discussed in literature. For what concerns the statistics primitives some solutions for histogram and co-occurrence matrix computation can be found respectively in /9/ for the array of processor and in /10/ for the pyramid case. In particular the "ad hoc" hardware proposed for the CSM computation /8/ is essentially an array of P.E.s working in SIMD mode that can be simulated efficiently with the usual general purpose array processor.

LINEAR TRANSFORM PRIMITIVES

One of the topics in low level vision is the calculus of the linear transforms. Many of them find application in the frequency domain analysis and in the linear filtering: Fourier transform, Walsh and Hadamard transforms. Some are used in communication and coding problems: Karounen-Loewe transform, Fourier, cosine, Haar and Walsh transforms. In particular the Haar transform is useful to elaborate planning strategies because of the hierarchical structure of the functions forming their kernel /11/.

We can classify the transforms above mentioned in several ways depending on the properties of the kernel. They are separable if the calculus can be performed in two different steps, one on the set of the rows and the other on the set of the columns (Fourier, Walsh, Hadamard). They may need the use of real or complex weights (Fourier), integer (Haar), or even only the values 1 and -1 (Walsh, Hadamard). Moreover a comparison can be done on the physical meaning of the components of the transform.

On sequential machines many transforms are computed by fast algorithms. On the other hand, on array processors and pipeline machines the computation is performed following the definition of the transform (sum of products between the data and the weights). In this way the parallelism offered by these architectures is completely exploited. A particular hint is due to the two-dimensional Haar transform. Its computation is achieved on array processors in a relatively simple way although this transform is not separable. On pyramidal machines, however, the Haar transform calculus is almost immediate. This topic is treated in another paper presented in this conference /1/.

We shall illustrate now an algorithm for the computation of the Walsh and Hadamard transforms and their inverse transforms. They use only weights 1 and -1; differently, Fourier and cosine transform use the real arithmetic for computing the inner product between the data and the weights, that normally needs a computation time much greater than integer arithmetic. So, parallel array machines working in SIMD mode allow an easy computation of Walsh and Hadamard transforms because no multiplication is required. This algorithm extensively exploits the near-neighbor operations among adjacent PE's and the possibility of enabling the single PE setting the mask-register. The procedure uses the Walsh or Hadamard functions codified with 1 (for the value 1) and 0 (for -1). They are stored inside the base-plane in the local memory of the PE's: the processor of position (i,j) has the j-th value (1 bit) of the i-th function. Moreover the rows and the columns of the array must be arranged in "wrap-around" way, with the first and the last processors connected.

The procedure is composed by four phases: 2 for the computation of the partial transform on the rows and two for the columns. The first phase is performed by repeating N times the following operations (N being the number of rows or columns):

- propagations along the columns of the coefficients situated on the diagonal line of the array;

- the matrix obtained in this way is loaded in the mask-register of the processors;

- the enabled processors sum the datum to the value contained in a partial result accumulator;

- all processors are enabled;

- the matrix of the coefficients rotates towards East;

- also the matrix of the data rotates towards East;

After the first phase in which only the processors having weight 1 work, the data are complemented and the same routine as before run except that the mask register is loaded with the complement of the coefficient so that the processors with weight -1 perform the sum between the partial result and the complement of the datum. At the end of the phase 2 the partial results in the accumulators are the transforms along the rows. These, normalized, are the data for the last 2 phases performing the transform along the columns. Now the data rotates towards South, while the coefficients propagate from the diagonal line along the rows. So it is not necessary to transpose the matrix of the coefficients.

CONCLUSION AND ACKNOWLEDGEMENTS

In this paper a non exhaustive list of parallel image processing primitives has been introduced with no reference to a specific system. Several peculiar primitives are needed in every machine together with the management and I/O ones.

The authors thank A. Machi' for several useful comments that led to an improvement of this paper.

REFERENCES

1. L. Carrioli: A Pyramidal Haar Transform Implementation, see these Proc.

2. A. Peled,B. Liu: A New Hardware Realization of Digital Filters, IEEE Trans. Acoust. Sp. Sig. Proc. ASSP-22,pp. 456-462

3. J. Serra': "Image Analysis and Mathematical Morphology", Academic Press, London (1982)

4. A.P. Reeves: A Systematically Designed Binary Array Processor, IEEE Trans. Computers, Vol C-29, N.4, April 1980

5. V. Cantoni,S. Levialdi: Contour Labeling by Pyramidal Processing, 7nth Workshop on Languages, Architectures and Algorithms for Image Processing, Chateau de Bonas, May 1985, in press

6. A. Rosenfeld,A.C. Kak:"Digital Picture Processing", Academic Press, London (1982)

7. K.S. Fu: Recent Developments in Pattern Recognition, IEEE Trans. on Computers, Vol. C-29, N. 10, October 1980

8. A.P. Reeves: A Parallel Mesh Computer, Proc. 6st International Conference on Pattern Recognition, pp. 465-476, Muenchen, October 1982

9. V. Cantomi,M. Ferretti,S. Levialdi,R. Stefanelli: PAPIA Pyramidal Architecture for Parallel Image Analysis, Proc. 7nth Symposium on Computer Arithmetic, pp. 237-242, Urbana, 1985

10. V. Di Gesu',A. Machi': Some examples of I.P. Algorithms for Pyramidal Architectures, see these Proc.

11. K.G. Beauchamp: "Walsh Functions and their Applications", Academic Press, London (1975)

SOME EXAMPLES OF IP ALGORITHMS FOR PYRAMIDAL ARCHITECTURE

V. Di Gesù[1] and A. Machì[2]

[1]Istituto di Matematica, Univ. di Palermo, Italy
[2]Istituto di Fisica Cosmica ed Applicazioni
   dell'Informatica del C.N.R., Palermo, Italy

ABSTRACT

Aim of the paper is to present a class of parallel algorithms for
Image Processing (IP) implemented in a pyramid machine architecture. The
complexity of the algorithms and their performance as regards to a serial
processor is also given.

INTRODUCTION

The request for new parallel architectures has become pressing in
several applications, due to the increasing rate of the data (mono and two
dimensional) which require real time or fast processing (<1h).

Many data analysis problems deal with data organized in array structures as in the case of time series of events or images from detectors. Often
the analysis requires the application of the same computation on each element of the array and the algorithm itself involves local operations on
its near neighbours. The results of the computation is still an array.
Examples are the algorithms for noise suppression, restoration by means
of filtering and enhancement by means of deconvolution.

Several parallel machines have been built with different architectures
and functional principles. For example the pipeline configuration is implemented in the Cytocomputer[1], while mesh connection is present in the CLIP
(Cellular Logic Image Processor) series[2], the MPP (Massive Parallel Processor)[3] and the DAP[4] machines.

Pyramid machines, defined as cellular array having hierarchical interconnections[5,6,7,8], seem to be very promising tools for IP and planning.
As S. Tanimoto underlined[9]:

"...The pyramid machine architecture is motivated by several
considerations:
a) The hierarchical structure of the mammalian visual pathway
   starting at the retina and ending in the deepest layers
   of the visual cortex;

b) the possibility of computing many function of N variables in O(logN) time;

c) the ease with which tree algorithms may be implemented;

d) the ease of image noise suppression..."

The present paper describes three algorithms for the analysis of some typical statistical IP problems, often present in the analysis of astronomical and biomedical images, texture analysis and robotic vision. The algorithms are the deconvolution, the median filter and the cooccorrence matrix ones.

In serial machines their time complexity is increasing with power $\geqslant 2$ of the input size and their implementation on pyramid architecture seems to be very promising.

Section two describes the main features of the pyramid machine, where the algorithms will be implemented[6]. In section three is given their description and the time complexity. Section four is devoted to final remarks.

THE PYRAMID PROCESSOR

The algorithms analized will be implemented in the pyramid machine PAPIA[8]. In this section a short description of it is given.

The pyramidal architecture of the machine may be considered as a three dimensional extension of a binary tree. It is composed by several cellular arrays of processors hierarchically connected, which operate on an array of data represented in decreasing solution.

The parallel CPU is composed of 8 arrays of Processing Elements (PE). The lower array is formed by 128x128 PE's. To allow the management of big image the array connections may be reconfigured.

Memory registers on the array edges take care of the contiguity among the various sections of the image subsequently loaded and allow also the hardware implementation of an 'image scroll' function.

A separate parallel channel is provided for the data I/O on the base plane, in column parallel bitplane format. The parallel pyramidal CPU operates on fixed size bitplanes.

Each PE is connected to 9 neighbour processors 4 'brothers' in the same plane, one 'father' in the upper plane and 4 'sons' in the lower one.

Each processor has various boolean registers, two variable length shift registers, a boolean ALU and 256 bits of local memory. It may performs bit transfer and boolean operations between its memory and registers as well between its registers and a selected subset of its neighbour ones[10].

The machine Control System[11] performs all the hard-software function required to emulate a SIMD/MSIMD machine operating on multi-gray-level images of decreasing size, by means of a powerful set of operations. The set will include operations between scalar and images and between images, coded in integer and floating point formats, program flux control instructions and primitive operations on the images[12].

DESCRIPTION OF THE ALGORITHMS

In the following the time analysis is performed in terms of the operations of sum, product, scroll, wraparound, comparison and propagation. The notation is the following:

Ta = time unit to perform a sum;
Tp = time unit to perform a product;
Tc = time unit to perform a comparison;
Ts = time unit to perform an image scroll/wraparound;
Tpr= time unit to propagate a value from the father to its suns;
c = time unit for comparison in a serial processor;
s = time unit for sum in a serial processor;
p = time unit for product in a serial processor.

All the images are considered square with size NxN. The pixel values may belong to a finite set of integer G=$\{1,2,...,g\}$ (gray levels) or to a set of real numbers.

Deconvolution

Many deconvolution algorithms have been studied for parallel architectures. Per-Erik Danielson gives an example for a systolic machine, under the hypothesis that x and y directions may be considered indipendent[13]. In the following a general deconvolution operator is considered.

The algorithm performs the deconvolution of an image M of real values by means of a kernel K of dimension DxD. The results is the deconvolved image M'. The algorithm is based on the discrete deconvolution formula:

$$M'(i,j) = \sum_{k,l=-D/2}^{D/2} M(i-k,j-l) \times K(k,l)$$

The values of N and D may be assumed, without loosing generality, to be power of 2 with D < N.

The input data of the algorithm are the image M, the deconvolution kernel K and their sizes. In order to speed up the computation $(N/D)^2$ copies of the kernel are reproduced in an image W of the same size of M, see Fig.1.

The computation of the product terms is straightforward, the sum of the products is performed by partitioning the pyramid in $(N/D)^2$ subpyramids of height Ll=Log2(D) and calculating the sum of the pixel-values with a bottom-up algorithm, see fig. 1.

The pyramid is iteratively used to accumulate in each father (root) PE the sum of its son values. At the process end the deconvolved value is obtained in each subpyramid vertex. The value then is propagated top-down to the pixel (i,j), that is the center of the deconvolution window. The computation is performed for each pixel of M by scrolling it in x and/or y directions, using an appropiate sequence. Therefore the computation time is proportional to the kernel size.

The algorithm may be outlined as follows:

STEP1:
    assign to M' the product MxW;
    sum the pixel values of M' bottom up;
    /*
        the vertex of each subpyramid contains the value of
        the corresponding pixel (i,j) of M'

```
*/
```
        propagate the value from the vertex of each
        subpyramid to the central pixel of its base;
REPEAT STEP1 D^2 times scrolling M in x and y directions.

The number of products is D^2; the number of sum is $L1xD^2$, the number
of step to propagate the value stored in the subpyramid vertex is also
$L1xD^2$, the number of scrolls is D^2.
It follows that the total computational time is:

$$PTcpu = O((Ts + Tp + (Ta+Tpr)xLog2(D))xD^2)$$

In the case of a sequential processor, assuming N=Log2(D)xD, the time
to perform the deconvolution is:

$$STcpu = O(Log2(D)^2xD^4x(p+s))$$

The ratio between parallel and serial implementation is:

$$\frac{PTcpu}{STcpu} = \frac{(Ts+Tp+(Ta+Tpr)xLog2(D)}{(p+s)xD^2xLog2(D)^2}$$

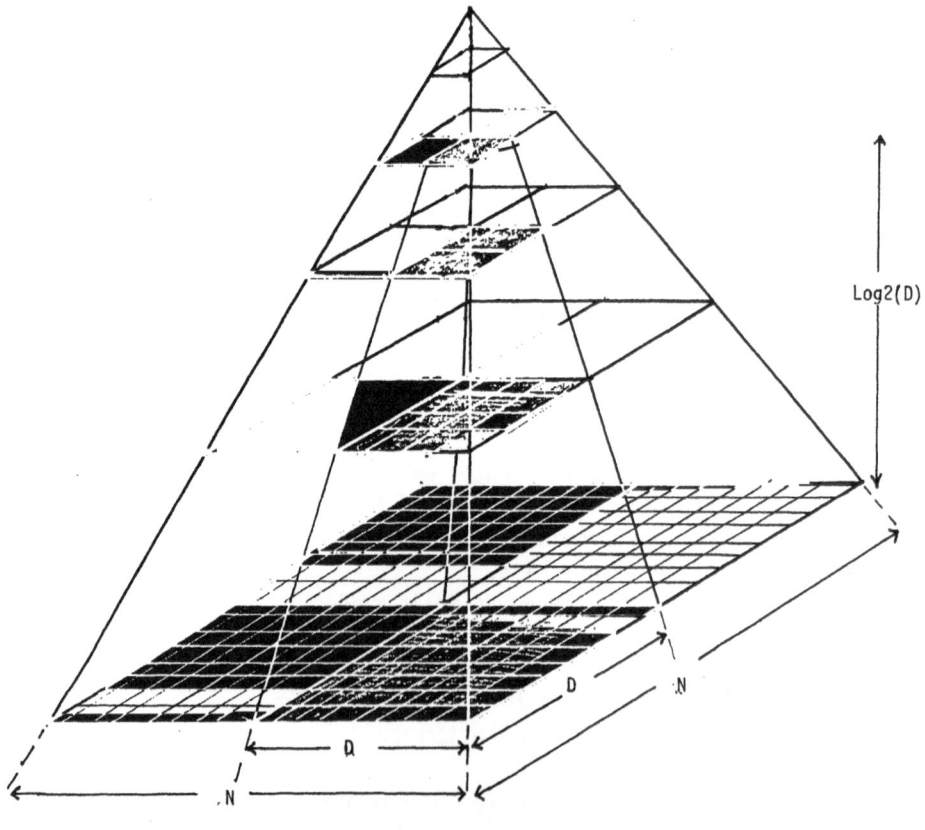

Fig. 1

Median Filter

A median filter of order k assigns to a pixel (i,j), of an image M, the kth maximum among pixel-intensities belonging to a window of size DxD centered in (i,j). It may be defined as follows:

$$M'(i,j) = \underset{k}{Max} \left\{ M(r,s) \mid i-D<r<i+D, \ j-D<s<j+D \right\}$$

Where M' is the filtered image. If the space is isotropous the result does not depend from the position of the pixel (i,j) into the window. In many applications the most used value for k is $D^2/2$.

S.Tanimoto reported[9] an example of algorithm for the computation of the median filter. The version proposed in this paper is addressed to the processor described in section 2 used in SIMD may.

The input data are M and k. Temporary image data are stored in MT, k' and MAX, a bitplane masks MK1 and MK2 are utilized.

The algorithm consists in sorting for each pixel (i,j) the elements of the surrounding window and setting its value to the kth maximum.

As in the deconvolution algorithm the pyramid is logically partitioned in $(N/D)^2$ subpyramids of base size equal to the dimension of the window (DxD) and height L1=Log2(D), see Fig. 1.

The algorithm may be outlined as follows:

```
STEP1:
    STEP2:
        compares each processor M-value with its neighbours
        M-values and transfers the maximum (MAX) to the father,
        until the vertex of each subpyramid is reached;
        /*
           after Log2(D) steps the first maximum reaches the
           subpyramid vertex
        */
           propagate MAX from each vertex to the base and store
           it in MT;
           where (MT=M) do
               assign - ∞ to M;
               assign TRUE to MK1;
           count the TRUE pixel in MK1 and put the result in k';
           assign to MK2 (k'<k)
           propagate MK2 from the vertex to the base;
           load MK2 in processor MASK register;
        /*
           the results is that where k' ≥ k
           the subpyramid processors are disabled
        */
    REPEAT STEP2 k times;
    enable all pyramid processors;
    transfer MAX from the subpyramid vertex to the base and assign it
    to M';
REPEAT STEP1 D² times scrolling M in x and y directions.
```

The computation of the kth maximum is performed D^2 times. The computa-

tion requires 4xlog2(D) comparisons, 2xLog2(D) sums, 4xLog2(D) propagations k times, Log2(D) transfers at the end to assign MAX to M' and D^2
scroll. Therefore the time required to compute the median filter is:

$$PTcpu=O(D^2x(Log2(D)x(kx(Tc + Tpr + Ta) + Tpr) + Tsr))$$

In the case of a sequential processor, setting N=FxD and using quick
sort algorithm, the optimal time is:

$$STcpu = O(F^2xD^4xLog2(D)xc)$$

The ratio between parallel and serial implementation is:

$$\frac{PTcpu}{STcpu} = \frac{Log2(D)x(kx(Tc+Tpr+Ta)+Tpr)+Tsr}{F^2xD^2xc}$$

It follows that the computation gain depends from the wideness of
the filtering window (usually F≫1).

Cooccurrence matrix

The cooccurrence matrix, C, of an image M defined on the set G contains
in the element C(i,j) the frequency of the occurrence in M of the couple
of values i and j at distance D along the direction . Therefore C is a
gxg square matrix.

$$C(i,j)= \left| \{ ((k,1),(m,n)) | M(k,1)=i \text{ and } M(m,n)=j \text{ and} \right.$$
$$\left. \sqrt{((k-n)^2+(1-n)^2} =D \text{ and } (k-m)/(1-n)=\tan \theta \} \right|$$

The input data are the image M, the angle θ and the distance D. Temporary values are stored in the image M' and bit-plane mask MK1. The algorithm may be described as follows:

```
copy M in M'
rotate the image M' of θ degree;
perform a scroll of M' of D columns on the right and
disable D processor columns in the left side;
STEP1:
    STEP2:
        where (M=i and M'=j) assign TRUE to MK1;
        count the TRUE pixels in MK1;
        /*
          The result is obtained in the vertex of the pyramid
        */
        propagate form the vertex to the top left PE
        on the base and assign the value to C;
        scroll C of one step in x direction on the left;
    REPEAT STEP2 for j=1,2,...g;
    scroll C of g steps in x direction on the rigth;
    scroll C of one step in y direction upward;
REPEAT STEP1 for i=1,2,...g;
```

perform a scroll of M' of 2xD columns of the left and disable D
processor columns in the right side;
STEP3:
    STEP4:
        where (M=i and M'=j) assign TRUE to MK1;
        count the TRUE pixels in MK1;
        /*
            The result is obtained in the vertex of the pyramid
        */
        propagate form the vertex to the top left PE
        on the base and sum the value to C;
        scroll C of one step in x direction on the left;
    REPEAT STEP4 for j=1,2,...g;
    scroll C of g steps in x direction on the rigth;
    scroll C of one step in y direction upward;
REPEAT STEP3 for i=1,2,...g.

The algorithm is composed of two main loops, where gxg times one sum,
one propagation and one comparison are made. Two scrolls are made g times,
3xD scrolls are performed outside the loops. The computation time is:

$$PTcpu = O(g^2 x(Tc + Log2(D)x(Ta+Tpr)) + (g+3xD)xTs))$$

For a serial processor the time required is:

$$STcpu = O(N^2 x g^2 x(c + s))$$

The ratio between parallel and serial implementation is:

$$\frac{PTcpu}{SRcpu} = \frac{g^2(Tc + Log2(D)x(Ta+Tpr)) + (g+3xD)xTs}{g^2 X N^2}$$

CONCLUDING REMARKS

The algorithms described may be considered as paradigm for many
computations in image and processing analysis.
Other straightforward algorithms could have been shown to compute
several statistical quantity as average, variance, histogram... of an
image. They have been omitted because the implementation make use of the
same kind of computational tools (sum, counting, propagation,...).
The examples shown underline how the hierarchical architecture allows
both a natural formulation of the algorithms and a reduction of one order
of the time complexity as regards to the the serial ones.

REFERENCES

1. S.R.Stemberg, 'Pipeline Architectures for Image Processing', in:Multi-
        computer and Image Processing (Algorithms and Programs),Ed.K.Preston,
        L.Uhr, Academic Press, London,(1982).

2. M.J.Duff, 'Review of the CLIP image processing system', Proc.Nat.Conf. Anaheim, USA, (1981).
3. V.E.Batcher, 'Design of the Massively Parallel Processor', IEEE Trans. on Computers, Vol C.29, (1980).
4. S.F.Roddaway, 'DAP-A distributed processor array', First Annual Symp. on Computer Architecture, Florida, (1973).
5. A.Rosenfeld , Multiresolution Image Processing and Analysis', Springer Verlag, New York, (1983).
6. V.Cantoni, L.Carrioli, L.Cinque, M.Ferretti, S.Levialdi, A.Perone, 'Image Processing in Hierarchical computer structure', Int.Conf. on Digital Signal Processing, Florence, Italy, (1984).
7. S.L.Tanimoto, 'A Pyramidal approach to parallel processing', Tenth Annual Symp.On Computer Architecture, Stockolm, (1983).
8. V.Cantoni, L.Carrioli, O.Catalano, L.Cinque, V.Di Gesù, M.Ferretti, G. Gerardi, S.Levialdi, R.Lombardi, A.Machì, R.Stefanelli, 'The PAPIA Pyramidal Machine: General Description and Applications', Convegno Nazional ASTRONET, Roma, (1985).
9. S.Tanimoto, 'Sorting, Histogramming, and Other Statistical Operations on a Pyramid Machine', A.Rosenfeld ed., Multiresolution Image Processing and Analysis, Springer Verlag, New York, (1983).
10.V.Cantoni, M.Ferretti, S.Levialdi, F.Maloberti, 'A Pyramid Project using Integrated Technology', in: Integrated technology for Parallel Image Processing, S.Levialdi ed., Academic Press, New York, 1984.
11.O.Catalano, G.Gerardi, R.Lombardi, A.Machì, 'The PAPIA Control System (Hardware Design)', III Int.Conf. on Image Analysis and Processing, Rapallo, (1985).
12.V.Cantoni, L.Carrioli, L.Cinque, V.Di Gesù, M.Ferretti, S.Levialdi, 'Parallel Image Processing Primitives', III Int.Conf. on Image Analysis and Processing, Rapallo, (1985).
13.Per-Erik Danielson, 'Implementation of the Convolution Operator', NATO ASI on Computer Architectures for Spatially Distributed Data, Cetraro, (1983).

A PYRAMIDAL HAAR-TRANSFORM IMPLEMENTATION

Luigi Carrioli

Dipartimento di Informatica e Sistemistica
Pavia University
Pavia, Italy

INTRODUCTION

The one-dimensional Haar functions set, used to built the homonymous transform, is defined in the interval (0,1) in this way:

$$HAR(0,x) = 1$$

$$HAR(2^p+n,x) = \begin{cases} 2^{p/2} & \text{for } \dfrac{n}{2^p} \le x < \dfrac{(n+1/2)}{2^p} \\[2ex] -2^{p/2} & \text{for } \dfrac{(n+1/2)}{2^p} \le x < \dfrac{n+1}{2^p} \\[2ex] 0 & \text{elsewhere} \end{cases}$$

$$p = 1,2,\ldots \quad n = 0,1,\ldots,2^p-1$$

This is a complete set formed by orthonormal functions /1-2/ assuming only three values. They take values different from zero only on a limited part of the interval (0,1). Moreover their integral is always zero except for the first function.

If we defined the two-dimensional Haar-functions like:

$$HAR2(u,v,x,y) = HAR(u,x)\,HAR(v,y)$$

we would miss the peculiarity of the one-dimensional Haar-functions, that is their "locality" property.

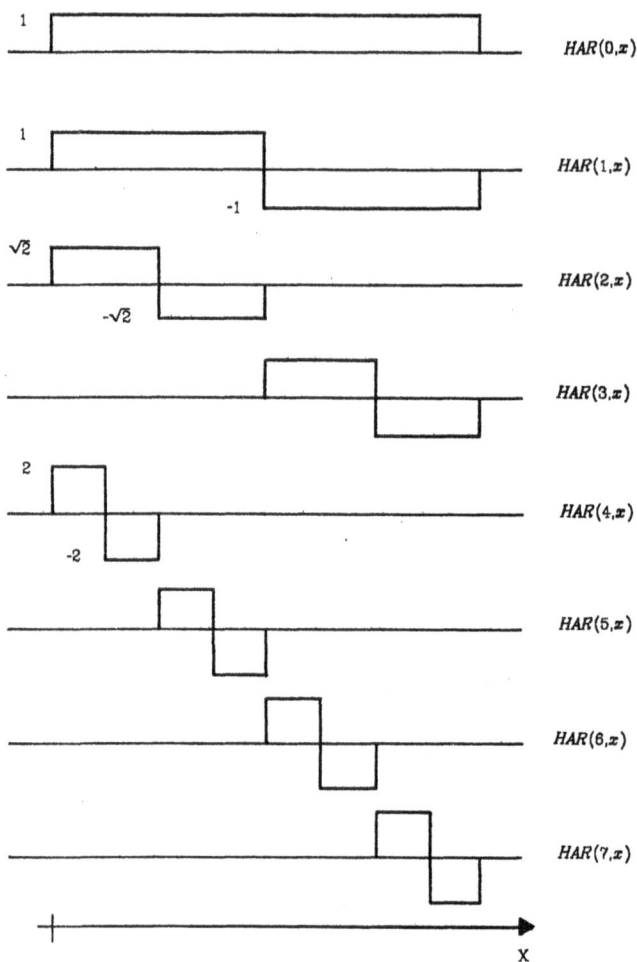

Fig.1: The first 8 Haar-functions.

A better approach to define the two-dimensional Haar-functions has been proposed by Shore /6/. He found a complete system of orthonormal two-dimensional functions having characteristics similar to the one-dimensional ones: in particular, they are non-zero only on squares contained in the set (0,1) x (0,1).

They are based on three fundamental types of blocks, shifted and scaled on the whole definition set:

$$f_1(x,y) = \begin{bmatrix} 1 & -1 \\ 1 & -1 \end{bmatrix} \quad f_2(x,y) = \begin{bmatrix} 1 & 1 \\ -1 & -1 \end{bmatrix} \quad f_3(x,y) = \begin{bmatrix} 1 & -1 \\ -1 & 1 \end{bmatrix} \quad 0 \le x,y \le 1.$$

Each function is identified by four indexes: one (h) furnishing the exten-
sion of the non-zero part $(1, -\frac{1}{4}, --\frac{1}{16}, \ldots, ------\frac{1}{2(h-1)}$ of the total area$)^{\frac{1}{2}}$; a second
(k) indicating the kind of the block (vertical, horizontal, diagonal); and
a couple of indexes (i,j) giving the position of the block inside the
square (0,1) x (0,1):

$$HAR2(0,0,0,0,x,y) = 1$$

$$HAR2(h,k,i,j,x,y) = \begin{cases} 2^{h-1} f_k(2^{h-1}x-i, 2^{h-1}y-j) & \text{for } \dfrac{i}{2^{h-1}} \le x \le \dfrac{i+1}{2^{h-1}}, \quad \dfrac{j}{2^{h-1}} \le y \le \dfrac{j+1}{2^{h-1}} \\[2ex] 0 & \text{elsewhere} \end{cases}$$

with

$$0 \le x, y \le 1 \qquad h = 1, 2, \ldots \qquad k = 1, 2, 3 \qquad i, j = 0, 1, \ldots, 2^{h-1} - 1$$

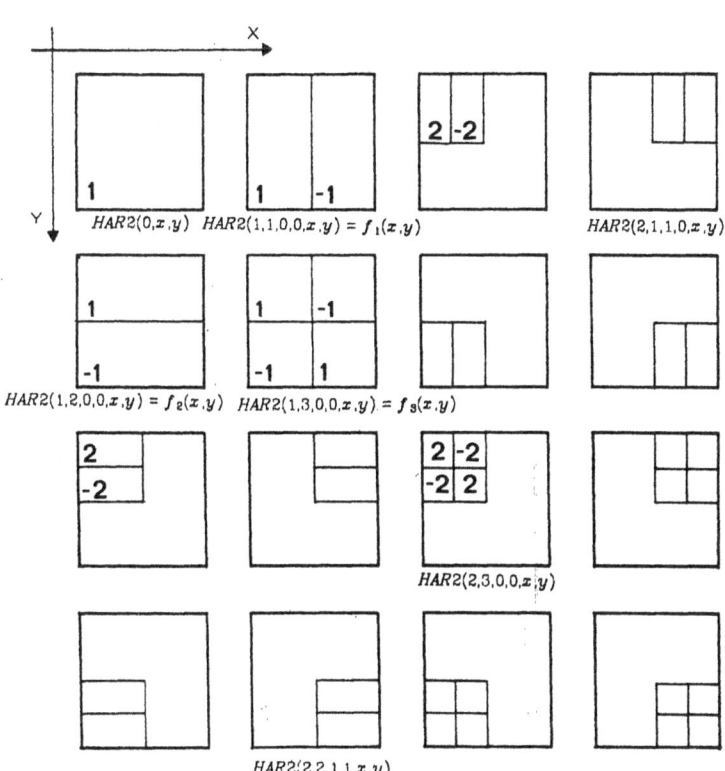

Fig.2: Two dimensional Haar-functions until h=2; the amplitudes are power of 2.

The templates (f_1, f_2, f_3) may be considered as gradient like operators along three directions: vertical, horizontal and diagonal. So, the
components of the two-dimensional Haar-transform give local information
about the variation of the signal.

However, the templates are applied with different sizes on the image, so
that the "locality" of the informations contained in the components of the
transform is associated to a scale factor.

From another point of view we can apply the templates on images with different resolution levels, obtained from the original image by local averag-
ing. This is the way for computing the two-dimensional Haar-transform on
pyramidal machines where different resolution images, quickly computed, are
all present at the same time, one for each plane of the pyramid.

The Haar-transform, because of these characteristics, is useful for ela-
borating planning strategies. In particular it can be used for localizing
areas of interest inside the image on the basis of the region descriptors
hierarchically organized.

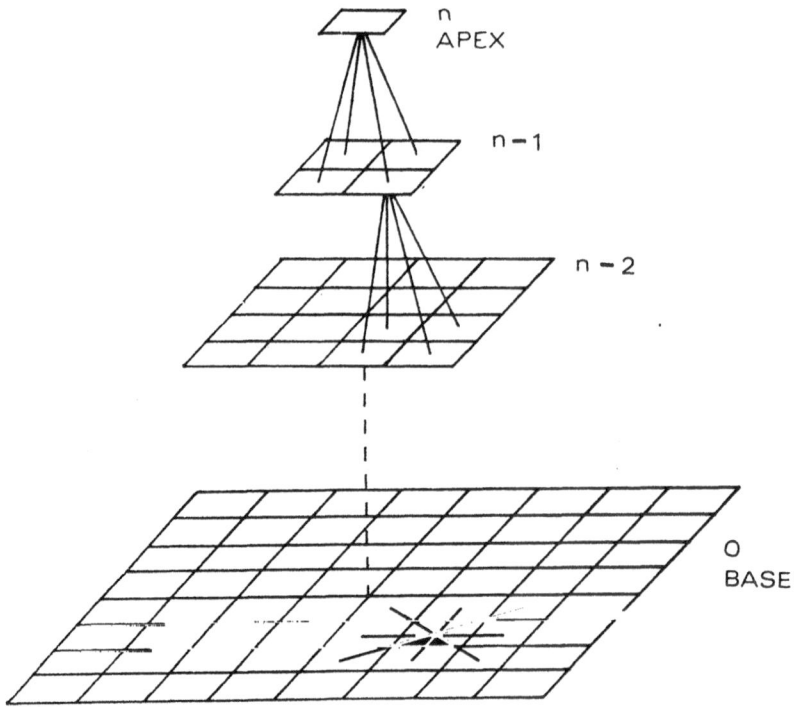

Fig.3: Connections among the processors of the pyramid: each of them
exchanges data with 4 (or 8) "brothers" on the same plane, 4 "sons" on
the lower plane and with the "father" on the higher plane.

THE ALGORITHMS

Let us show now the algorithms performing the computation of the
direct and inverse transforms.

They are built for a pyramidal architecture of SIMD kind, in which each
processor is physically connected to the four "sons" situated on the lower

plane, to the four (or eight) "brothers" on the same plane and to the "father" on the upper plane. For simplicity we refer to the case in which the base of the pyramid and the image to transform have the same dimension.

Direct transform

The procedure works on a set of images containing the original image to transform (it is stored on the base of the pyramid) and its copies at lower resolutions, stored one for plane. They are easily obtained from the original image performing a local average operation on the four pixels connected to the same father. This operation is repeated in all planes until the apex of the pyramid is reached. All data so obtained have the same format.

The transform is immediate: on the whole pyramid (except the apex) the four processors sons of the same father accomplish the following operation (elementary transform) on the four data belonging to them:

$$\begin{bmatrix} A & B \\ C & D \end{bmatrix} \longrightarrow \begin{bmatrix} W & X \\ Y & Z \end{bmatrix}$$

where

$$W = (A+B+C+D)/4$$
$$X = (A-B+C-D)/4$$
$$Y = (A+B-C-D)/4$$
$$Z = (A-B-C+D)/4$$

Denoting with $\bar{V}$ the vector $\begin{bmatrix} A \\ B \\ C \\ D \end{bmatrix}$ and with $\bar{U}$ the vector $\begin{bmatrix} W \\ X \\ Y \\ Z \end{bmatrix}$ we have:

$$\bar{U} = \frac{1}{4} H_4 \bar{V}$$

where H_4 is the Hadamard's matrix of rank 4:

$$H_4 = \begin{bmatrix} 1 & 1 & 1 & 1 \\ 1 & -1 & 1 & -1 \\ 1 & 1 & -1 & -1 \\ 1 & -1 & -1 & 1 \end{bmatrix}$$

Remembering that

$$(H_4)^{-1} = -H_4$$

we have:

$$\bar{H}_4 U = -H_4 \bar{H}_4 \quad V = (\bar{H}_4)^{-1} \bar{H}_4 V = V.$$

All Xs, Ys, Zs of each plane and the datum of the apex are the values of the two-dimensional Haar-transform apart from a multiplying coefficient depending on the plane: the values situated on the k-th plane are divided by 2^{k+n+1}; the value of the apex (the dc component of the image) is an exception because it is diveded by 2^{2n} instead of 2^{2n+1}.
The data format equals the original image data format.
The significative values are located like in figure: the values placed on the plane m are referred to the functions with h=n-m.

Porcedure direct transform


```
      begin

            for I:=1 step 1 until n-1 do
            begin
                A   := (A    + B    + C    + D   ) / 4;
                 I      I-1    I-1    I-1    I-1
            end
      end
      begin
            W := (A + B + C + D) / 4;
            X := (A - B + C - D) / 4;
            Y := (A + B - C - D) / 4;
            Z := (A - B - C + D) / 4;
      end
end
```


Inverse transform

    The inverse transform procedure works on data located inside the pyramid in the same position where they were created by the direct transform algorithm.
It is formed by the following steps:
- let W=0 for all Ws except on the 2x2 plane;
- calculus of:

$$\begin{bmatrix} W & X \\ Y & Z \end{bmatrix} \longrightarrow \begin{bmatrix} A & B \\ C & D \end{bmatrix}$$

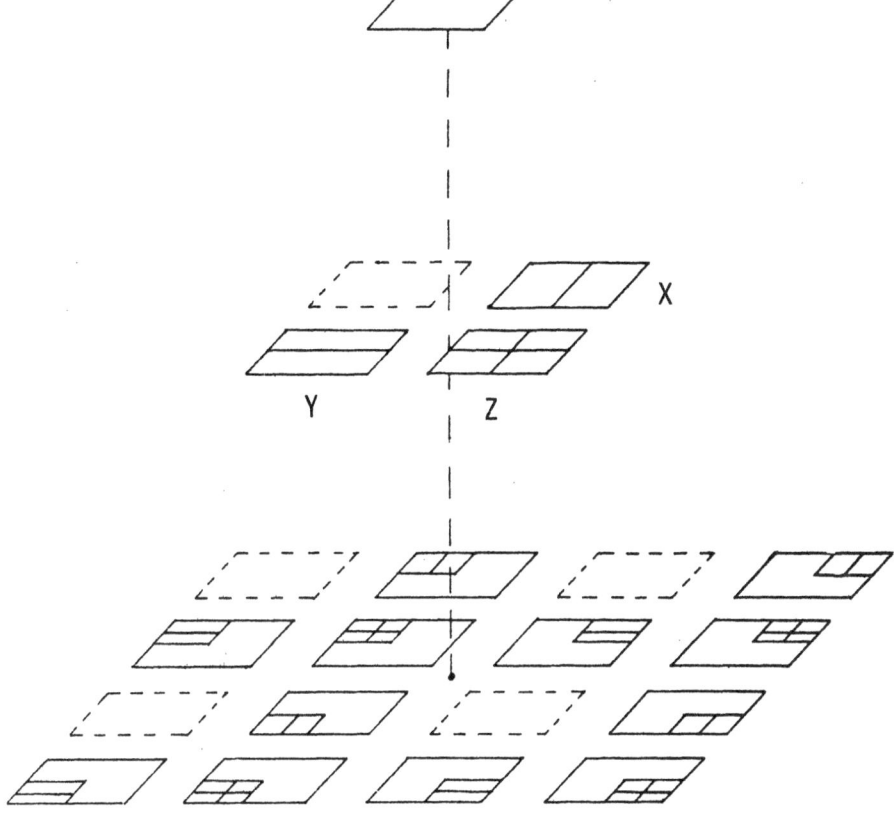

Fig.4: Final position of the values of the transform inside the pyramid: the processors being at North-East of their fathers have the values relative to the functions with k=1 (vertical), those at South-West have the values obtained from the functions with k=2 (horizontal), and those at South-East with k=3 (diagonal). A quarter of the processors have non significative data.

or

$$\overline{V} = \overline{H}\ \overline{U};$$
$$4$$

but, having W = 0:

$$A = X+Y+Z$$
$$B = -X+Y-Z$$
$$C = X-Y-Z$$
$$D = -X-Y+Z$$

- beginning from the 4x4 plane until the pyramid's base is reached each processor adds its father's value (A,B,C,D) to that belonging to it.
At the end of this operation we have again the set of different resolution images, placed one for plane.

The direct and inverse algorithms are dual: in the first there is a
propagation phase in which the data flow from the base to the apex (computation of the reduced resolution images). This is followed by a global
phase (elementary transform) where all the planes perform the same instructions. On the other hand, the inverse transform procedure shows first the
global phase, then the propagation one from the apex to the base.

Procedure inverse transform

```
    begin
        MASK := 1;
        MASK        := 0;
            (n-1)
        W := 0;
        begin
            A := (W + X + Y + Z);
            B := (W - X + Y - Z);
            C := (W + X - Y - Z);
            D := (W - X - Y + Z);
        end
        begin
            for I:=n-2 step -1 until 0 do
            begin
                A   := A  + FATHER;
                 I      I
                B   := B  + FATHER;
                 I      I
                C   := C  + FATHER;
                 I      I
                A   := D  + FATHER;
                 I      I
            end
        end
    end
end
```

IMPLEMENTATION ON PAPIA 1

Now we report the procedures implementing the algorithms above
described on the MSIMD pyramidal architecture PAPIA 1 /4-5/.
Among the multiresolution architectures proposed /11/, PAPIA 1 is a pyramid
formed by 8 planes of processors, the greatest of which has 128 x 128 elements. Two are the kinds of connections among the processor elements: horizontal and vertical (fig.3). Considering only the vertical connections
PAPIA 1 can be seen as a tree whose sub-trees are disjoined.

Direct transform

The procedure achieving the direct transform calculus needs, on each plane except the apex, the following data:
- data matrix (in complement to 2) stored in the shift register 2 (SR2)
- two binary matrix, stored in the memory locations M1 and M2: M1 is 1 in all the processors situated at North-West and South-West respect to their fathers; it is 0 for the processors of North-East and South-East; M2 is 1 for the processors of North-West and North-East, it is 0 for the others.
The calculus of W, X, Y, Z is performed by the four processors "brothers" in two steps: first the two processors of NW and SW compute A+B and C+D, while the processors of NE and SE compute A-B and C-D; then, with analogous technique, the processors of North compute A+B+C+D and A-B+C-D, while the others A+B-C-D and A-B-C+D.

Inverse transform

The data on which this procedure works are the same used by the direct transform one:
- data matrix stored in SR2;
- binary matrixs M1 and M2.
While the direct transform algorithm leads to data having uniform format, the inverse transform algorithm can provoke the dilation of some values. Generally, if the data on which the inverse transform algorithm works have a format of n bits in complement to 2, the results can be codified in n+h bits, where h depends on the plane of the pyramid: 2 for the 2x2, 3 for the 4x4, 4 for the three following plane, 5 for the 64x64 and 128x128.

REFERENCES

1. G.E. Paglia: "Rappresentazione ed elaborazione numerica dei segnali (III parte)", RIDIS, Universita' di Pavia, 1981.

2. K.G. Beauchamp: "Walsh functions and their application", Academic Press, 1975.

3. R.C. Gonzalez, P. Wintz: "Digital Image Processing", Addison-Wesley, 1977.

4. V. Cantoni, M. Ferretti, S. Levialdi, F. Maloberti: "A Pyramid Project using Integrated Technology", in Integrated Technology for Parallel Image Processing, ed. Levialdi, Polignano workshop (Italy), June 1983, Academic Press.

5. V. Cantoni, M. Ferretti, S. Levialdi, R. Stefanelli: "Papia: Pyramidal Architecture for Parallel Image Analysis", 7-th symposium on Computer Arithmetic, June 4-6 1985, Urbana, Illinois.

6. J.E. Shore: "A two dimensional Haar-like transform", NRL Report 7472 AD 755433, 1973.

7. J. Lifermann: "Les methodes rapides de transformation du signal", Masson et Cie, Paris, 1977.

8. N. Ahmed, K.R. Rao: "Orthogonal transforms for digital signal processing", Springer-Verlag, Berlin, 1975.

9. W.K. Pratt: "Digital image processing", Wiley, N.Y., 1977.

10. H.F. Harmuth: "Transmission of information by orthogonal functions", Springer-Verlag, Berlin, 1970.

11. A. Rosenfeld: "Multiresolution image representation", Digital Image Analysis, Pitman Book 1983, S. Levialdi ed., 18-28.

IMAGE PROCESSING
TECHNIQUES

FORM FEATURE REPRESENTATION IN A STRUCTURED BOUNDARY MODEL

S. Ansaldi[1], L. De Floriani[2], and B. Falcidieno[2]

[1]Politecnico di Milano, Milano, Italy
[2]Istituto per la Matematica Applicata, C.N.R.
Genova, Italy

ABSTRACT

A relational boundary model of a solid object, based on a structured graph representation is presented, and its application to the description of form features is discussed. In this hierarchical graph structure, called Structured Face Adjacency Graph, the global shape of an object is represented at the highest level of abstraction, while its representation details can be described at lower levels of specification. In the paper, we show how explicit topological form features, grouped into three main categories, namely through holes, protrusions or depressions, and connections, can be represented in this graph model as lower level attributes of the main object shape. We define also two basic transformations on the structured face adjacency graph, termed refinement and abstraction, which allow local modifications of its hierarchical structure, especially useful to reorganize object descriptions during the process planning step.

1. INTRODUCTION

The representation of the geometric characteristics of solid objects is a primary component in any geometric modeling system, since algorithms do not manipulate objects, but symbol structures, which define volume models. A representation scheme is the relation between a mathematical modeling space, whose elements are abstract solids, and the collection of all syntactically correct representations. Until now, the emphasis, in the development of representation schemes, has been on the provision of a geometry which allows the representation of the largest possible number of solid objects. Although this topic is a current field of interest in solid modeling, the attention of the researchers has recently turned to its engineering applications.

In this view, we have developed a relational structure based on a boundary representation of solid objects, called Face Adjacency Graph /3,8/. This relational model encodes faces as primary defining entities of an object and the edge-face and vertex-face relations as the fundamental relations between primitive object entities. Edges and vertices

111

are also explicitly represented by graph entities: edges as arcs connecting pairs of nodes, and vertices as hyperarcs connecting the set of nodes corresponding to the faces of the object concurrent into them. This model can be organized hierarchically, thus giving rise to a hierarchy of relational models, termed Structured Face Adjacency Graph, which provides a representation of objects at successively finer levels of detail. Different surface-based relational models of solid objects have been recently proposed in the literature /2,10/, some of which are basically an extension of the widely used winged edge structure /8/. The various models differ in the relations between the primitive topological entities they explicitly encode, and thus can be evaluated in terms of their storage requirements and of the time complexity of the algorithms for retrieving the topological information not stored in the model. All these structures, however, represent all the parts forming the boundary of an object at the same level of specification, without the capability of decoupling the description of the main shape of the object from its lower level attributes.

In this paper we show the capabilities of this hierarchical relational model for representing an object together with its form features. In fact, the boundary model of an object is structured as a two-level hierarchy, already during the design phase, by inserting the description of its global shape at the highest abstraction level and putting the definition of its topological form features at the second level. The model structured in this way is transferred to the process planning step, which specifies how the object must be manufactured by defining the so-called manufacturing features. If some new features are identified in the process planning step or, conversely, some parts of the object, previously defined as second level attributes, must be considered as parts of the main shape of the object, the model can be reconstructed, before the manufacturing step, by applying two transformations, called abstraction and refinement, which will be defined in section four.

2. A STRUCTURED GRAPH-BASED MODEL OF A SOLID OBJECT

In this section we define a relational model of the boundary of an object in which the three primitive topological entities defining its boundary, namely faces, edges and vertices are explicitly and unambiguously represented by elements of the graph model. In this model, called Face Adjacency Graph, nodes represent faces and arcs correspond to the relations among faces induced by the edges and vertices of the object. The face adjacency graph represents a further development of the edge-face graph we defined in a previous paper /2/, in which only the adjacency relation between pairs of faces defined by the edges was made explicit.

In the face adjacency graph, we represent two adjacency relations induced over the faces of an object S by its edges and vertices. In fact, two faces f_1 and f_2 of S are termed edge-adjacent if they share a common edge, and, similarly, two faces are called vertex-adjacent if they have at least a vertex in common. These relations can be suitably represented in the form of a hypergraph, which is a graph whose arcs may connect an arbitrary number of nodes /4/. Hence, the face adjacency graph /3/ of an object S is a hypergraph G = (N,A,H), where N, A and H denote, respectively, the set of nodes, arcs and hyperarcs of G, such that:

(i)   for every face f of S, there exists a unique node of G corresponding
       to f;

(ii)   for every edge e of S, shared by two of its faces, f_1 and f_2, there
       exists a unique arc in A connecting the two nodes of N corresponding
       to f_1 and f_2;

(iii) for every vertex of S, there exists a unique hyperarc in H con-
       necting all the nodes corresponding to the faces of S incident into
       V.

Fig. 1 shows a cube and its face adjacency graph representation. In the
diagram, dashed lines represent the hyperarcs of G, whereas continuous
lines its arcs.

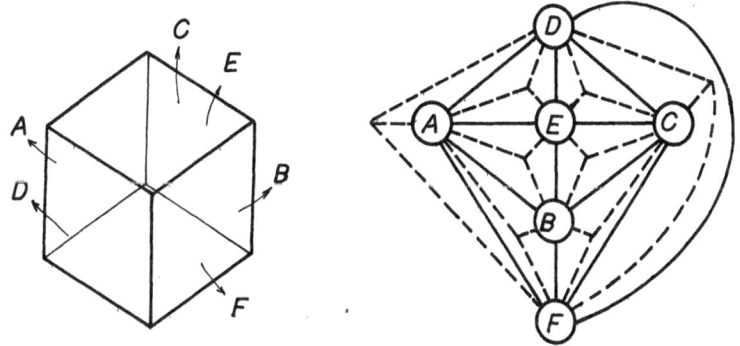

Fig. 1   A cube and its face adjacency graph representation

In the above definition, we distinguish between arcs and hyperarcs,
because of their different semantics when related to the topological
entities of the object. In fact, the arcs of G correspond to the edges
of S, while its hyperarcs encode the vertices of S. Since two faces of
S may share more than one edge, the face adjacency graph may have multiple
arcs. Also, the vertices bounding a given face are represented by the
hyperarcs incident into the corresponding node of G. Since the nodes of
the graph represent the object faces, this relational model is consistent
with the intrinsic hierarchy of the geometric information, according to
which surfaces are considered defining entities and curves and points
second level ones. Four relations between pairs of primitive are explicitly encoded in the face adjacency graph, i.e. the face-edge, the
edge-face, the edge-vertex and the vertex-face relations. The graph is
stored in a modified adjacency list form in which each arc e is encoded
as a pair of nodes (f_1, f_2) and a pair of vertices (v_1, v_2), which represent
the two exteme vertices of the edge corresponding to e. The set N of the
nodes of G is encoded into a linked list, in which each record describing
a node f contains the pointer to the sublist of the arcs incident into f.
Similarly, the set H of the hyperarcs of G is encoded in a list form, in
which each record describing a hyperarc v contains the pointer to the
sublist of its extreme nodes (which correspond to the faces of S concurrent
into vertex v).

The face adjacency graph of an object can be organized into a hier-

archical form in order to represent the object at successively finer
levels of details. In such a hierarchical representation, called
<u>Structured Face Adjacency Graph</u>, the root gives a description of the
object at the highest abstraction level, whereas any other node contains
a face adjacency graph providing a more detailed specification of a part
of the object. More formally, a Structured Face Adjacency Graph is
defined as a pair $\gamma = (G,T)$ where T is the tree describing the structure
of γ and G a family of face adjacency graphs, such that each component G_i
of G is associated with a unique node of t, denoted t_i. The component of
G associated with the root of T is the face adjacency graph representation
of the boundary of the global shape of the object. Any other component
G_i is a graph description of a collection of faces of S, which forms the
boundary of an attribute attached to an entity of S represented in its
direct ancestor graph. Every G_i, except for the root graph, is hence
associated with an element (node, arc, or hyperarc) or with a suitably
defined subgraph of the parent graph G_j of G_i in γ. G_i is called
<u>expansion graph</u> of such an element or subgraph of G_j.
The association between G_i and the element (or subgraph) of G_j expanded
into G_i is defined by a set of nodes, which belong to both G_i and G_j and
are called <u>boundary nodes</u> of G_i. The set of boundary nodes of G_i is
denoted by BN_i. BN_i corresponds to the set of faces in the subset of the
boundary of S represented by G_j to which the subset described by G_i is
attached. When G_i is associated with an element of G_j (hence, called
<u>macroelement</u>), three different cases arise depending on the kind of
element. If G_i is the expansion graph of a node f of G_j, then $BN_i = \{f\}$.
If G_i expands an arc or a hyperarc, then BN_i is the set of extreme nodes
of such an arc or hyperarc. If G_i is the expansion graph of a subgraph
of G_j, called <u>macrosubgraph</u>, then the set of boundary nodes of G_i is
strictly dependent on the subgraph itself. Fig. 2 shows the structured
face adjacency graph representation of an object with a protrusion and
a through hole. Graph G_o is the specification of the global shape of the
object. Graphs G_1 and G_2 represent respectively the face adjacency graphs
describing the protrusion on face E and the through hole involving faces
E and F. Note that G_1 is the expansion graph of the dummy arc in G_o
connecting nodes E and F.

The structured face adjacency graph γ is encoded as a tree structure
in which each element corresponds to a component G_i of γ. Each component
is stored in the modified adjacency list form described before with a
head record containing the link to its parent graph G_j and to the elements
of G_j expanded into G_i. The parent-child relation is maintained also by
associating with each macroelement a pointer to its expansion graph.

114

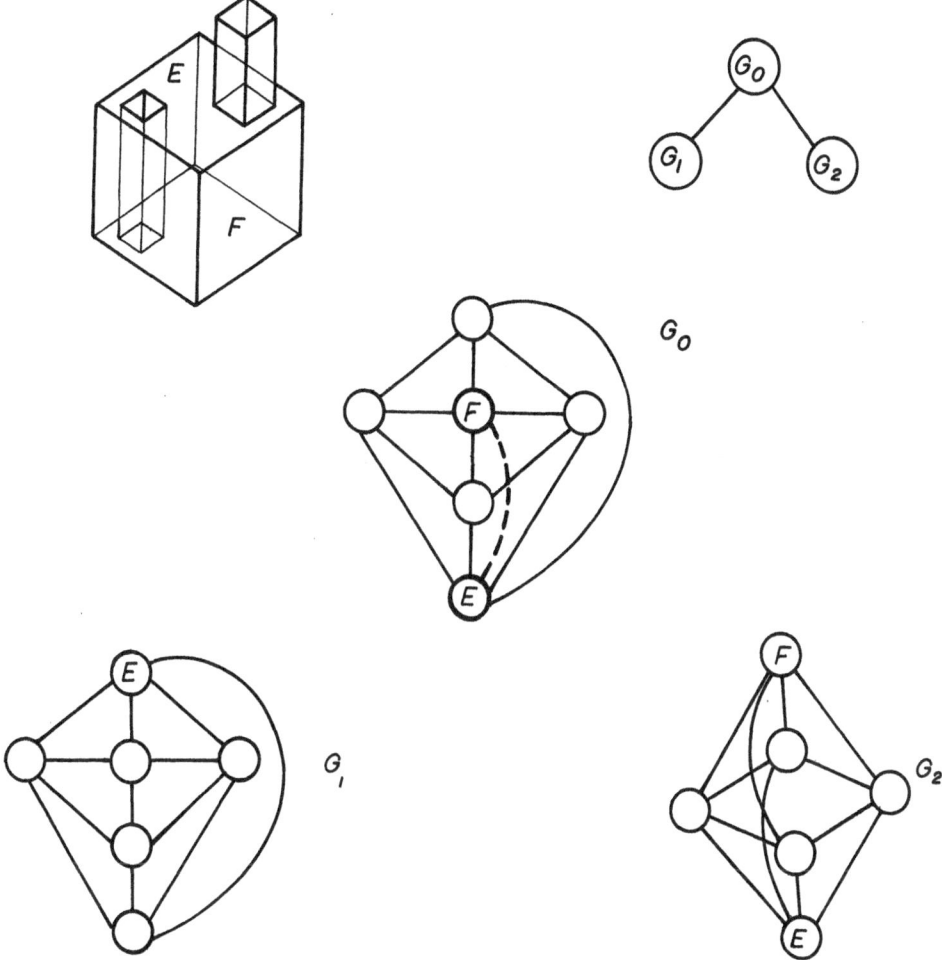

Fig. 2 Structured face adjacency graph representation of an object with a protrusion and a through hole.

3. FACE ADJACENCY GRAPH REPRESENTATION OF FORM FEATURES

In the hierarchical graph structure defined in the previous section the main shape of an object can be represented at the first level, while its attributes can be described at lower levels of specification. In this section, we apply the structured face adjacency graph to describe three-dimensional objects and their form features.

People devoted many hours in discussing what a form feature is, and so far the only definition, on which everybody agrees, is that "a feature is a region of interest on the surface of a part" /9/. Such a definition is so general in order to encompass the myriad of items that different users of a modeller (designers, engineers, manufacturers,...) consider to be a feature of a part /5,7,9/. In a CAD/CAM system a component is designed in its overall shape and also in its details to meet certain

functional requirements. These details are usually defined in terms of
functional features, and are considering as parts of the representation
of the object. When this representation is transferred from the design to
the process planning step, it must be specified how each single part must
be manufactured. This specification is usually done by considering the
manufacturing features of the part. In many cases, these latter will be
the same as the design ones. In some other situations, when, for instance,
the overall size of the features and the tolerances specified are taken
into consideration, a different classification of the design features
could be necessary, or parts of the model must be specified as features,
which have not been considered so during the design step.

In the following, we will show how to define form features as a part
of our structured relational model based on boundary representation. In
a boundary model, a feature is defined as a "connected set of faces
forming part of the boundary surface of an object" /9/. The features in
a boundary model can be subdivided into two major categories: <u>profile</u> and
<u>topological</u> features. Profile features, such as, for instance, blends,
fillets or knurls, produce slight changes to the boundary of the component.
They do not alter the topology of the model, but modify only its geometry.
Topological features, on the other hand, affect the topology of the model
by increasing the number of its faces, edges and vertices. In our boundary
model we consider only features of this second type.

According to Wilson's classification /9/, we can group topological
features into three major categories:
(i)   through holes
(ii)   protrusions or depressions
(iii) connections
These three categories of topological features can be represented in terms
of a structured face adjacency graph, as described in the following
subsections.

3.1 <u>Protrusion or depression on a face</u>

This category includes depressions like bores, pockets and slots and
protrusions like bosses, pads and beads.
A protrusion or depression is represented by a component of the structured
face adjacency which expands a node of its parent graph. By denoting by
f both the face of the solid S on which the protrusion of the depression is
done and the corresponding node in a component G_j of the SFAG γ representing S, the expansion graph G_i of f is the face adjacency graph representation of the object obtained by considering face f as part of the
boundary specification of the feature. Also, $BN_i = \{f\}$ and node f is a
macronode in G_j. Fig. 3 shows the structured face adjacency graph represen
tation of a cube with a protrusion on a face.

3.2 <u>Through hole</u>

This categories includes all through holes.
A through hole is represented by a component G_i expanding a dummy arc of
a graph G_j in γ, which connects two faces f_1 and f_2 of object S. G_i is the

face adjacency graph of the object obtained by adding both f_1 and f_2 to the boundary specification of the feature. Also, $BN_i = \{f_1, f_2\}$.

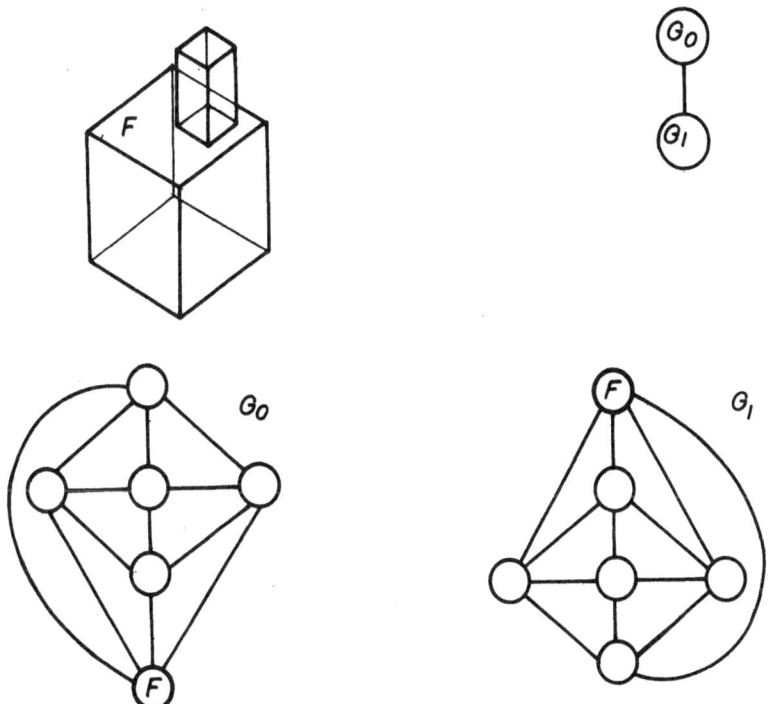

Fig. 3 SFAG representation of a cube with a protrusion on face F.

Fig. 4 shows the structured face adjacency graph representation of a cube with a through hole defining a holeloop on two adjacent faces F and B. Graph G_1 is the expansion graph of the dashed arc connecting nodes F and B in the diagram.

3.3 Connections

This category includes all area features, like chamfers or bevels, which connect two or more object faces by inserting one or more new faces. In the following, we present only the description of vertex chamfering, as representative of this category.

3.3.1 Vertex-chamfering

This feature is represented by a graph component G_i of the structured face adjacency graph which expands the hyperarc of a graph G_j of γ corresponding to the vertex v of S, which must be replaced with a new face f. If we denote by v that hyperarc of G_j and by E(v) the set of extreme nodes of v in G_j (which correspond to the faces of S concurrent into v), the expansion graph $G_i = (N_i, A_i, H_i)$ is completely defined, i.e. $N_i = E(v) \cup \{f\}$, where f denotes the new node corresponding to face f, A_i is the collection of the arcs connecting f with the nodes belonging to

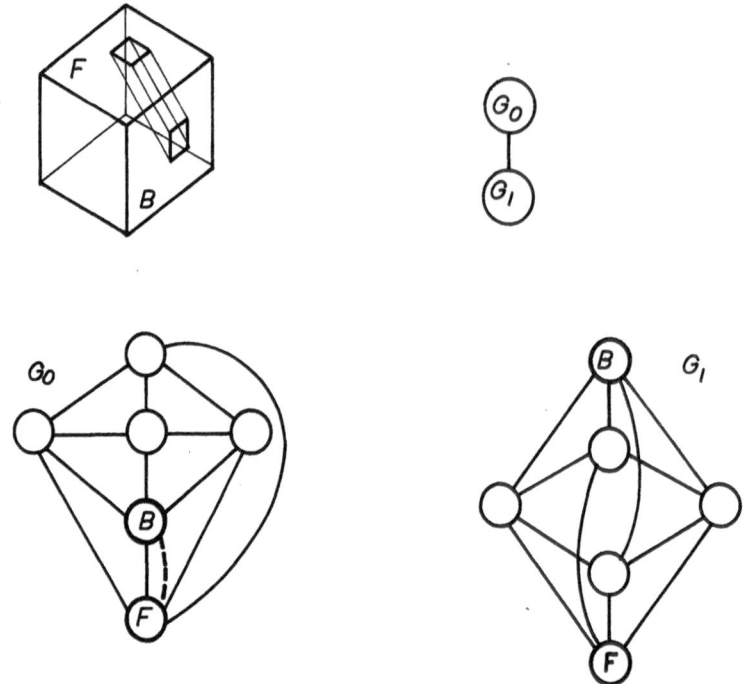

Fig. 4   SFAG representation of a cube with a through hole

$E(v)$ and H_i is the collection of the hyperarcs connecting node f with all edge-adjacent pairs of nodes belonging to $E(v)$, i.e.
$H_i = \{(f,f_1,f_2)$, for every f_1, f_2 in $E(v)$ and f_1 edge-adjacent to $f_2\}$.
Fig. 5 shows the two-level SFAG representation of a cube with a vertex replaced by a face H. In this example, the hyperarc connecting faces A,B and E, is expanded into graph G_1 in which the new face H is vertex- and edge-adjacent to A,B and E.

4. BASIC TRANSFORMATIONS ON THE STRUCTURED FACE ADJACENCY GRAPH

In our application, we construct the boundary of an object by inserting the graph description of the global characteristics of the object at the first level in the structured face adjacency graph and the specification of its design features at the second level. This information is transferred to the process planning, which specifies how such a part must be manufactured, usually by defining its manufacturing features. Manufacturing features are often the same as design ones, but, in some cases, some parts of the model not described as features by the designer must be considered like this in the manufacture, and, conversely, some design features, defined at the second level, are to be regarded as global attributes of the model and thus must be included into its first level description. Hence, in our modeling system, we define two basic transformations, termed <u>refinement</u> and <u>abstraction</u>, which perform local modification of the SFAG by operating on two of its components at a time /11/.

A refinement applied to a macroelement or to a macrosubgraph of a component G_i of a structured face adjacency graph and to its

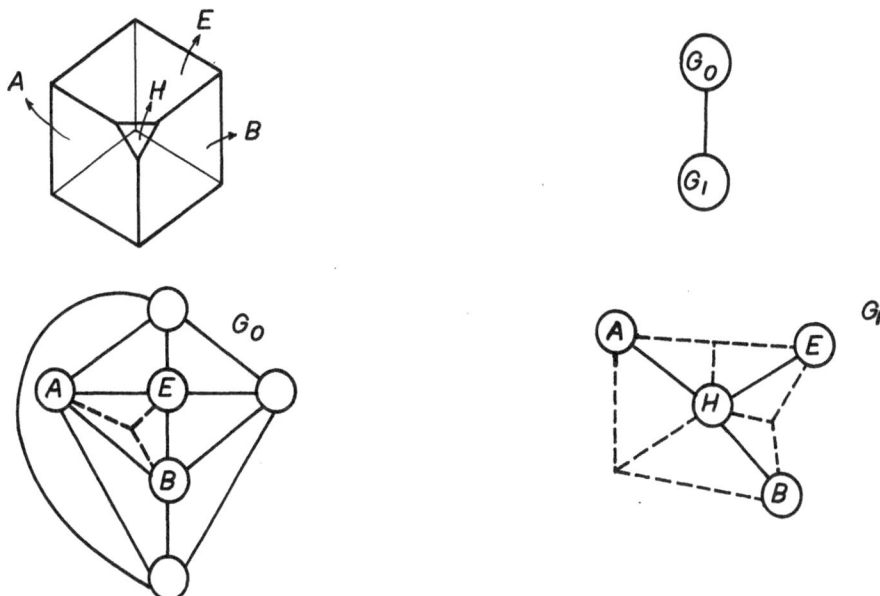

Fig. 5 Two level SFAG representation of a cube with a vertex replaced by a face (example of vertex-chamfering)

expansion graph G_j consists of replacing such an element or subgraph in G_i with its expansion graph G_j and deleting G_j from the hierarchical structure describing the SFAG. For instance, a refinement applied to a macroelement m of a component G_i and to its expansion graph G_j consists of inserting all nodes, arcs and hyperarcs of G_j into G_i, except for those nodes of G_j belonging to BN_j.

An abstraction applied to a subgraph G_i' of any component G_i of a structured face adjacency graph consists of replacing G_i' with a macro-element or a macrosubgraph in G_i and inserting G_i' into the hierarchy as child of G_i and expansion graph of such a macroelement or macrosubgraph.

5. CONCLUDING REMARKS

We have shown how a hierarchical boundary model has been used to represent solid objects and their form features. The use of this model provides many important benefits. First of all, it completely reflects the object design process which is intrinsically hierarchical, since the designer builds the object model by specifying first its general shape and then inserting the description of its form features.

This latter information, of great importance in the manufacturing step, cannot be generally identified within classical boundary models, in which all the parts of the model are represented at the same level of specification, or descriptions of the features are attached only as notations to the object representation. Moreover, our model has not a rigid hierarchical organization, in the sense that the Structured Face Adjacency Graph can be restructured, by applying abstraction and refinement, so as to adapt it to the new object description, expressed in terms of manufacturing features, developed during the process planning step.

ACKNOWLEDGEMENTS

The authors are grateful to Sandra Burlando for her help in typing this manuscript.

REFERENCES

1. Ancona,M., De Floriani,L., 1982, Structured Graphs and their Applications, Proceedings Second IASTED Applied Simulation Symposium, Paris.
2. Ansaldi,S., De Floriani,L., Falcidieno,B., 1984, Edge-face Graph Representation of Solid Objects, Proceedings Workshop on Computer Vision, Representation and Control, Annapolis, Md., pp. 164-169.
3. Ansaldi,S., De Floriani,L., Falcidieno,B., 1985, Geometric Modeling of Solid Objects by Using a Face Adjacency Graph Representation, Computer Graphics, 19, 3, pp. 131-139.
4. Berge,C., 1977, "Graphes et Hypergraphes", Dunod, Paris.
5. Braid,C., 1982, Form Features and Generic Shapes, CAM-I Report.
6. Hanranan,P.M., 1982, Creating Volume Models from Edge-vertex Graphs, Computer Graphics, 16, 3, pp. 77-84.
7. Pratt,M.J., 1984, Solid Modeling and the Interface Between Design and Manufacture, IEEE Computer Graphics and Applications, pp. 52-59.
8. Weiler,K., 1985, Edge-based Data Structures for Solid Modeling in Curved-Surface Environment, IEEE Computer Graphics and Applications, 5, 1, pp. 21-40.
9. Wilson,P.R., 1983, Features, CAM-I Interim Report III.
10. Woo,T.C., 1985, A Combinatorial Analysis of Boundary Data Structure Schemata, IEEE Computer Graphics and Applications, 5, 3, pp. 19-27.

3D RECONSTRUCTION FROM MULTIPLE STEREO VIEWS

P. Morasso and G. Sandini

DIST - University of Genoa
Via Opera Pia 11a - 16145 Genoa Italy

ABSTRACT

This paper describes a method to obtain a volumeric representation of objects from multiple stereo pairs. The procedure is based on a robust stereo algorithm solving the correspondence problem in an indirect way and providing, for each stereo pair, a disparity map of low resolution. The integration of the depth information computed from stereo pairs acquired from many positions in space, allows the extraction of a 3D description of the objects present in the scene. Such description is a volumetric image whose elements (voxels) represent a 3D portion of space. The relevance of such explicit 3D representation with respect to image understanding is also discussed.

INTRODUCTION

Understanding images is a complex process aimed at building a volumetric representation of the scene from bidimensional images. Moreover, the analysis of a visual scene is based very often on exploration strategies providing 3D information by means of active movements of the observer within the environment. To this extent, the information content of a single image (or stereo pair) provides, at best, only a bas-relief of the scene and in spite of the fact that even this reduced information may be sufficient to perform common visual tasks, a single stereo pair is not sufficient to generate an accurate and complete volumetric representation of the scene. On the contrary, multiple views provide hidden surface information beyond the occlusion limitation of a single stereo pair. As a consequence, the use of multiple views and active exploration strategies require a volumetric, object-centered, representation storing and integrating the 3D information acquired from different points of view. Many sources of information can be used to produce a volumetric representation. Among them: occluding contours[1,2] and motion[3,4] The aim of this paper is to present a way of obtaining a

Acknowledgements: The present work was partly sponsored by an ESPRIT grant (Project P419) and from a Grant of the Special Project on Mechanical Technology of the Italian National Council of Research. We thank Mr. M. Parodi and Mr. M. Pellissetto for the programming help and for their contribution to this project.

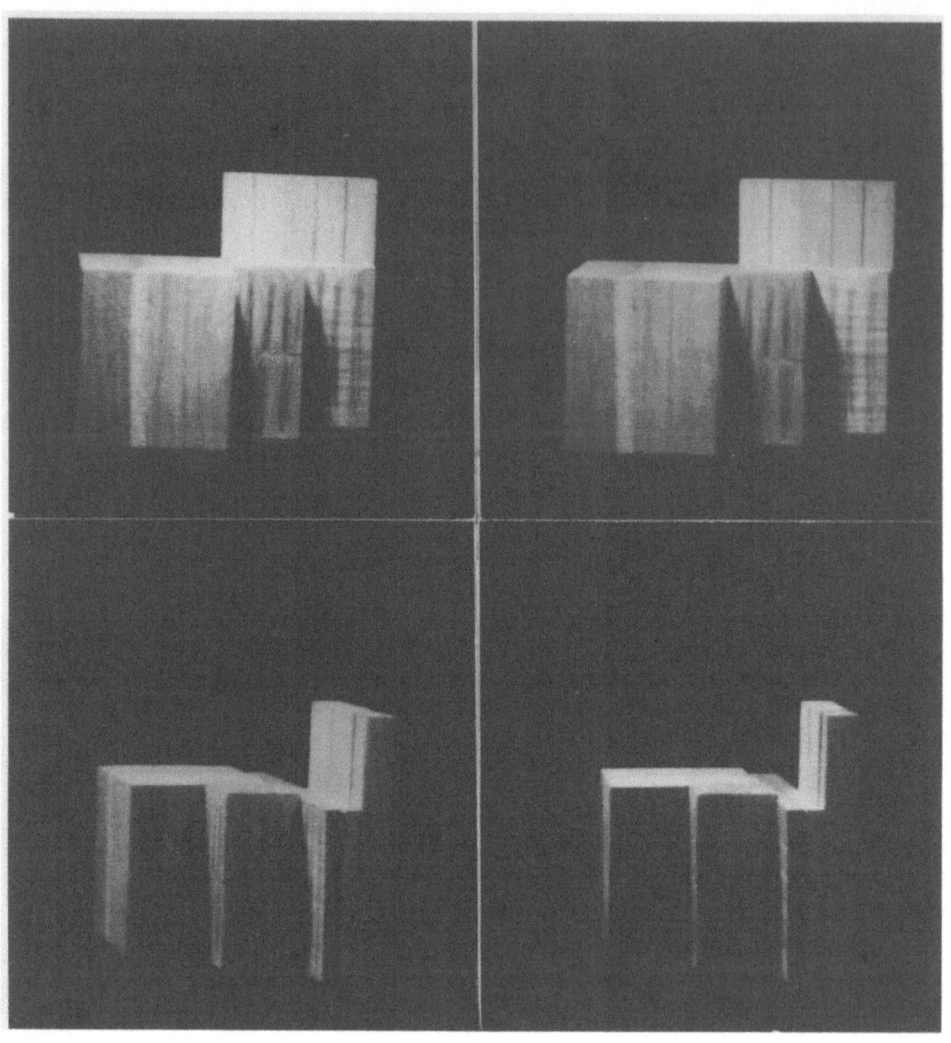

Fig. 1. Original images. Top row: stereo pair of the first view, Bottom row: stereo pair acquired from the second view.

volumetric representation of the scene from multiple stereo images. The stereo algorithm used is a modification of the PRISM system[5] and is based on the correlation between corresponding image patches of the stereo pairs. This algorithm does not use a correspondence procedure and is capable of providing rough but robust range information. The use of a pyramidal, multiple-resolution structure has the advantage of providing range information at a speed inversely proportional to the resolution necessary for a given task[6] The volumetric representation is obtained by integrating the depth information computed from each stereo pair into a 3D memory whose elementary components represent a solid portion (voxel) of the scene.

EXTRACTION OF DEPTH INFORMATION FROM A SINGLE VIEW

The main advantage of the PRISM system[5] is the fact that the stereo matching is not based on point features, like the zero-crossings of a band-pass filtered image, but it is based on the signs between zero-crossings. By this technique the sensitivity to noise is greatly reduced at the expenses of a lower precision in the computation. The process is organized into the following steps:

a) A stereo pair of images is acquired (see Fig. 1.) using two cameras and stored into two image buffers of 256x256 pixels (8 bit per pixel).

b) Each image is filtered with a Laplacian of Gaussian operator at three different scales of resolution. The filtering is performed using a pyramidal convolution scheme providing images with a size inversely proportional to the size of the convolution mask[6]
The output of the process is a set of 3 images from each image of the stereo pair (see Fig. 2). In the examples presented below, the sizes of the convolution masks are 41, 21, and 11 for the coarse, medium and fine resolution images, respectively. Due to the pyramidal organization, the size of the filtered images are 64x64, 128x128 and 256x256.

c) Each of the convolved images is clipped to produce a binary sign representation which is used afterward to perform the matching.

d) The left and right sign representations, at the coarse, medium and fine scale, are matched pair-wise to produce coarse, medium and fine disparity measures, respectively. The matching is performed first at the coarse scale (Fig. 3a), to obtain a coarse 4x4 disparity map (disparity is defined as a measure of the translation required to "register" corresponding patches of the stereo pair). The disparity information obtained at the coarse scale is used to guide the computation at the medium scale (Fig. 3b). The same matching algorithm is applied at the medium scale to produce an 8x8 disparity map. The latter is used, again, to guide the matching algorithm at the fine scale (Fig. 3c) and to produce the final disparity map composed by a 16x16 array. It is worth noting that the use of a pyramidal structure greatly reduces the computation at the coarse scale. The size of the image patches is in fact constant at all the scales whereas the number of patches decreases from fine to coarse

Fig. 2. Output of the pyramidal convolution. From left to right the standard deviations of the Gaussian operator are: 3, 6, and 9.

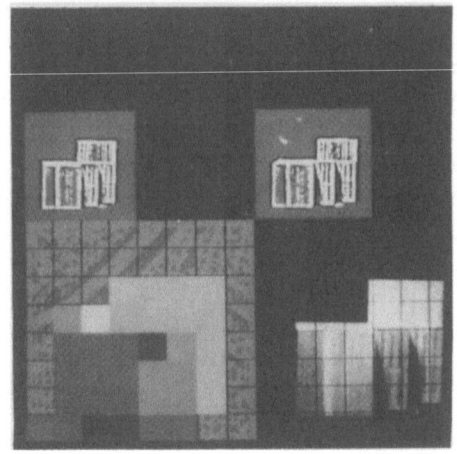

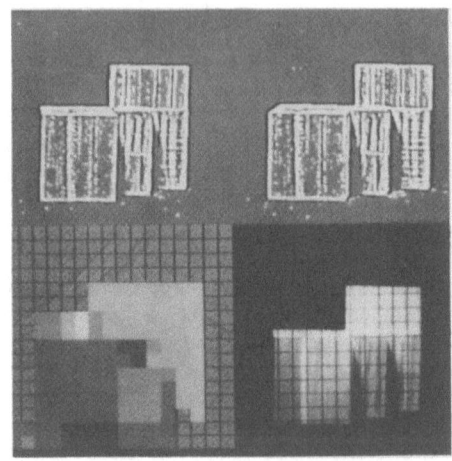

Fig. 3. Correlations and disparity maps. For each image the upper part
represent thresholded convolutions, lower right the original image, lower left the disparity map. a) Coarse resolution, b) middle
resolution, c) fine resolution. The gray levels of the disparity
maps code the range measure (darker meaning closer to the camera).
From the fine disparity map (c) the range map is computed

(being 256, 64 and 16 respectively). As a consequence, the basic
correlation procedure is exactly the same at all the resolution
scales and the computation time decreases from fine to coarse
proportionally to the number of patches. Moreover, the fact that the
information at the low scale is used to guide the correlation at the
high scale assures that the proportional dependence of the computation
load represents the "worst case" situation.

e) Computation of depth measurement from the disparity map. The
resolution in depth near the fixation point is a function of the
camera parameters which can be adjusted to achieve the desired
precision. In the example presented in this paper, we used a focal
length lens of 50 mm. with a distance between the cameras of 23 cm.
and the fixation point at about 1.5 m from the cameras. This resulted
in a depth resolution of less than 2 cm. with a 256x256 stereo pair.

The entire procedure is depicted in Fig.s 1 to 3. After the last step, the information obtained is the distance of the camera from the nearest object within the portion of the image "covered" by each patch. The next paragraph describes the integration of such information extracted from different views.

INTEGRATION OF RANGE MEASUREMENTS FROM MULTIPLE VIEWS

In the previous section the extraction of range information from a single view was described (a single view is actually composed by a stereo pair). This section describes how a common volumetric representation is used to store and integrate the range information computed from many views. This volumetric representation map a portion of the scene into a 3D array whose coordinate system is independent of the camera position. To integrate the information derived from multiple views the only information required about the position in space of the cameras is the position of the fixation point with respect to the origin of the coordinates system. At the beginning of the process, the solid array is "filled", i.e. each voxel is set as if is were occupied by a solid object. From each view each patch of the range map is projected in space generating a pyramid, with the aim of computing the intersection between the pyramid and the solid array. This intersection, obtained with a ray casting procedure, "carves" a pyramidal volume out of the solid array. In fact the depth information computed from each patch defines the distance of occupied scene locations from the point of view. All voxels closer than this distance, and lying within the pyramidal volume previously defined, are removed from the solid array. At the end of each step all the voxels can assume one of three different states: "empty", "filled" or "not scanned" (if they have not been "seen" by any of the previous view). Because of possible errors coming from a single view, the information about how many times a voxel has been seen empty and/or filled is also retained. In the example presented here, two views were selected in such a way that their fields of view completely defined the object (the optic axes formed an angle of about 90 degrees). The size of the solid array was set to 25x25x25 voxels. The depth resolution achieved, which dependents on the camera parameters, the parameters of the convolution and the size of the solid array, was 1.5 cm. The procedure is depicted in Fig. 4.

DISCUSSION

The use of a volumetric representation of the scene, far from being simply a sophisticated way of representing in natural form a 3D information, may, in our opinion, significantly influence the processing of visual information The predominant value of 3D information compared with other "bidimensional image features" is universally recognized. For example, the extraction of intrinsic images in the Barrow and Tenenbaum approach requires the knowledge about surface orientation. Many different methods have been proposed to derive such information from single images (the "shape from..." approach) but the totality of them fail to provide the system with the necessary generality to solve even common volumetric problems in unrestricted environment. On the other hand, the 3D structure of the scene is an intrinsic characteristic itself and it may be better to determine the 3D structure of the scene before attempting to segment and describe the images. For example the problem of determining the physical nature of the edges could be greatly simplified even by a rough knowledge about the 3D structure of the world. The "shape from .." approach could be considered a way of obtaining further knowledge about surface orientation in order to enrich (and possibly modify) the solid knowledge

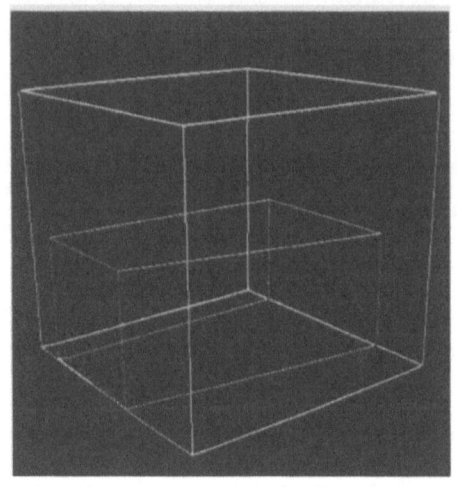
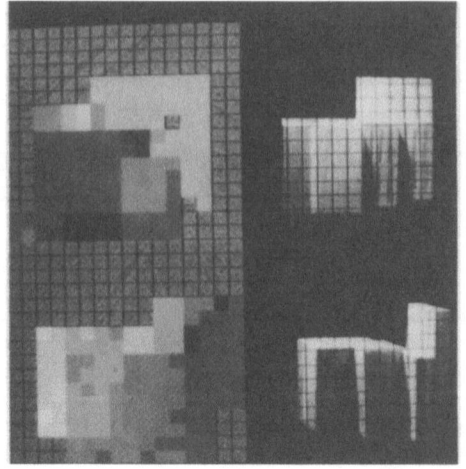

a b

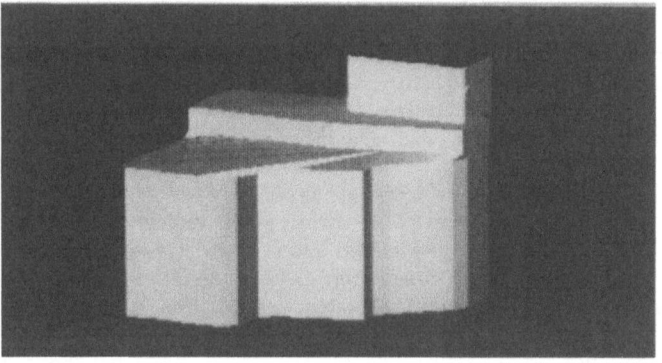

c

Fig.4: Integration of the two views into a volumetric storage. a) Schematic representation of the work volume. The large cube depicts the work volume, while the pyramidal outline inside represent the boundary of the intersection between the field of view and the work volume. b) Disparity maps computed from the two views. The range information computed from each map is used to remove from the work volume the empty voxels (i.e. to remove the portions of the 3D representation of the scene which are not occupied by objects). c) Computed volumetric model seen from a "virtual" point of view.

about the scene. To this extent, the volumetric representation could be thought of as the common representation used to integrate different sources of spatial visual and cognitive information and to refine the solid model. Following this reasoning, the first information which should be extracted from the scene is its volumetric representation. At this preliminar stage, the most important requirement is not a very high precision, but a robust extraction of information. If a more detailed representation is required, other finer computations could be carried out which could be based on the results of the previous steps. The features of the method of stereo matching described above, are, in our opinion, well suited to provide such rough, initial information about the solid structure of the scene. An additional motivation to our approach comes from the study of human vision, in particular the emphasis which has been put by Gibson[7] on the "ecological nature" of vision, which implies a strong integration between active exploration and image processing, and on the "direct perception" of the three-dimensional structure of objects, which implies the egemonic role of a three-dimensional representation. Even if the Gibson approach has been contrasted to that of Marr[8] as a typical non-computational point of view[9] we think, on the contrary, that the rigorous computational methodology advocated by Marr can well fit with the visionary, "Copernican" framework of Gibson, away from the traditional retino-centric formulation of vision.

REFERENCES

1. L. Massone, P. Morasso, and R. Zaccaria, "Shape from Occluding Countours", S.P.I.E Symposium "Intelligent Robots and Computer Vision", , Cambridge - USA (November 4-8, 1984).

2. Y. F. Wang, M. J. Magee, and J. K. Aggarwal, "Matching Three-Dimensional Objects Using Silhouettes", IEEE Trans. PAMI Vol. **PAMI-6 No.4** pp. 513-518 (1984).

3. N. J. Bridwell and T. S. Huang, "A Discrete Spatial Representation for Lateral Motion Stereo", CVGIP Vol. **21** pp. 33-57 (1983).

4. D. T. Lawton, "Processing Translational Motion Sequences", CVGIP Vol. **22** pp. 116-144 (1983).

5. H.K. Nishihara, "PRISM: a practical real-time imaging stereo matcher", A.I. Memo 780, MIT A.I. Laboratory, Boston, Mass. (May, 1984).

6. A. Giordano, M. Maresca, G. Sandini, T. Vernazza, and D. Ferrari, "A Systolic Convolver for Parallel, Multiresolution Edge Detection", Proc. of IEEE Computer Society Conference on "Computer Vision and Pattern Recognition, , San. Francisco (June 9-13, 1985).

7. J. J. Gibson, "", in The Ecological Approach to Visual Perception, Houghton Mifflin, Boston (1979).

8. D. Marr, "", in Vision, Freeman and Co., San Francisco (1982).

9. S. Ullman, "Against Direct Perception", The Behav. and Brain Sciences Vol. **3** pp. 373-415 (1980).

A STEREO ALGORITHM FOR FLAT OBJECTS

F.Masulli and M.Straforini

Dept.of Physics - University of Genoa
Via Dodecaneso 33 - 16146 Genova, Italy

G.Sandini

DIST - University of Genoa
Via All'Opera Pia - 16145 Genova, Italy

ABSTRACT

This paper describes a method for determining the attitude of a flat object in the space on the basis of the images taken with two cameras. The algorithm reduces the correspondence problem to the match of the zero-curvature points (that are perspective invariants) on the conjugated epipolar lines. The algorithm can solve the stereo problem even if the ordering constraint is not satisfied (i.e. in the case of an object lying in the so-called "ambiguous" zone). The gained precision is about 99%.

INTRODUCTION

Measurement of depth is a critical problem in robotic vision. Depth information can be obtained by motion[1], shading[2,3], or through stereographic vision. The key problem of stereo is to match the points in the two images that correspond to the same physical location (correspondence problem). The correspondence problem requires the search for the image primitives on which the matching is based, and for the rules to be followed in the matching procedure.

Examples of image primitives are edges [4,5,6,7,8], and patches of the convolution sign[9] or surface[10]. The above mentioned techniques yeld good results when the two images are similar, that is when they are taken from two close points of view.

As illustrated in a previous paper[11], in order to minimize the error in the depth measurement, we have to solve the correspondence problem using rather different images of the same scene. Therefore, it is necessary to look for image primitives or features that are preserved under perspective projection.

By using standard techniques of differential geometry[12], it is possible to show that the zero-curvature points (ZCPs) of planar or quasi-planar curves are perspective invariants. Using this propriety, we have developed a stereo algorithm to find the attitudes of flat objects in space with a relative error of less then 1%[11].

The use of other possible perspective invariants would be a major step to obtain efficient stereo algorithms.

It is worth noting that, if the size and attitude of flat objects in space are known, the proposed procedure can be used to measure the positional orientation of stereo cameras in space for example, to measure the trajectories of self-moving systems.

STEREO GEOMETRY

Let (Xl,Yl,Zl) and (Xr,Yr,Zr) be two systems of coordinates, the former being fixed in the left camera, the latter in the right one, so that their origins coincide with the intersections of the optical axes with the camera targets and the planes $Zl=0$ and $Zr=0$ coincide with the target. The related stereo geometry is described by the focal length f of the camera optics, by the displacement vector $D=(Kl,Ll,Ml)$ between the centers of the targets (of the origins of the system of coordinates), and by Euler angles φ, δ, ψ determined by the two systems of coordinates[12]. Note that Yl and Yr stand for the axes of abscissas.

We assume that the two optical axes are coplanar, and that the two cameras have been rotated around the optical axes so that we have $\varphi=0$, $\psi=0$, and $Kl=0$. Under perspective projection the point $P=(Xl,Yl,Zl)$ in the left system of coordinates is projected on

$$Xlp = \frac{f}{f+Zl} \; Xl \tag{1}$$

$$Ylp = \frac{f}{f+Zl} \; Yl \tag{2}$$

and on the second screen(i.e., in the right system of coordinates)

$$Xrp = \frac{f}{f+Zr} \; Xr \tag{3}$$

$$Yrp = \frac{f}{f+Zr} \; Yr \tag{4}$$

If the point(Xlp,Ylp) on the first screen is matched with the point (Xrp,Yrp) on the second screen the absolute depth Zl is:

$$Zl= f \; \frac{(Yrp \cdot \sin\delta + f \cdot \cos\delta)(Ll-Ylp)+(f \cdot \sin\delta - Yrp) \cdot Ml + Yrp \cdot f}{(Yrp \cdot Ylp + f^2) \cdot \sin\delta + f \cdot (Ylp-Yrp) \cdot \cos\delta} \tag{5}$$

STEREO ALGORITHM FOR PLANAR OBJECTS

We have implemented a stereo algorithm for planar and quasi-planar objects lies on a MICRO PDP 11 computer connected with a VDS 701 image-pro

cessing system (512x512 pixels with 256 grey level.
    The algorithm consists of six step:
a) - measurement of the camera parameters
b) - acquisition of the images and extraction of the shape contours
c) - detection of zero-curvature points of shape contours
d) - epipolar transformation
e) - matching of ZCPs on conjugated epipolar lines
f) - geometrical recontruction of the object plane.

    We tested this algorithm using a pair of scissors lying
in a well-known plane. Figures 1A and 1B show the stereo images acquired by the two cameras. The origin of the coordinate
system is fixed in the center of the vidicon tube of the left
camera, with the x and z axes lying on the optical plane determined by the optical axes of the two cameras. The equation
of the lying plane was:

$$z = ax + b \qquad \text{where:} \quad a = 1.51 \quad b = 70.2 \qquad (6)$$

Measurement of the camera parameters

    The displacement vector D and the angle   between the ca-
meras are:

$$L1 = 66.2 \text{ cm} \qquad M1 = 46.9 \text{ cm} \qquad \delta = 1.23 \text{ rad} \qquad (7)$$

The focal length of the lenses is 16 mm which correspond
to the "equivalent" focal length f=1307 expressed in pixels.
This value was obtained by measuring the size (in pixels) of a
known object placed at two different distances from the cameras. Let R be the size of the object (in cm), X1 the size (in
pixels) of the image of the object at the distance L1 (in cm)
from the camera and X2 the size at the distance L2, so that
the focal length is:

$$f = \frac{(D2-D1) \cdot X1 \cdot X2}{R \cdot (X1-X2)} \qquad (8)$$

This conversion is necessary to use equation (5).

Extraction of the shape contour

    The images were filtered with a two-dimensional symmetri-
cal Gaussian (σ = 4 pixels) and the zero crossings of the Laplacian of the filtered images[13] were extracted. The resulting
contours are shown in Figs. 2A and 2B.

Detection of zero curvature points on the shape contours

    To extract zero-curvature points we used a contour-follow-
ing algorithm that computes the curvature according to the
algorithm proposed by Freeman and Davis[14]. The identified ZCPs
are indicated with black dots in Figs. 3A and 3B.

Epipolar transformation

    When the viewing geometry is known it is possible to re-
duce the two-dimensional problem of matching points to a much
simpler one-dimensional problem. This simplification is obtained
by searching for matching points along conjugated epipolar
lines into horizontal lines with the same ordinate.

The degree of image distortion introduced by epipolar transformation increases with the distance of the epipole from the camera. Large distortions occur whenever the epipole is on the vidicon target, or just outside. Negligible distortions occur when the epipole is far from the camera at least 10 times the size of the vidicon tube. In this case, the two images are already "registered" and matching can be performed on the horizontal lines with the same ordinate.

The results of the epipolar transformation are shown in Figs.4A and 4B. The correspondence between the left and right ZCPs is graphically shown by the horizontal lines drawn from the ZCPs of the left image to the ones of the right image. Such correspondence is evident in both the original and transformed images particularly for the points lying on epipolar lines distant from the main epipolar line.

Matching of zero-curvature points

If there are few zero-curvature points in the shape contour, it is rather unlikely that more than a single ZCP will lie on the same epipolar line. If two or more ZCPs lie on the same epipolar line, the matching of the corresponding ZCPs can be performed according to the ordering contraint or other rules. In robotic vision the use of the ordering contraint may be misleading. Since the two cameras must be far apart in order to reduce the depth error Z1, the ordering contraint may often be violated. In fact, if a planar object lies on a plane intersecting the line between the camera foci, it will be in the so-called "ambiguous" zone. For lines, curves, segments in the ambiguous zone, the ordering constraint is not a good matching rule.

When more than one ZCPs were found on the same epipolar line, matching was performed following rules based on the qualitative kind of such ZCPs. By these procedures, it is possible to determine, in many cases, whether or not the planar object is in the ambiguous zone. However, it is possible to obtain patterns that remain ambiguous and whose 3-D structures are not uniquely determined.

Geometrical reconstruction of the object plane

By using eqs. (1),(2) and (5) we computed the 3-D locations of the matched ZCPs. For the shape shown in the Figs.2A and 2B, 12 ZCPs were detected and 8 ZCPs corresponded in the two images. Table 1 shows the computed values (x,y,z) for the ZCPs along with their distances (dist) from the original plane. The values are expressed in cm. From this table we can see that the computed points are always within 2 mm from the original plane.

The plane computed by a best fit of the ZCPs is:

$$z = ax + by + c$$

where

$a = 1.47$

$b = -0.11$

$c = 70.12$ (10)

In our case, L_1, $M_1 \gg X_{1p}$, Y_{1p}, X_{rp}, Y_{rp}; then to evaluate the error we can use the equation (11)

$$\Delta Z_1 = \frac{1}{|\tan \delta|} \, \Delta L_1 + \Delta M_L + \frac{L_1}{|\sin \delta|^2} \, \Delta \delta \qquad (11)$$

By using the values given in eq.(7) and $\Delta L_1 = \Delta M_1 = .1$ cm, $\Delta \delta = .0019$ rad, we obtain $Z_1 = .27$ cm.

It is worth noting that if $\delta = 10°$, the resulting error would be $\Delta Z_1 = 4.8$ cm, and accuracy of the Z_1 evaluation would decrease from 99% to 90%.

TABLE 1

ZCPs	X1	Y1	Z1	dist.
1	7.8	8.0	58.6	-.11
2	7.2	8.5	59.4	-.07
3	7.7	5.8	58.5	.01
4	7.4	3.8	59.2	-.08
5	3.5	1.0	65.0	-.04
6	2.5	.2	66.4	.02
7	7.3	-2.8	59.5	-.18
8	7.6	-4.2	58.9	-.08

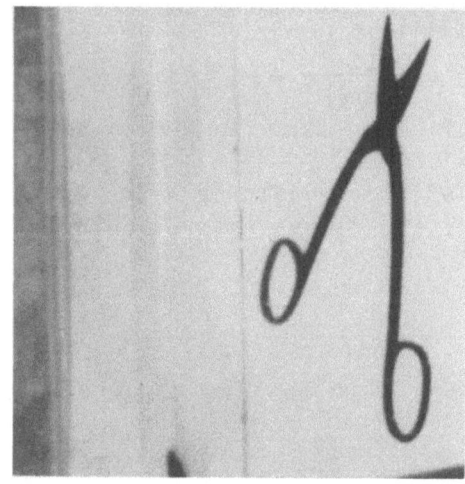

FIG 1A

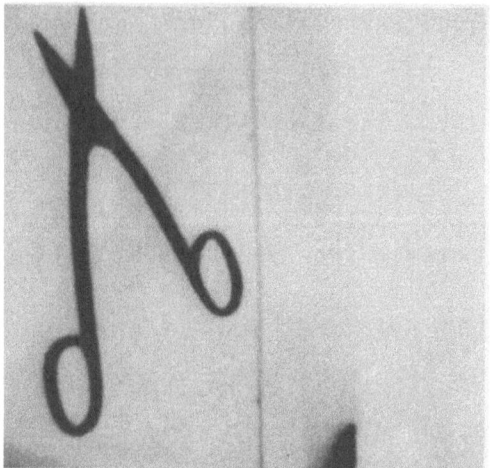

FIG 1B

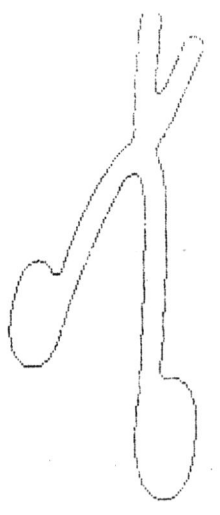

FIG 2A

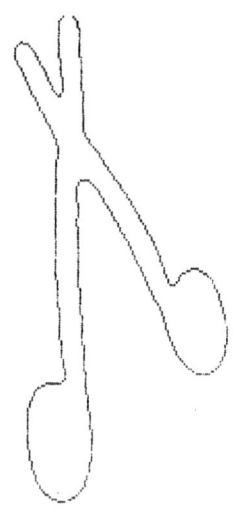

FIG 2B

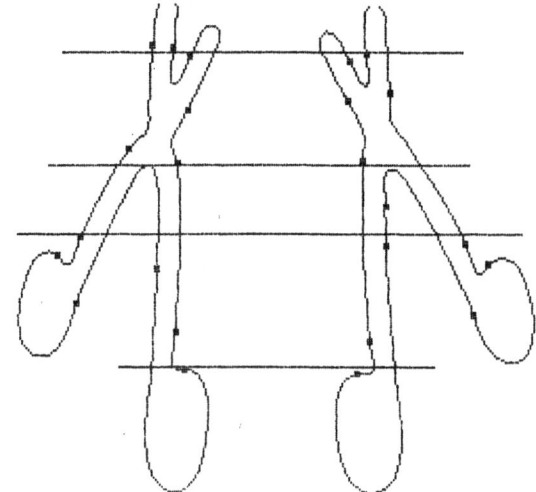

FIG 3A   FIG 3B

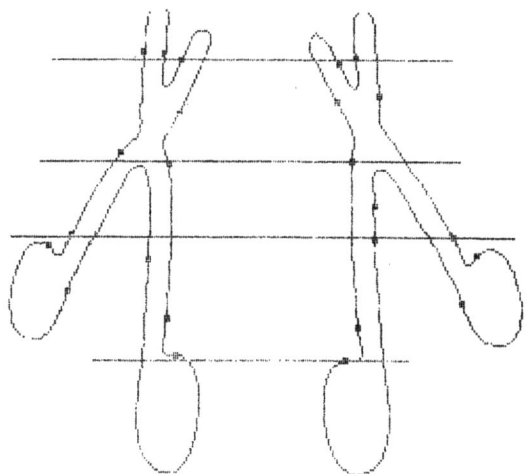

FIG 4A   FIG 4B

REFERENCES

1. S.Ullman, The Interpretation of Structure from Motion, Proc.R.Soc.London B, 203; 405 (1979)
2. B.K.P.Horn, Obtaining shape from shading information, in: "Psychology of Computer Vision", P.H.Winston ed., McGraw-Hill Publ. New York (1975).
3. K.Ikuechi and B.K.P.Horn, Numerical Shape from Shading and Occluding Boundaries, Artificial Intelligence 17: 141 (1981)
4. D.Marr and T.Poggio, A Computational Theory of Human Stereo Vision, Proc.R.Soc.London B., 204: 301 (1979)
5. W.E.L.Grimson, A Computational Theory of Visual Surface Interpolation, Phil.Trans.R.Soc.London B, 298:395(1982)
6. R.D.Arnold and T.O.Binford, Geometric Constraints in Stereo Vision, Proc.S.P.I.E. San Diego 238: 281 (1980)
7. H.H.Backer and T.O.Binford, Depth from Edge and Intensity Based Stereo, in "Proc.6th Int.Conf.Al.", Tokyo (1981)
8. J.E.W.Mayhew and J.P.Frisby, Psychophysical and Computational Studies towards a Theory of Human Stereopsis, Artificial Intelligence 16: 349 (1981)
9. K.Nishihara, PRISM: A Practical Real-time Imaging Stereo Matcher, in: "Intelligence Robots: 3rd Int.Conf. on Robot Vision and Sensory Controls", Society of Photo-Optical Instrumentation Engineers, Cambridge MA (1983)
10. O.Faugeras and U.Herbert, A 3-D Recognition and Position Algorithm Using Geometrical Matching Between Primitive Surface, in "Proceedings of the Conference an Artificial Intelligence", Karlsruhe (1983)
11. G.Sandini, M.Straforini, V.Torre and A.Verri, 3-D Reconstruction of Silhouettes, in: "Proceeding of the 4th Conference on Robot Vision and Sensory Controls", Society of Photo-Optical Instrumentation Engineers, London (1985)
12. A.Verri, Metodi Matematici per la Visione Stereografica, Ph.D. Thesis, Dept. of Physics, University of Genoa, Italy (1984)
13. D.Marr and E.C.Hildreth, Theory of Edge Detection, Proc. R.Soc.London B, 207: 187 (1980)
14. H.Freeman and L.S. Davis, A Corner-Finding Algorithm for Chain-Code Curves, IEEE Transactions on Computers C-26: 297 (1977)

FINDING MULTIPLE PIXELS

C. Arcelli and G. Sanniti di Baja

Istituto di Cibernetica del CNR

80072 Arco Felice, Naples, Italy

INTRODUCTION

When the shape of a digital figure is of interest, suitable procedures may allow one to find contour subsets from which a satisfactory description of the figure silhouette can be derived, e.g., see /1/ and the references listed therein. For instance, significant contour subsets can be found by using information regarding curvature and geometry.

This paper is concerned with the detection of the contour pixels (multiple pixels) located where distinct contour arcs of the continuous figure are so close to each other that their digital counterparts either coincide or result to be adjacent to each other.

In the past, finding multiple pixels in 8-connected contours has been faced by Pavlidis /2/: contour tracing was used as a guideline to investigate the contour structure and to point out which conditions have to be satisfied in order to reveal multiple pixels. The approach proposed in this paper is based on the structural equivalence between digital contours and digital (closed) curves. A definition of simple contour is given in analogy with the definition of simple curve, and interactions among contour parts are assumed to occur only when a contour fails to be simple. In particular, the notion of regular pixel is introduced to characterize the pixels where no interactions occur, and the multiple pixels are identified with the pixels which result not to be regular. Conditions to detect the regular pixels in case of both 8-connected and 4-connected contours are proposed, which can be implemented by simply using 3x3 local operations.

BASIC NOTIONS

In a binary picture P digitized on a square grid, let $F = \{1\}$ and $\bar{F} = \{0\}$. Both the 8-metric and the 4-metric, respectively involving the chessboard distance D8 and the city block distance D4, must be considered to deal correctly with P. If the 4-metric holds in F, then the 8-metric must be used for its complement $\bar{F}$, and viceversa. In the sequel, we will indicate with DF and D$\bar{\text{F}}$ the distance functions respectively chosen for F and $\bar{F}$, and we will assume that no pixel of F lies on the frame of P, i.e., on the first and on the last row or column of P.

The neighborhood $N(p) = \{n_k \mid k=1,8\}$ of a pixel p is the set of pixels surrounding p as shown below:

$$
\begin{array}{ccc}
n_2 & n_3 & n_4 \\
n_1 & p & n_5 \\
n_8 & n_7 & n_6
\end{array}
$$

The neighbors of p are the pixels having unit distance from p according to the metric chosen for the set including p. Thus, if the 4-metric (8-metric) is chosen for such a set, the neighbors of p are the n_k's with k odd (all the n_k's). A neighbor n_k, k odd, is also termed D-neighbor.

A path in F is a sequence of pixels of F such that each pixel, except the first, has distance DF=1 from the preceding pixel. The set F is connected if for any two pixels in F there exists a path in F joining them. A connected subset of F which is not properly included by any other connected subset of F is termed a component of F.

The contour C of F is the subset of F, every pixel of which is neighbor of some pixel of $\bar{F}$. This contour definition is in agreement with the natural requirement that the metric adopted for a given set equally holds for any of its subsets. Consequently, C turns out to be structured either as an 8-connected curve, or as a 4-connected curve depending on the distance function chosen for F (DF = D8 or DF = D4).

Unless C coincides with F, the detection of C transforms P into a ternary picture. The two sets $F \cap \bar{C}$ and $\bar{F}$ will be respectively mentioned as the inside and the outside of C. The inside of C may consist of more than one component. Since the same metric selected for F

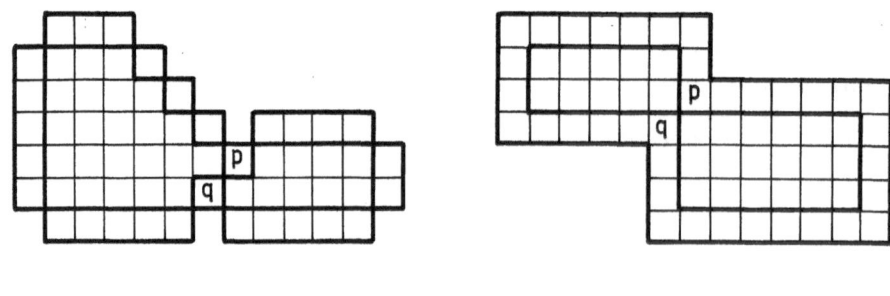

a   b

Fig. 1 - Topological ambiguities in correspondence of pixels p and q, in case of an 8-connected contour a), and of a 4-connected contour b).

is used for the set $F \cap \bar{C}$, topological ambiguities, as those shown in Fig. 1 may arise. In case of an 8-connected F (see Fig. 1a), the pixels p and q, though neighbors of each other, do not divide $F \cap \bar{C}$, which is indeed an 8-connected set. On the contrary, in case of a 4-connected F (see Fig. 1b), p and q, though not neighbors of each other, divide $F \cap \bar{C}$ into two 4-connected components. The definition of simple contour will provide a way to overcome this problem.

MULTIPLE PIXELS

Multiple pixels are located wherever contour arcs, expected to be distinct, either coincide or are adjacent to each other. It is known that when a similar interaction affects the arcs of a curve, the curve results to be not simple. Thus, since a structural equivalence exists between contours and curves, we give a definition of simple contour in analogy with the definition of simple curve, and we say that a contour includes multiple pixels whenever it fails to be simple.

Several definitions of simple curve can be found in the literature, see for instance /3/, so that several definitions of simple contour are possible. In our opinion, the definition which better agrees with the intuitive idea of simple contour, i.e., one where no interactions among contour arcs occur, is the following.

Definition 1. A contour is simple iff i) the inside has exactly one component, and ii) for every contour pixel, its removal causes a local disconnection of the contour.

We note that, by using Definition 1, the topological ambiguities mentioned in the previous Section are overcome. Independently of the metrical relations among contour pixels, p and q do not interact with each other in Fig. 1a, as the contour depicted therein results to be simple. In turn, contour pixels interacting with each other and causing the inside to consist of two components, must be detected as multiple in the not simple contour of Fig. 1b.

Multiple pixels are present in a contour as soon as either of the conditions i) and ii) is not satisfied. However, the adopted Definition 1, which is clearly effective to decide whether a contour is simple, is not adequate to detect all the multiple pixels present in a not simple contour. First of all, condition i) requires a global analysis which does not involve the contour pixels, but only those belonging to the inside. Therefore, the detection of the contour pixels causing violation of condition i) cannot be achieved (e.g., see Fig. 1b). Moreover, it is easy to verify that also condition ii), though based on a local property of contour pixels, cannot be used to distinguish pixels which are not multiple from pixels expected to be multiple. Indeed, such a property is not peculiar exclusively of the not multiple pixels. For instance, some of the pixels located where contour arcs coincide are likely to satisfy condition ii).

In our opinion, by inspecting the neighborhood of pixels belonging to a simple contour, it should be possible to find suitable local properties, which can be simultaneously satisfied exclusively by the not multiple pixels. Therefore, a new definition of simple contour should be possible which, besides providing an answer about contour simplicity in agreement with Definiton 1, allows the identification of all the multiple pixels present in a not simple contour. To achieve this goal, different local properties, respectively for the 8-connected and the 4-connected contour, are found, and the pixels for which such properties are satisfied are termed regular pixels. Then, a new definition of simple contour is given in terms of regular pixels, and the multiple pixels turn out to coincide with the not regular pixels.

REGULAR PIXELS

For the sake of simplicity, we will assume that both F and $\bar{F}$ consist of exactly one component, and that $F \cap \bar{C}$ is a not empty set. The set $\bar{C}$ includes all the pixels not in the contour, i.e., pixels belonging to the outside $\bar{F}$ and pixels belonging to the inside $F \cap \bar{C}$. Due to the different metrics respectively holding in $\bar{F}$ and in $F \cap \bar{C}$, the components of $\bar{C}$ are connected according to different metrics. For every pixel p in C, at least one component including a pixel at distance $D\bar{F}=1$ from p will constitute the set $N(p) \cap \bar{F}$. On the contrary, the set $N(p) \cap (F \cap \bar{C})$ may or may not be empty.

A pixel p belonging to an 8-connected contour C is termed a regular pixel if the set $S(p) = N(p) \cap \bar{C}$ can be characterized as follows:

a)   S(p) consists of two components made up of pixels respectively belonging to the outside and to the inside of C.

b)   S(p) includes at least a pair of D-neighbors n_k and n_j, j=k+4 (modulo 8), respectively belonging to the outside and to the inside of C, or viceversa.

In turn, if C is a 4-connected contour, then p is termed a regular pixel if

c)   S(p) consists of two components made up of pixels respectively belonging to the outside and to the inside of C.

d)   p has exactly two neighbors in C.

We now prove the following:

Theorem.   The contour C of a simply connected figure F is simple, iff it entirely consists of regular pixels.

Proof.   Suppose that property b) holds for every p in an 8-connected contour C, then deletion of p causes a local disconnection of C. The same is true if both properties c) and d) hold for every p in a 4-connected contour. Therefore, condition ii) of Definition 1 is satisfied in both cases of 8- and 4-connectedness.

Suppose that condition i) does not hold. Due to property b) or to property c) (depending on the selected metric), the set $F \cap \bar{C}$ is for sure not empty. Then, it should consist of at least two components and a connected set, entirely made up of contour pixels, must be placed in between them, as F is a connected figure. It is easily verified, by examining all the possible cases, that for at least one among such pixels either of properties a) and b), in case of an 8-connected contour, or either of properties c) and d), in case of a 4-connected contour, is not satisfied, while every contour pixel is regular. Contradiction.

Suppose now that C is a simple 8-connected contour. Since p is a contour pixel, S(p) includes a D-neighbor of p, say n_1, belonging to $\bar{F}$. Hence, at least one component exists in S(p). Such a component cannot be the only one present in S(p), otherwise p could be deleted without locally disconnecting the contour, while condition ii) is verified for p. Therefore, at least two components exist in S(p). However, only one component including pixels of $\bar{F}$ can be present in S(p). Otherwise p would belong to a contour part where arcs, expected to be distinct, coincide, which cannot happen because C is a simple contour. Thus, at least one component of pixels belonging to the inside exists in S(p). Moreover, as n_1 belongs to $\bar{F}$ and the 8-metric holds in $F \cap \bar{C}$, at most two components made up of pixels of $F \cap \bar{C}$, say I_1 and I_2, are likely to be present in S(p). If this is the case, necessarily n_5 is a contour pixel, and as such it has a D-neighbor in $\bar{F}$. Either such a D-neighbor or n_1 should belong to a hole of F, if a path, made up of pixels all belonging to the inside and connecting I_1 with I_2, could be built up. Since F is simply connected such a path cannot be built, and consequently I_1 and I_2 are placed in two distinct components of the inside, so violating condition i). Then, S(p) includes exactly two components, one is a subset of $\bar{F}$, the other is a subset of $F \cap \bar{C}$, and property a) is verified.

If n_5 belongs to $F \cap \bar{C}$, property b) holds. Otherwise, n_5 belongs either to $\bar{F}$ or to C. In the first case, as the component of $N(p) \cap \bar{F}$ is connected according to the 4-metric the only possible configurations for N(p) are the following

$$
\begin{array}{ccc}
0 & 0 & 0 \\
0 & p & 0 \\
C & I & C
\end{array}
\qquad
\begin{array}{ccc}
C & I & C \\
0 & p & 0 \\
0 & 0 & 0
\end{array}
$$

where the letters O, I and C are respectively used to indicate pixels belonging to the outside, to the inside and to the contour. For both configurations property b) holds.

In the second case, i.e., when n_5 belongs to the contour, the neighborhood configurations

$$
\begin{array}{ccc}
0 & 0 & \bullet \\
0 & p & C \\
\bullet & C & I
\end{array}
\qquad
\begin{array}{ccc}
\bullet & C & I \\
0 & p & C \\
0 & 0 & \bullet
\end{array}
$$

where the dots cannot belong to $F \cap \bar{C}$, are prevented because p satisfies condition ii). Thus, only the configurations

$$
\begin{array}{ccc}
0 & 0 & \bullet \\
0 & p & C \\
C & I & *
\end{array}
\qquad
\begin{array}{ccc}
C & I & * \\
0 & p & C \\
0 & 0 & \bullet
\end{array}
$$

where the stars do not belong to $\bar{F}$, are possible. Also in these cases property b) holds.

Let us suppose now that C is a simple 4-connected contour. Since p is a contour pixel, $S(p)$ includes at least an n_k, $k=1,8$, belonging to $\bar{F}$ and, consequently, at least one component of pixels in the outside. No more than one component of pixels belonging to $\bar{F}$ can be present in $S(p)$, otherwise p would be placed where contour arcs coincide, which cannot happen as C is a simple contour. Moreover, at least two components must be present in $S(p)$, otherwise p could not satisfy condition ii). Therefore, at least one component of pixels belonging to $F \cap \bar{C}$ must be present in $S(p)$. Since the 4-metric holds in $F \cap \bar{C}$ as well as in C, the only basic configurations of $N(p)$ such that $S(p)$ includes more than two components are the following

```
 •  C  |        O  C  |        O  C  |        O  C  +

 O  p  C        C  p  C        C  p  C        C  p  +

 •  C  |        |  C  |        +  +  +        |  C  +
```

where at least one fo the crosses belongs to the inside (the remaining ones belong either to $F \cap \bar{C}$ or to C), and the dots are not in the inside. Any other possible configuration for $N(p)$ could be obtained by assigning to $\bar{F}$ any n_k, $k \neq 1,2$.

Let us recall that contour pixels are neighbors of pixels of $\bar{F}$. Then, whichever configuration, a path made up of pixels all belonging to the inside and connecting two components of pixels belonging to $F \cap \bar{C}$ present in $N(p)$ could be built up, only provided that F have a hole. Since F is a simply connected figure, this cannot happen and no path can be built, so violating condition i). Therefore, exactly one component of pixels belonging to the outside, and one component of pixels belonging to the inside are present in $S(p)$, and property c) holds.

Every p in C has at least two D-neighbors in C, otherwise $S(p)$ could not include two components. On the other hand, p cannot have more than two D-neighbors in C. In fact, suppose for instance that n_1, n_3 and n_5 are in C. Since only two components exist in $S(p)$, necessarily either of n_2 or n_4, say n_2, belongs to C. As n_2 is a contour pixel, it satisfies property c). Thus, in the neighborhood of n_2, besides a component of pixels of $\bar{F}$, also a component of pixels of $F \cap \bar{C}$ is present. A path, made up of pixels all belonging to the inside, can be built up to connect such a component with the component of the inside present in $S(p)$, only if a hole exists in F. As F is simply connected, no path can be built, and the inside turns out to be not connected. Contradiction.$\square$

For a pixel p whose removal does not locally disconnect the contour, only two events turn out to be possible. The first is common to both 8-connected contours and 4-connected contours. Precisely, $N(p)$ includes just one component made up of pixels not belonging to the contour. If this is the case, either property a) or property c) is not satisfied, depending on the metric chosen for F. The second event can only happen for an 8-connected contour and, particularly, it occurs in correspondence of pixels located in corner configurations of the contour. In fact, any such a pixel, having in the contour a couple of D-neighbors 8-connected to each other (say n_1 and n_3), is superfluous from the point of view of preserving the local connectedness of the contour. If this is the case, property b) is not satisfied. Thus, the set of the not regular pixels includes all the superfluous pixels, i.e., the ones detectable as multiple due to violation of condition ii) of Definition 1.

Pixels lying where the local thickness of the figure is so small that contour arcs coincide, are expected to be multiple. For such pixels either property b) or property c) does not hold and, consequently, they are not regular. Still, contour pixels, multiple as preventing the inside to consist of exactly one component, turn out to be not regular. This could be seen by examining all the possible cases. Therefore, the set of the not regular pixels includes all the pixels expected to be multiple.

On the other hand, a not regular pixel is one for which at least either of the properties a) and b) (or either of the properties c) and d)) is not satisfied. This guarantees that a not regular pixel can only be present wherever an interaction among contour arcs occurs.

In conclusion, the set of the not regular pixels turns out to coincide with the set of the multiple pixels. For illustrative purposes, refer to Fig. 2 where both contours are not simple, and the multiple pixels (dotted) are recognized as not regular.

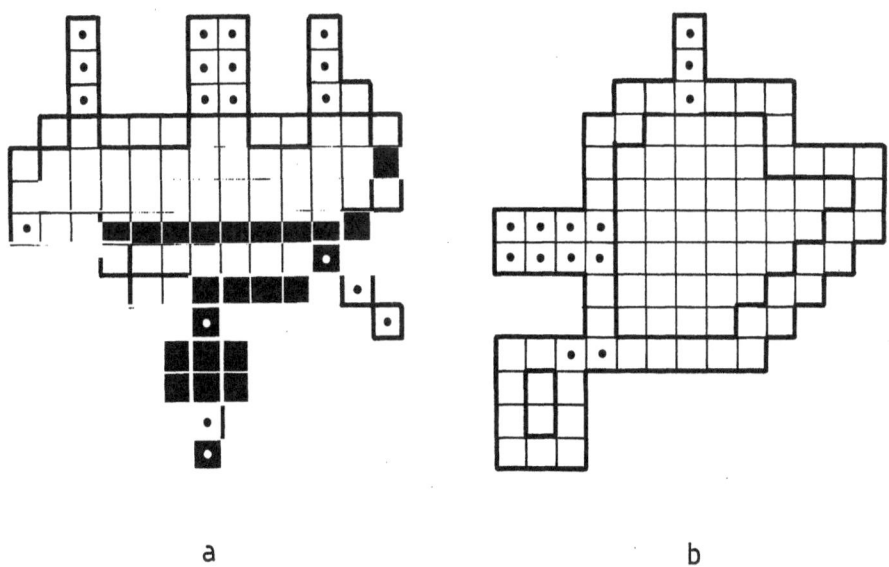

a   b

Fig. 2 - Dots indicate multiple pixels in case of an 8-connected contour a), and of a 4-connected contour b).

CONCLUSION

The multiple pixels have been identified as those located where some interaction among distinct arcs of a digital contour occurs. The local conditions to be satisfied in order that a contour pixel be regular have been given both in case of 8-connected and of 4-connected contours, and a definition of simple contour in terms of regular pixels has been proposed. Our definition allows to find the pixels where interactions among contour arcs occur, while this was not possible by using Definition 1. This contour characterization results to be particularly convenient when parallel processors are at disposal, since only 3x3 local operations are sufficient to find the multiple pixels.

ACKNOWLEDGMENTS

The authors wish to thank Mrs. Anna Maria Mazzarella for her skillful assistance in preparing the manuscript, as well as Mr. Umberto Cascini for providing the illustrations.

REFERENCES

1. T. Pavlidis, Algorithms for shape analysis of contours and waveforms, IEEE Trans. Pattern Analysis and Machine Intelligence 2: 301 (1980).

2. T. Pavlidis, "Algorithms for Graphics and Image Processing", Chapter 7, Springer-Verlag, Berlin (1982).

3. A. Rosenfeld, "Picture Languages", Chapter 2, Academic Press, New York (1979).

ON EDGE DETECTION OF TRIHEDRICAL VERTEXES

Enrico De Micheli(*) and Giulio Sandini(**)

(*) Department of Physics,University of Genoa

(**) D.I.S.T.,University of Genoa

ABSTRACT

In this paper we analyse,for an ideal trihedical vertex,geometrical and topological properties of edges detected with the Marr and Hildreth approach. On the basis of this properties,it would possible to identify and eliminate spurious edges originating from the adopted edge detection procedure.

INTRODUCTION

Vision starts with the transformation of a flux of photons into a set of intensity values. The first step of this process is to obtain a compact description of the raw intensity values. Primitive elements of the initial description should be complete and meaningful. Physical edges,for instance, are among the most important properties of objects,since they correspond to objects' boundaries or to changes in surfaces' orientation. Three dimensional edges are often mapped by the imaging process into critical points of the two dimensional intensity profile formed in the eye.

Edge detection is the process that attempts to detect and localize such sharp changes in intensity. Edges are therefore candidates to be good primitives for later processing. A great deal of effort has been invested in developing algorithms for edge detection. An historical survey of edge detection can be found in Davis(1975). Marr and Hildreth(1980)have suggested identifying edges with zero-crossings of the image filtered with Laplacian of a symmetrical Gaussian ($\nabla^2 G(x,y)$). In this scheme spurious edges can be present in a noise-free image because of topological properties of zero-crossing contours.

Torre and Poggio(1984) have shown that zero-crossing contours,obtained by filtering the image with $\nabla^2 G(x,y)$ are either closed curves or curves terminating at the image boundary. As a consequence important features of images as trihedrical vertexes are incorrectly detected by the Marr and Hildreth algorithm even in a noise-free image.

In this paper, using a mathematical procedure derived from Berzins(1984) we analyse, for an ideal trihedrical vertex, geometrical and topological properties of edges detected with the Marr and Hildreth algorithm.

THE TRIHEDRICAL VERTEX

A trihedrical vertex with unending edges and step intensity variation is represented by the intensity function:

$$I(x,y) = A\,U(-x)\,U(-y-mx) + B\,U(x)\,U(mx-y) \qquad (2.1)$$

with $m = \operatorname{tg}\vartheta$ and $0 < \vartheta < \pi/2$. A and B are the intensity values at the sides of the vertical edge (see Fig.1).
Now let be:

$$g(x) = 1/\sqrt{2\pi}\,\exp(-x^2/2) \qquad (2.2)$$

the unit Gaussian distribution, which will be used as filter.
To simplify the equations, we use a coordinate system where the unit of measurement is equal to the size of Gaussian filter. We can convert into a more general coordinate system (X,Y) with a size σ using the transformation:

$$\begin{cases} x \longrightarrow X/\sigma \\ \\ y \longrightarrow Y/\sigma \end{cases} \qquad (2.3)$$

Let Φ define:

$$\Phi(x) = \int_{-\infty}^{x} g(t)\,dt \qquad (2.4)$$

and let G(x,y) denote two dimensional symmetrical gaussian distribution:

$$G(x,y) = g(x)\,g(y) \qquad (2.5)$$

Let U be the unit step function:

$$U(x) = \begin{cases} 1 & x \geqslant 0 \\ \\ 0 & x < 0 \end{cases} \qquad (2.6)$$

The filtered trihedrical vertex is:

$$F(x,y) = I(x,y) * G(x,y) = A + (B-A)\,\Phi(x) - A\int_{x}^{\infty} g(t)\Phi(y+mx-mt)\,dt -$$
$$- B\int_{-\infty}^{x} g(t)\Phi(y-mx+mt)\,dt \qquad (2.7)$$

with laplacian:

$$f(x,y) = \nabla^2 F = (A-B)x\,g(x)\Phi(-y) - A\,\bar{u}\,g(\bar{u})\Phi(-\bar{v}) - B\,u\,g(u)\Phi(v) \qquad (2.8)$$

146

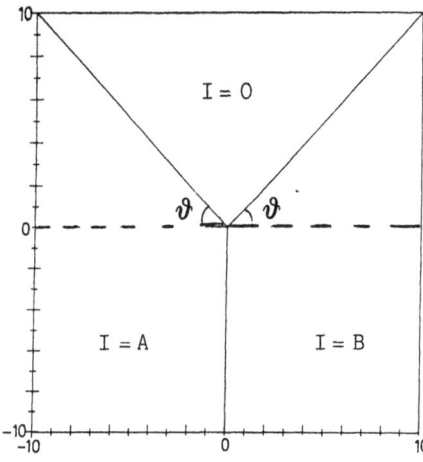

Fig.1 Trihedrical vertex

where:

$$u = x \sin\vartheta - y \cos\vartheta \qquad\qquad \bar{u} = -x \sin\vartheta - y \cos\vartheta$$

$$v = x \cos\vartheta + y \sin\vartheta \qquad\qquad \bar{v} = x \cos\vartheta - y \sin\vartheta$$

$$(\; 2.9 \;)$$

are the coordinates in two cartesian coordinate systems rotated, respectively, by ϑ and $-\vartheta$. Note that to obtain (2.8) we used:

$$\Psi(s) = g(s) + \int_{-\infty}^{s} t \, g(t) \, dt \; = 0 \qquad \forall s \qquad\qquad (\; 2.10 \;)$$

Edges are defined by points $P = (x,y)$ such that

$$f(x,y) = 0 \qquad\qquad (\; 2.11 \;)$$

The slope of the zero-crossing in P is $\left| \text{grad} \, f(x,y) \right|_P$ where:

$$\left| \text{grad} \, f(x,y) \right| = \sqrt{f_x^2 + f_y^2} \qquad\qquad (\; 2.12 \;)$$

with:

$$f_x = (A - B) \, g(x) \, \Phi(-y) \, (1 - x^2) - A \, g(\bar{u}) \left[\Phi(-\bar{v}) \, (\bar{u}^2 - 1) \sin\vartheta - \bar{u} \, g(\bar{v}) \cos\vartheta \right] -$$

$$- B \, g(u) \left[\Phi(v) \, (1 - u^2) \sin\vartheta + u \, g(v) \cos\vartheta \right] \qquad (\; 2.13 \;)$$

$$f_y = (B - A) \, x \, g(x) g(y) - A \, g(\bar{u}) \left[\Phi(-\bar{v}) \, (\bar{u}^2 - 1) \cos\vartheta + \bar{u} \, g(\bar{v}) \sin\vartheta \right] -$$

$$- B \, g(u) \left[\Phi(v) \, (1 - u^2) \sin\vartheta + u \, g(v) \cos\vartheta \right] \qquad (\; 2.14 \;)$$

From eq. (2.8) it is obvious that for every σ the vertex $V = (0,0)$ always satisfy equation (2.11). Therefore its spatial position does not change when the size of the gaussian filter is varied.

Furthermore, we have:

$$\left| \text{grad } f(x,y) \right|_{V} = \sqrt{2}/8\pi \; (A - B)^2 \sqrt{1 + \sin\vartheta} \; \neq 0 \quad \forall \vartheta \qquad (2.15)$$

then the surface $S = [x,y,z = f(x,y)]$ meets transversally the surface $S_1 = [x,y,0]$ in $V = (0,0,0)$. Then, for the Isotopy Theorem (Thom, 1954), the zero-crossing in V is structurally stable.

Equation (2.11) can be solved numerically and result are shown in Fig.2 for ϑ small (less than 40°) and Fig.3 for ϑ large (greater than 40°). Fig.2.a and 3.a show the original image, while the zero-crossings computed for $A = 5$ and $B = 10$ are shown in Fig.2.b and 3.b.

As it can be noticed, the zero-crossing contours are two curves terminating at the boundary of the image, and in both cases a spurious edge is present which does not correspond to an intensity change in the image, but it is a consequence of the topological properties of $\nabla^2 G$ zero-crossing.

However, analysing the asymptotic values of $\left| \text{grad } f(x,y) \right|$ we note that the spurious edge has a different behavior compared with others. In fact, we have:

$$\lim_{y \to -\infty} \left| \text{grad } f(0,y) \right| = \left| A - B \right| / \sqrt{2\pi} \qquad (2.16)$$

$$\lim_{x \to \infty} \left| \text{grad } f(x,mx) \right| = B/\sqrt{2\pi} \qquad (2.17)$$

$$\lim_{x \to -\infty} \left| \text{grad } f(x,-mx) \right| = A/\sqrt{2\pi} \qquad (2.18)$$

and along the other direction:

$$\lim_{x,y \to \infty} \left| \text{grad } f(x,y) \right| = 0 \qquad (2.19)$$

Since the asymptotic direction of the zero-crossing contours are the same of the trihedrical vertex lines (as can be easily proved from (2.11)),

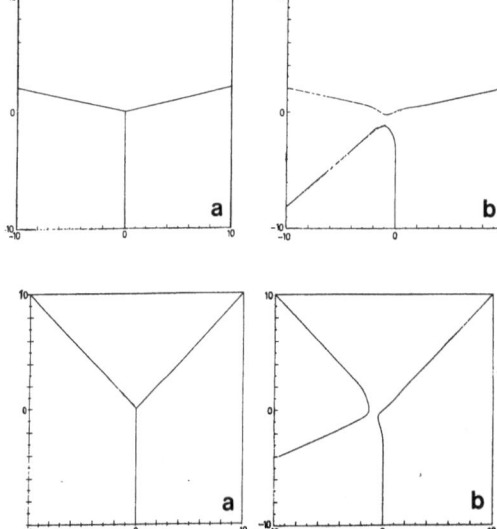

Fig.2.a and 2.b

Fig.3.a and 3.b

the slope of the true edges approaches contrast (disregarding the constant $1/\sqrt{2\pi}$), while the slope of the spurious one goes to zero as the distance from V increases.

In order to define the geometrical features of the point V,we can compute the elements of the hessian matrix of the surface S:

$$f_{xx} = (A - B)(x^3 - 3x) g(x)\Phi(-y) - A g(\bar{u})\Big[(\bar{u}^3 - 3\bar{u})\Phi(-\bar{v})\sin^2\vartheta +$$

$$+ \bar{u}\,\bar{v}\,g(\bar{v})\cos^2\vartheta\Big] - B g(u)\Big[(u^3 - 3u)\Phi(v)\sin^2\vartheta + 2g(v)(1 - u^2)\sin\vartheta\cos\vartheta -$$

$$- u v g(v)\cos^2\vartheta\Big] - 2Ag(\bar{u})g(\bar{v})(1-\bar{u}^2)\sin\vartheta\cos\vartheta \qquad (2.20)$$

$$f_{xy} = (A - B) g(x) g(y)(x^2 - 1) - A g(\bar{u})\Big[1/2\Phi(-\bar{v})(\bar{u}^3 - 3\bar{u})\sin 2\vartheta +$$

$$+ g(\bar{v})(1-\bar{u}^2)\cos 2\vartheta - 1/2\,\bar{u}\,\bar{v}\,g(\bar{v})\sin 2\vartheta\Big] - B g(u)\Big[1/2\Phi(v)(3u - u^3) \cdot$$

$$\cdot \sin 2\vartheta + g(v)(u^2 - 1)\cos 2\vartheta - 1/2 u v g(v)\sin 2\vartheta\Big] \qquad (2.21)$$

$$f_{yy} = (A - B) x y g(x) g(y) - A g(\bar{u})\Big[\Phi(-\bar{v})(\bar{u}^3 - 3\bar{u})\cos^2\vartheta + 2g(\bar{v})(\bar{u}^2 - 1) \cdot$$

$$\cdot \sin\vartheta\cos\vartheta + \bar{u}\,\bar{v}\,g(\bar{v})\sin^2\vartheta\Big] - B g(u)\Big[\Phi(v)(u^3 - 3u)\cos^2\vartheta + 2g(v) \cdot$$

$$\cdot (u^2 - 1)\sin\vartheta\cos\vartheta - u v g(v)\sin^2\vartheta\Big] \qquad (2.22)$$

Then in $V = (0,0)$ we have:

$$f_{xx} = - (A + B)/2\pi \sin 2\vartheta \qquad (2.23)$$

$$f_{xy} = (B - A)/2\pi (1 + \cos 2\vartheta) \qquad (2.24)$$

$$f_{yy} = (A + B)/2\pi \sin 2\vartheta \qquad (2.25)$$

Hessian determinant is:

$$H\Big|_V = - 1/2\pi^2\Big[(A^2 + B^2)(1 + \cos 2\vartheta) - AB (\cos 4\vartheta + 2\cos 2\vartheta + 1)\Big] \qquad (2.26)$$

The eigenvalues of Hessian matrix are:

$$L_1 = - L \qquad (2.27)$$

$$L_2 = L \qquad (2.28)$$

where:

$$L = \sqrt{- H}\Big|_V \qquad (2.29)$$

Since $L_1 + L_2 = 0$ for all ϑ,the trace C of hessian in V is always zero,that is:

$$C\Big|_V = 0 \qquad\qquad \forall \vartheta \qquad (2.30)$$

and the gaussian curvature K in V is:

$$K\Big|_V < 0 \qquad \forall \vartheta \qquad\qquad (\,2.31\,)$$

that is,the vertex V is an hyperbolic point.

Fig. 4   Original Image

EXPERIMENTAL RESULT

    To test the relevance of the above described properties for the
detection of trihedrical vertexes in real images,a simple algorithm was
implemented based on the processing of the slope of the zero-crossing
contours. The image was then filtered using a Laplacian of Gaussian operator
with $\sigma = 3$,the location of the zero-crossing point was detected,and the slope
and local orientation for each zero-crossing point was computed. As describe
in the previous paragraph,the slope of a point along a zero-crossing contour
changes,near a trihedrical vertex,from zero,along the spurious edge,to the
value corresponding to the contrast of the luminance discontinuity. For
this reason the location in space of trihedrical vertexes can be attemped
by computing the maxima of the slope trend. In Fig. 5 the result of this
operation is presented. As it can be seen,in spite of the relatively simple
algorithm,all the trihedrical vertexes are correctly identified by
thresholding the slope trend.

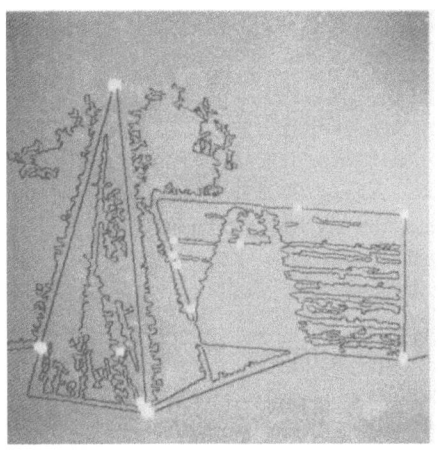
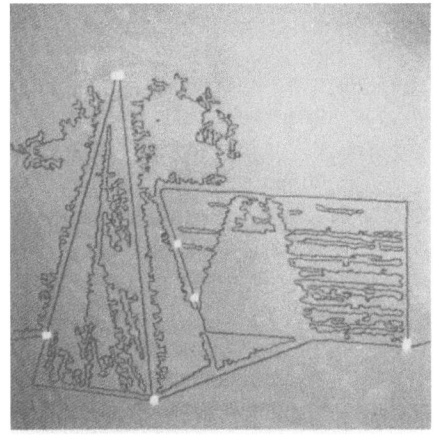

Fig.5.a   Fig.5.b

Fig.5.a and Fig.5.b : Zero-crossing detected after convolution with Laplacian of Gaussian;white marks identify the location of the points whose slope trend was higher than 12 (Fig.5.a) and 18 (Fig.5.b). The maximum slope trend for this image is 20.

CONCLUSION

The relevance of trihedrical vertexes for image understanding was extensively studied within the framework of the so called "block world" for the reason that trihedrical vertexes are often tied to 3D features. Certainly the fact that the zero-crossing contours incorrectly detect trihedrical vertexes, may be a strong limitation to the use of this method of edge detection. To this extent the use of some of the properties described in the present paper could help to solve the problem by locating trihedrical vertexes independently from the location of the zero-crossing.

We will now summarize the main results of our analysis of a noise-free trihedrical vertex.

   A) The vertex V has the following properties:
i   : It is always detected at every scale,therefore it does not move
      when the size of gaussian filter is varied.

ii : It is an hyperbolic zero-crossing structurally stable.

   B) Edges detected are constituted by two curves with these properties:
i : The slope of the spurious edge goes to zero when the distance from
      V increases.

ii : The slope of the true edges approaches asymptotically the contrast.

REFERENCES

Ballard,D.H. and Brown,C. Computer Vision,
    Prentice-Hall,Englewood Cliffs,New Jersey,1982.
Berzins,V. "Accuracy of Laplacian edge detectors."
    Computer Graphics and Image Processing,27,195-210,1984.
Binford,T.O. "Survey of model-based image analysis systems."
    Int.J.Robotics Res.,1,no.1,18-64,1982.
Binford,T.O. "Inferring surfaces from images."
    Art.Int.,17,205-244,1981.
Brady,J.M. "Computational Approaches to Image Understanding."
    Computing Surveys,14,3-71,1982.
Hildreth,E.C. "Implementation of a theory of edge detection."
    A.I. Memo 579,M.I.T.,1980.
Marr,D.C. and Hildreth,E.C. "Theory of edge detection."
    Proc.R.Soc.Lond.B,207,187-217,1980.
Rosenfeld,A. and Kak,A.C. Digital Picture Processing,second edition
    Academic Press,New York,1982.
Torre,V. and Poggio,T. "On Edge Detection."
    A.I. Memo 768,M.I.T.,1984.

ACKNOWLEDGEMENT

The present work was partially sponsored by an ESPRIT contract
(project P419) and by a grant of the Special Project of Mechanical
Technology of the Italian.

A TECHNIQUE FOR OBJECT RECOGNITION BASED ON SUBPART CLASSIFICATION

V.Cappellini

Dipartimento di Ingegneria Elettronica, University of Florence
and IROE - C.N.R., Via Panciatichi, 64 - 50127 Firenze, Italy

M.T.Pareschi and C.Raspollini

Centro Scientifico IBM, Via Santa Maria, 67 - 56100 Pisa, Italy

INTRODUCTION

This paper describes a technique, developed within a joint research project between the IBM Pisa Scientific Center and the Faculty of Engineering of the University of Florence, to analyze and recognize complex objects in bidimensional grey images.
Many efforts have been made in the field of 2-D recognition of mechanical objects. Usually, the first step is the extraction of the boundaries of the objects present in the scene. This edge-point information may be successively used in different ways. To cite some examples:
- computing the spectrum (FFT) of the distances between the centroid of the object and its contour pixels. If the difference between object and model spectrum is smaller than a given threshold, the object is recognized (Cappellini and Del Bimbo, 1983; Borghesi et al., 1984);
- expressing the boundary in terms of tangent angle versus arc length and then evaluating the FFT of this function (Pavlidis, 1977);
- fitting the edge points to a connected set of straight lines and circular arcs obtaining a "concurve" and then matching the concurve data of the model to the concurve data of the image finding a suitable transformation from model coordinates to image coordinates (Perkins, 1978);
- computing central moments of the pixels inside the boundaries and then performing the classification using a Bayes decision rule and a distance-weighted k-nearest-neighbor rule (Dudani et al, 1977);
In all these methods the objects are regarded as a single part, that is they are not constituted by several adjacent subparts.
The technique here described does not consider the boundaries in the scene but, by a region-growing segmentation algorithm, isolates every subparts from the background and, considering the adjacency relationships existing among them, allows the recognition of complex objects.
The objects, which can be constituted by different subparts, are recognized by means of their models, previously computed and stored. The input image, after a preliminary nonlinear smoothing to reduce random noise, is segmented into a set of regions characterized by nearly uniform brightness (the number of obtained regions is possibly reduced by merging too small areas into neighbour larger ones of similar brightness). The characteristics and the contiguity relationships for each region are then computed and compared with those of the prestored subpart models. If a subpart is not recognized, the procedure merges it into one of its not yet classified neighbour regions and tries to form a known subpart. At the final step, the complex object is recognized only if all its subparts have been correctly classified.

Figure 1 shows a diagram of the recognition procedure.
By means of this technique, different scenes with complex mechanical objects have been successfully analyzed.

PREPROCESSING

As first step, a nonlinear smoothing of the image is performed. This preprocessing is necessary to reduce the noise, introduced during the acquisition of the image by means of a TV camera, and to make the image more homogeneous in view of the successive segmentation step. The digital filter utilized to smooth the image is a 3x3 nonlinear operator which substitutes a pixel by the average value of the pixel itself and those of its eight neighbours whose grey level difference with respect to the pixel under consideration is less then a fixed threshold (Rosenfeld and Kak, 1982; Borghesi et al., 1984). If, as shown in Figure 2, P_o is the grey level of a generic pixel of the image, $P_{1,2...8}$ are the corresponding values of its eight neighbours, and the prime indicates the updated value, the nonlinear smoothing is given by the formula:

$$P'_o = 1/n \sum_{P_i \varepsilon S} P_i$$
$$S = \{P_i : | P_i - P_o | \le k \} , i=0...8$$
$$n = \text{number of } P_i; \ k \text{ threshold value}$$

The threshold k is chosen in such a way as to reduce the noise without blurring the edges; in fact, near a boundary whose grey level difference is greater than k, the pixels are smoothed on both sides of the edge, but

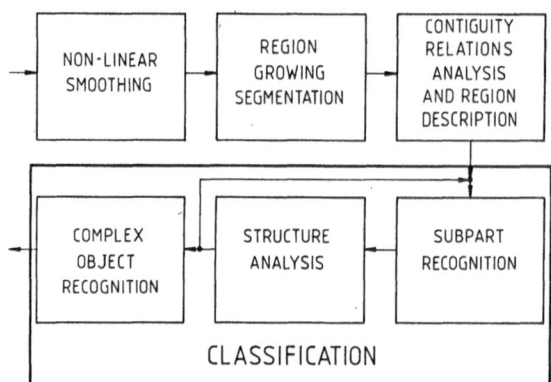

Fig.1 Block-diagram of the recognition procedure

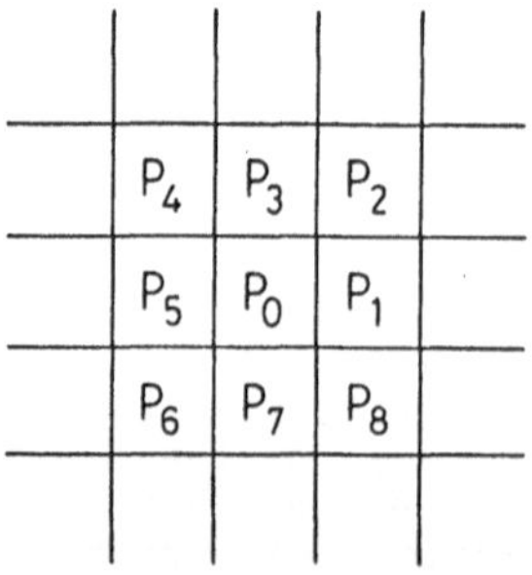

Fig.2 Grey-level definition of a 3-3 pixel block

the filtered value is obtained without considering the pixels laying on the other part of the boundary. To this purpose, the threshold value must be chosen conveniently inferior to the difference existing on the average between the object grey value and the background grey value, In the experimental tests the pixels have values in the range 0-255 and a good experimental value of k is 20.

SEGMENTATION

The second operation performed on the smoothed image is a segmentation based on a region growing technique.

Region growing algorithms look for groups of pixels of similar brightness. The standard way to proceed is to start with one pixel and then to examine its neighbors in order to decide whether they have similar brightness. If they do, then they are grouped together to form a region.

In our technique, the first top-left pixel of the image is considered and its grey level is the initial one of the first region. A 3x3 "search window" is centered on this pixel and each pixel grey level inside the window is compared with grey level values of the region which the central pixel belongs to. If the difference between these values is less than a given threshold, the neighbour pixel is marked as one of the region and the region grey level value is updated with that of the pixel, otherwise the pixel is ignored. When all the pixels inside the window have been examined, the window is moved and centered on the last pixel added to the region. If an edge of the image is reached or no new pixels have been added to the considered region, the search window is moved back to the first allowable pixel of the region which still has some open "search directions". If there is none, the region is considered completed and a new region growing process is started.

On the basis of experimental texts, a good threshold value for the segmentation algorithm is 30. This algorithm gives satisfactory results, that is there is a good agreement between object subparts in the input image and the segmented regions, if the former are fairly uniform[*] . In agreement with Pavlidis (Pavlidis, 1977) it is practically possible to obtain a good segmentation using a given threshold k, if the mean square error of the pixel grey level values is much smaller than k. This condition is more easily reached with a suitable choice of scene illumination and performing, before the segmentation phase, a smoothing operation to reduce random noise.

The minimum number of pixels in a region is obtained by knowing the number of subparts present in the observed scene (obviously not the exact number but only an approximation of it).

At the end of the segmentation phase, the region number obtained is reduced: areas which are too small are merged into the adjacent region with the nearest grey level value. The reduction operation allows to utilize in the segmentation step a low threshold value. This means to have a high sensibility to grey level changes and, as a consequence, a good agreement between the input image and the segmented one. The reduction operation only removes part of the noise or little details. As far as the successive classification procedure is concerned, only the main components of every object are considered and stored as models. Moreover, the reducing procedure has the advantage of considerably shortening the computational time of the successive step.

---

[*] A region is considered uniform if:

$$\max|f(P)-m| < k$$

$$m = 1/N \ \Sigma \ f(P) \qquad N : \text{number of pixels of the region}$$

where $f(P)$ is the grey level of the generic pixel P belonging to the region.

For each of the obtained regions, the procedure computes some quantities that are invariant to translation, rotation and scale changes. These quantities are:

1) TH : thinness (area/perimeter^2)
2) RAPT : ratio of the maximum to the minimum distance between the centroid and the region contour
3) HU1 : first Hu invariant
4) HU2 : second Hu invariant
5) BAY : total positive area subtended by the centroidal profile
6) PENINSULA : total negative area subtended by the centroidal profile

The first and second Hu invariants are function of the central normalized inertia momenta up to the second order. If f(x,y) is a bidimensional function, the inertia momenta of order p+q are given by the formula:

$$m_{pq} = \iint_{area} x^p y^q dx dy$$

and the central inertia momenta are:

$$\mu_{pq} = \iint_{area} (x-x_g)^p (y-y_g)^q dx dy$$

where the two values:

$$x_g = m_{10}/m_{00}$$

$$y_g = m_{01}/m_{00}$$

are the centroid coordinates. The normalized central momenta η_{pq} are function of μ_{pq}:

$$\eta_{pq} = \mu_{pq}/\mu_{00}^{\gamma}$$

$$\gamma = (p+q)/2 + 1 \qquad p,q = 0,1,2$$

From η_{pq} it is possible to obtain a set of seven quantities (called "Hu invariants") invariant to translation, rotation and scale changes (Hu, 1962; Gonzalez and Wintz, 1977; Reddi, 1981). Here only the first two Hu invariants are utilized (the other five, because of their dependence on η_{pq} of higher order, are greatly affected by noise). The first two Hu invariants are:

$$HU1 = \eta_{20} + \eta_{02}$$

$$HU2 = (\eta_{20} - \eta_{02})^2 + 4\eta_{11}^2$$

Other parameters utilized for recognition are the total positive and negative area subtended by the centroidal profile. The centroidal profile (Freeman, 1978) is a normalized graph of the distance from the boundary to the centroid of the region. Since the centroid coordinates are determined by the ratio between the first order momenta and the area, they are relatively insensitive to noise, and so the centroidal profile tends to be a stable curve. The profile values corresponding to clockwise angular rotation are considered positive and those corresponding to counterclockwise rotation negative. The total positive area is defined as the area between the positive centroidal profile and the contour curvilinear coordinate axis, while the negative area is that subtended by negative profile and curvilinear coordinate axis (Figure 3). These two quantities do not obviously depend on region orientation; to obtain scale

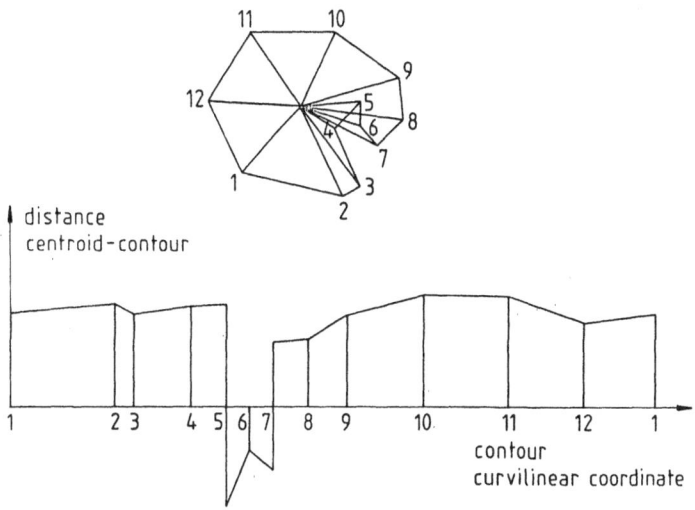

Fig.3 Centroidal profile and definition
of the positive-negative area

change invariance both areas are divided by the square of the perimeter.
The six parameters presented are representative of the shape of the
various objects only if these are clearly visible in the image; in other
words, the objects must not be overlapped.

CLASSIFICATION

The analyzed objects can be simple (that is formed by a single region)
or complex (that is made up by a set of subparts). The procedure tries to
recognize each subpart separately and, if a subpart is not recognized,
the procedure merges it into one of its neighbour regions not yet
classified and tries to form a known subpart. All the possible "merge"
combinations are tested, and, if this procedure fails, the subpart is
definitively not recognized. For each subpart a model exists which
consists of a set of identifiers: the six parameters mentioned in the
previous section with the corresponding "confidence radius"*, the number
of holes, and the adjacency relationship number (that is the number of
contiguous regions). Steps a)-f) describe in detail the recognition of a
generic subpart:

a) A generic subpart is considered and the parameters: TH, RAPT, HU1,
   HU2, BAY, PENINSULA, NH1 (numbers of holes), SP1 (adjacency
   relationship number) are computed. Then, for each subpart model, steps
   b)-d) are performed.

b) SP1 is compared with the adjacency relationship number of a model; if
   there is a match, step c) is performed, otherwise a new model is
   considered. If there is no correspondence with any model, the subpart
   is not recognized. In this case the procedure tries to merge the
   unknown region into one or more adjacent regions to form a new subpart
   and control comes back to step a);

c) NH1 is compared with the number of holes of a model; if they
   correspond, step d) is performed, otherwise the next model is
   inspected. The recognition fails if there is no match with any model;
   in this case, the procedure tries to merge the unknown region into one
   or more adjacent regions to form a new subpart and control comes back
   to step a);

---

* The parameters TH, RAPT, HU1, HU2, BAY, PENINSULA and the relative
confidence radius are obtained by a set of digitized images of the
subpart under consideration. More precisely, the parameters are given by
the arithmetical mean of the values extracted by each digitized image,
while the confidence radius is proportional to the relative mean square
error.

Fig.4 Input grey level image

Fig.7 Input grey level image

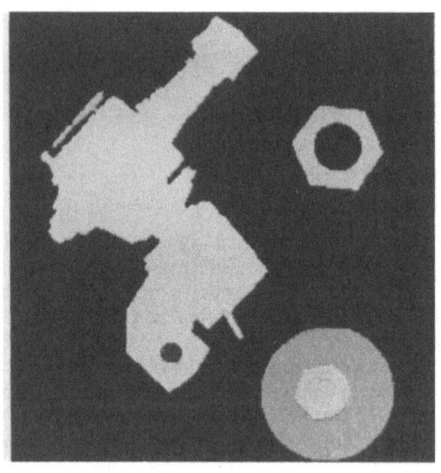

Fig.5 Segmented image

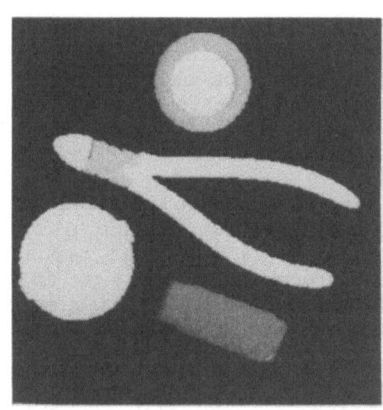

Fig.8 Segmented image

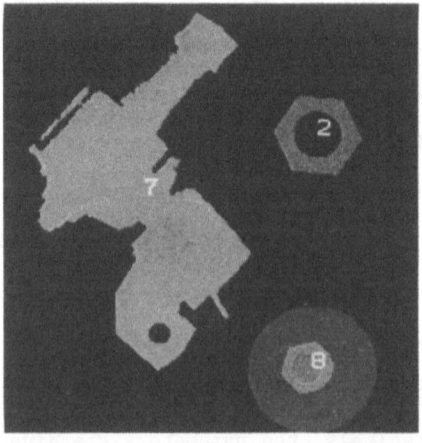

Fig.6 Recognition results

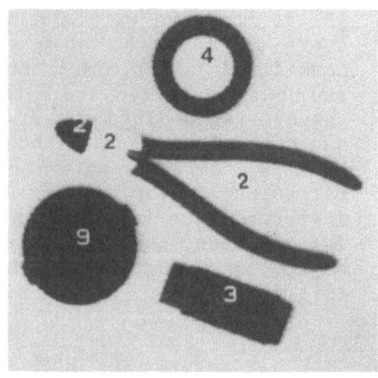

Fig.9 Recognition results

d) the differences between the parameters TH, RAPT, HU1, HU2, BAY, PENINSULA of the subpart under investigation and those of a model are computed and divided by the relative confidence radius;

e) for each parameter, the minimum value computed at step d) is considered and if it is less than one, the match between the region and the model which has originated that minimum value has been successful;

f) if there are at least four positive out of six possible matches, that is the absolute majority, for the same model, the region is considered recognized.

Among all the parameters, the previous identification operation privileges two of them: the adjacency relationship number and the number of holes. As a matter of fact, these two values are known with a precision which is much greater than that of the other parameters and, in addition, this choice allows to gain computational time in the classification step.

EXPERIMENTAL RESULTS AND CONCLUSIONS

The described technique performs a bidimensional scene analysis. 3-D objects which can be characterized by a single view (flat objects) can be successfully recognized.

The technique was tested on different digitized pictures. The digitized images are 256x256 pixel with 8 bit resolution. Figures 4-9 show some phases of the procedure for different kinds of objects. Figures 4 and 7 show input scenes taken by a monochrome TV Camera, Figures 5 and 8 are the corresponding segmented images. At the end, Figures 6 and 9 show the final results: different recognized subparts are shown as uniform color regions and the superimposed number indicates the type of object which they belong to.

The results obtained with this technique are greatly dependent on the segmentation effects, that is the better the segmentation, the faster and the more satisfactory the classification. To obtain a good image segmentation, it is very important to use suitable thresholds both in the smoothing and in the segmentation phase (however, it appears that these two values can be taken constant for a set of images acquired under the same illumination conditions). Very satisfactory results were obtained by taking account of illumination in the acquisition phase in order to minimize shadows and reflection effects (nevertheless, in the classification step, the merging algorithm manages to fuse fictitious subparts into real ones).

The procedure, implemented on an IBM 4341, takes about two minutes of CPU time (segmentation is the most expensive process, while classification is the fastest phase: it takes less than one second for a catalogue of ten subparts corresponding to five distinct objects). Input digitized images and resulting images are displayed on an IBM 7350.

REFERENCES

Borghesi P., Cappellini V., Carla' R., Del Bimbo A., Mecocci A., Pareschi M.T., Digital Image Processing Techniques for Object Recognition and Experimental Results, Proc. of the Int. Conf. on Digital Signal Processing, Florence, pp.764-769 (1984).

Cappellini V., Del Bimbo A., Digital Processing of Time Varying Images, NATO ASI Series F1, Issued in "Acoustic Signal Image Processing and Recognition", Chen C.H. ed., Springer Verlag, Berlin Heidelberg, pp.283-293 (1983).

Dudani S.A., Breeding K.J., Mc Ghee R.B., Aircraft Identification by Moments Invariants, IEEE Trans. on Computers, vol. c-26, n.1, pp.39-45 (1977).

Freeman H., Shape Description via the Use of Critical Points, Pattern Recognition, vol. 10, pp.159-166 (1978).

Gonzalez R.C., Wintz P., Digital Image Processing, Addison Wesley, Reading, Mass. (1977).

Hu M.K., Visual Pattern Recognition by Moment Invariants, IRE Trans. on Inf. Theory, pp.173-187 (1962).

Pavlidis T., Structural Pattern Recognition, Springer Verlag, Berlin Heidelberg, pp.154-156 (1977).

Perkins W.A., A Model-Based Vision System for Industrial Parts, IEEE Trans. on Computers, vol. c-27, n.2, pp.126-143 (1978).

Reddi S., Radial and Angular Moment Invariants for Image Identification, IEEE PAMI, vol. 3, pp.240-242 (1981).

Rosenfeld A., Kak A.C., Digital Picture Processing, Academic Press, New York (1982).

ABOUT AREA OF FIGURE COMPONENTS

Luigi P. Cordella[o] and Gabriella Sanniti di Baja[oo]

o Dipartimento di Informatica e Sistemistica, Università di Napoli
oo Istituto di Cibernetica del CNR, Arco Felice, Napoli

INTRODUCTION

Area is one of the features most widely used for figure description. The simplest way to evaluate it, is to count the pixels constituting the figure at hand. However, when data reduction techniques are employed for storage or description purposes, the figure itself is no longer available, and suitable methods for area measurement are needed.

In the past, methods to evaluate the area of figures represented by their contour have been proposed /1-3/.

In this paper, the problem of determining the area of a figure represented by its labeled medial line is faced.

For a connected single-valued figure F, its labeled medial line (LML, for short) is a subset of F having the following properties: 1) its pixels are labeled according to their distance from the background, 2) it is centered within F, 3) it has unit width, 4) it is connected and has the same connectivity order of F, and 5) it includes all the pixels having a locally maximal label (the so called local maxima) except for those removed to gain unit width.

A branch is a connected subset of the LML such that every pixel has just two neighbors except for the extremes which can be either end points or branch points. End points have only one neighbor, while branch points have more than two neighbors. Any connected subset of a branch will be called arc.

Including the local maxima turns out to be a very important feature of the LML, as it guarantees that the figure can be recovered and its area evaluated, if the reverse distance tansformation is applied to the LML. On the other hand, the LML transformation establishes a correspondence between medial line arcs and figure regions, in such a way that a suitable partition of the LML into arcs specifies a partition of the figure into partially overlapping component regions. Some methods for figure decomposition and description based on LML partitioning, have been proposed in the literature /4-6/. In this framework, the measure of the area of the region associated to an arc of the LML can be used, for instance, to contribute to the characterization of that figure component.

The method we propose here, allows to evaluate the area of the region corresponding to any arc of the LML without applying to it the reverse distance transformation. In fact, recovery seems to be unnecessary since the LML already possesses all the information required to achieve the goal.

According to our method, each arc is traced starting from either of its extremes, and the area of the corresponding region is obtained by iteratively adding the contributions provided by the local maxima.

The computational cost of the algorithm, as regards both computation time and memory occupation, is lower than that of alternative methods using the reverse distance transformation.

AREA EVALUATION

In what follows we will assume that the pixels of the LML are labeled according to their 8-distance from the background. Accordingly, a square-shaped neighborhood of size $(2L-1)^2$ is associated to every pixel labeled L. In particular, the region associated to each local maximum, called maximal neighborhood (MN), never completely overlaps any other MN. Conversely, the neighborhood associated to a pixel which is not a local maximum is completely included by some MN. Thus, only the contribution given to the area associated to an arc by the local maxima present on it, has to be taken into account.

Let M_i be any of the local maxima occurring along a given arc, and let L_i and MN_i be respectively its label and the associated maximal neighborhood.

Two local maxima M_i and M_k such that

$$d_8 (M_i, M_k) < L_i + L_k - 1$$

will be said to be "interacting" since MN_i and MN_k partially overlap. Thus, if for either of them, say M_k, the contribution to the area A associated to the arc has been already computed, the contribution of M_i to A will be restricted to that part of MN_i which protrudes from MN_k. This is better illustrated in Fig. 1, where $J_r(i)$ and $J_u(i)$ respectively indicate the rightward and the upward jut of MN_i with respect to MN_k. Then, the contribution A_i given by M_i to the area A, can be simply computed as:

$$A_i = (2L_i - 1) \cdot \left[J_r(i) + J_u(i) \right] - J_r(i) \cdot J_u(i)$$

In the general case however, M_i is likely to interact with more than one other local maximum. Thus, the contribution of M_i to A may be further reduced to just that part of MN_i which does not overlap with any other already considered maximal neighborhood, associated to a local maximum interacting with M_i. As an example, see Fig. 2 where M_i interacts with both M_k and M_h. If the contribution of M_k and M_h to A has been already computed, M_i contributes only for the dashed part of MN_i. In fact, the crossed portion of the rightward protrusion of MN_i with respect to

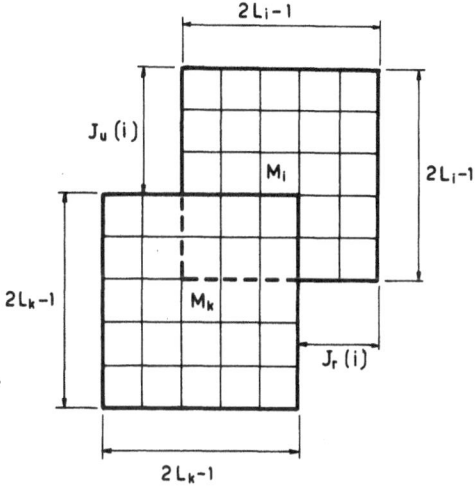

Fig. 1 - Two interacting local maxima and their associated overlapping maximal neighborhoods.

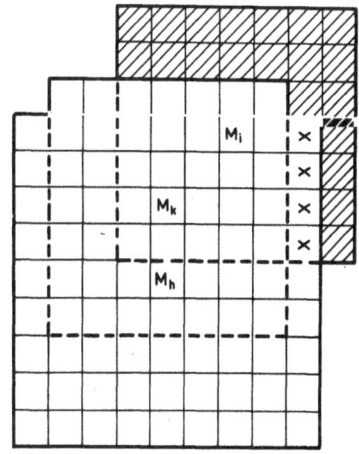

Fig. 2 - Only the dashed area of MN_i is not overlapped by either MN_k or MN_h.

MN_k is overlapped by MN_h. Consequently, the two sides of the crossed rectangular region must be evaluated and the corresponding area must be subtracted from A_i.

For the sake of generality, we will describe now the procedure for evaluating the area of the region associated to any 8-connected sequence of pixels labeled under the constraint that the difference in label between any pair of pixels is not greater than the 8-distance between them. Since this is not the only constraint for a sequence of pixels belonging to a labeled medial line, some simplifications of the procedure are possible, as it will be eventually pointed out.

According to our procedure, a connected sequence of pixels is traced starting from either of its extremes. Pixels whose label is smaller than that of some enighbor are skipped. In correspondence to the first encountered local maximum, say M_0, the value $(2L_0-1)^2$ is added to the register A, initially empty. For any successively traced M_i, $i > 0$, the following expressions are evaluated:

$$\Delta x(i) = x_i - x_{i-1}$$
$$\Delta y(i) = y_i - y_{i-1}$$
$$\Delta L(i) = L_i - L_{i-1}$$
$$J_r(i) = \Delta L(i) + \Delta x(i)$$
$$J_l(i) = \Delta L(i) - \Delta x(i)$$
$$J_u(i) = \Delta L(i) + \Delta y(i)$$
$$J_d(i) = \Delta L(i) - \Delta y(i)$$

The values of the above expressions are respectively assigned to the i-th elements of seven vectors. In the first three vectors the differences in coordinates and in label between the current local maximum M_i and the previously traced one, are successively stored. The values stored in the remaining four vectors respectively indicate the rightward, the leftward, the upward and the downward jut of MN_i with respect to MN_{i-1}.

The previous expressions can be verified with reference to the cases shown in Fig. 3, where M_i is encircled and M_{i-1} is the other extreme of each sequence of pixels. For instance it can be noted that the downward jut assumes positive value only in Fig. 3c, where MN_i protrudes downwards from MN_{i-1}. On the contrary, for a downward juxtaposition (Fig. 3a), $J_d(i)=0$ while for a downward "intrusion" (Fig. 3b), $J_d(i) < 0$.

Obviously, as only local maxima are taken into account, no more than three juts can simultaneously assume a positive value, i.e., any MN_i can protrude from MN_{i-1} towards at most three directions.

For every positive jut of MN_i with respect to MN_{i-1}, there is the possibility that part of the protrusion in that direction is overlapped by the maximal neighborhood associated to some already traced pixel (as it was for the rightward protrusion of MN_i in Fig. 2).

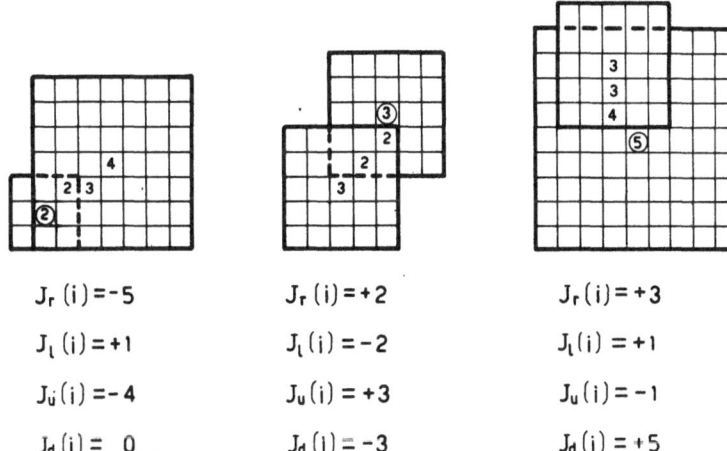

$$J_r(i) = -5 \qquad\qquad J_r(i) = +2 \qquad\qquad J_r(i) = +3$$

$$J_l(i) = +1 \qquad\qquad J_l(i) = -2 \qquad\qquad J_l(i) = +1$$

$$J_u(i) = -4 \qquad\qquad J_u(i) = +3 \qquad\qquad J_u(i) = -1$$

$$J_d(i) = \;\; 0 \qquad\qquad J_d(i) = -3 \qquad\qquad J_d(i) = +5$$

Fig. 3 – Three typical configurations. The current local maximum M_i is encircled. The value of the juts of MN_i with respect to MN_{i-1} depends on the relative position and labels of M_i and M_{i-1}.

Since the procedure to be followed in order to evaluate the amount of overlapping is almost the same, whichever jut has a positive value, we will discuss in detail the case in which $J_r(i) > 0$. The differences in case of a positive jut towards another direction will be pointed out later.

Now, let S_r represent the rightward jut of MN_{i-k} with respect to MN_{i-1}. Moreover, let T_r be the part of $J_r(i)$ not overlapped by MN_{i-k}, and Z_r a register where the area of that part of protrusion of MN_i from MN_{i-1} overlapped by MN_{i-k} is added.

The overlapping area is given by

$$\left[(2L_i - 1) - \left(\left| \sum_{h=i}^{i-k} \Delta y(h) \right| + \sum_{h=i}^{i-k} \Delta L(h) \right) \right] \cdot \min\left(T_r, |S_r| \right)$$

and its value is added to Z_r.

The reason for the factor $\min(T_r, |S_r|)$, is that MN_{i-k} could protrude from MN_{i-1} more than MN_i protrudes from MN_{i-k}. Moreover, in principle some further maximal neighborhoods may overlap the rightward protrusion of MN_i. Therefore, T_r is decremented by $\min(T_r, |S_r|)$, S_r is reset to zero, and the backwards inspection of the vector is continued possibly adding new terms to Z_r, until either of the following events occurs:

1) $T_r = 0$ (i.e., the sum of the rightward juts that any two successive maximal neighborhoods overlapping MN_i have with respect one another, is equal to $J_r(i)$).

2) $i-k=1$ (i.e., the first element of the vector has been reached).

At the end of the procedure, the area $A_{i,r}$ of the rightward protrusion of MN_i can be determined as:

$$A_{i,r} = (2L_i - 1) \cdot J_r(i) - Z_r$$

For a positive value of $J_l(i)$, the procedure to be followed to compute the area of the leftward protrusion is exactly the same. Conversely, for both downward and upward positive juts, $\Delta y(h)$ must be substituted by $\Delta x(h)$, while evaluating the terms to be added to Z_d and Z_u respectively.

Finally, the contribution provided by M_i to the whole area A, can be computed by adding the area of every protrusion of MN_i with respect to MN_{i-1}, and by subtracting the portion shared by each pair of protrusions (for instance, $J_r(i) \cdot J_u(i)$ when both rightward and upward protrusions of MN_i are present).

Tracing is then continued until the second extreme of the sequence of pixels is met and its contribution to the area is evaluated.

The performance of the algorithm is illustrated in Fig.4, where the sequence of pixels has been traced starting from the extreme labeled 9.

DISCUSSIONS AND CONCLUSIONS

As mentioned in the previous Section, the procedure we have illustrated can be simplified when it has to be applied to a connected sequence of labeled pixels that actually belong to an LML arc. The described procedure is effective even if a protrusion of MN_i with respect to MN_{i-1} is partially overlapped by more than one previously considered maximal neighborhood. However, it seems that a sequence of local maxima belonging to an LML arc, can never give place to such "multiple overlaps", so that in practice the procedure can be shortened. Specifically, it seems unnecessary to iterate the backward inspection of the previously defined vectors, after an overlapping maximal neighborhood MN_{i-k} has been detected for anyone of the protrusions. Moreover, in case of a unique positive value of the juts of MN_i, the procedure for detecting overlaps can be completely skipped.

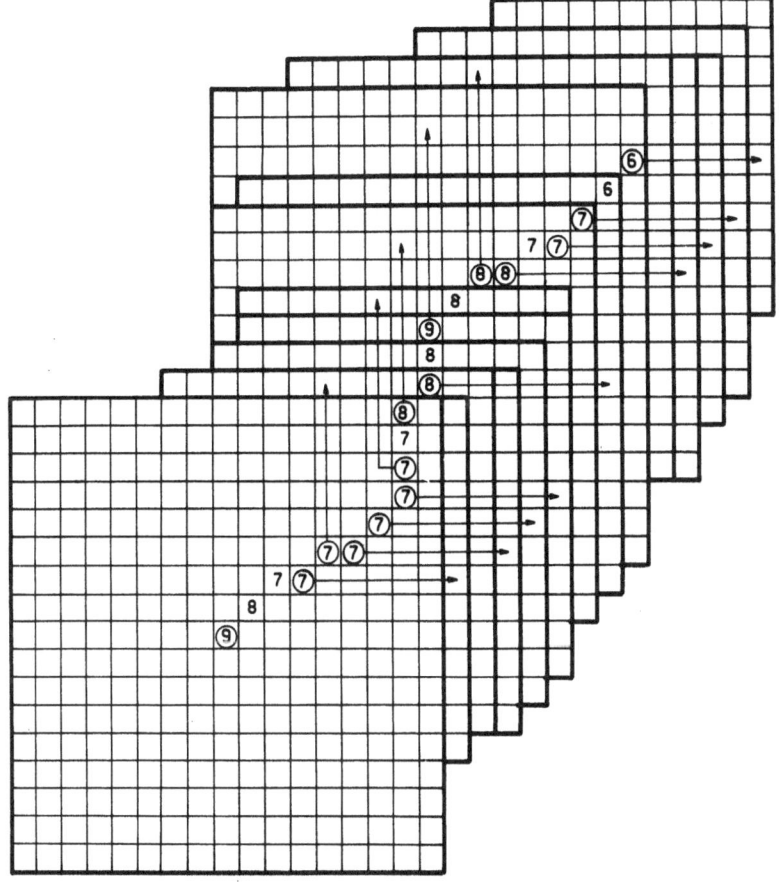

Fig. 4 – For each local maximum (encircled labels) the part of its maximal neighborhood (pointed by an arrow) contributing to figure area is outlined by bold lines.

Our algorithm is especially convenient in the framework of figure decomposition methods based on medial line partitioning, in order to eva-luate components area by saving time and memory space.

ACKNOWLEDGMENTS

The authors with to thank Mrs. Anna Maria Mazzarella for her skillful assistance in preparing the manuscript, as well as Mr. Umberto Cascini and Mr. Salvatore Piantedosi for providing the illustrations.

REFERENCES

1. H. Freeman, Computer processing of line drawing images, ACM Computing Surveys 6: 57 (1974).

2. L.P. Cordella, A method for evaluating features of outlined components of an image, Signal Processing 5: 485 (1983).

3. P. Zamperoni, A note on the computation of the enclosed area for contour-coded binary objects, Signal Processing 3: 267 (1981).

4. L.P. Cordella and G. Sanniti di Baja, Structural description of silhouettes, Proc. 3rd Scandinavian Conference on Image Analysis, Copenhagen: 73 (1983).

5. C. Arcelli and G. Sanniti di Baja, An approach to figure decomposition using width information, Computer Vision, Graphics, and Image Processing 26: 61 (1984).

6. T. Kasvand, Segmentation using thin lines, Proc. International Conference on Digital Signal Processing, Firenze (1984).

EXPERIMENTS USING THE GENERALIZED HOUGH TRANSFORM

FOR DETECTING CORRESPONDENCES IN A SEQUENCE OF SHAPES

Maria F. Costabile and Goffredo G. Pieroni

Dipartimento di Matematica
Universita' della Calabria
87036 Rende (Cosenza), Italy

ABSTRACT

The Hough transform is a technique for detecting curves in an image by exploiting the relationship between the set of points on a curve and the parameters of that curve. This method has been extended to the detection of arbitrary non-analytic shapes in gray level images. In this paper we show some experiments using this technique for detecting corresponding segments of shape boundary lines belonging to successive frames of a sequence which describes the modifications that occurred on the shape boundary in a time interval.

INTRODUCTION

The Hough transform is not a particular novel idea but one of its major attractions is that it can be implemented on the parallel hardware that is now becoming available more cheaply, with the wider use of VLSI techniques[1]. In its original version the Hough transform can be described as a technique for detecting lines in the image space by exploiting the relationship between the set of points on a line and the set of parameters defining the line. This method has been extended to the detection of arbitrary non-analytic shapes in gray level images. Ballard[2] shows how the boundary of an arbitrary non-analytic shape can be used to construct a mapping between image space and Hough transform space. Such a mapping can be exploited to detect instances of that particular shape in an image.

In this paper we apply the generalized Hough transform for detecting corresponding segments of shape boundary lines belonging to successive frames of a sequence which describes the modifications that occurred on the shape boundary in a time interval. The main motivation of this work comes from biomedical problems which deal with the analysis of the modifications of the boundary of a two-dimensional representation of an organ. Once the boundary of the organ has been determined at given time intervals, the variation of such a line during the time must be described. We examined this problem in previous papers[3,4]. In our approach a polygonal approximation of the boundary of the shape representing the object is considered; the polygonal is decomposed into segments with given attributes assigned to them. For each segment we find its corresponding one in

the following frame and the difference between the structure of corresponding segments is evaluated. Thus, the description of the modifications
occurring between two successive frames is provided.

The decomposition of the boundary into meaningful segments is a
delicate procedure regulated by thresholds which are frequently critical
to define. Under the hypothesis of slow variations, the generalized Hough
transform represents a valid tool for detecting corresponding parts of two
successive frames without considering the segmentation of the boundaries,
as we will show with the experiments.

GENERALIZED HOUGH TRANSFORM

The Hough transform was originally a method for detecting straight
lines in digitized images. It describes a mapping between points in image
space and points in parameter space. The parameter space is defined by the
parametric representation used to describe lines in the image space.
Hough[5] used the familiar slope-intercept parameters and thus his parameter
space was the two-dimensional slope-intercept plane. Because both the
slope and the intercept are unbounded, unnecessary complications arise in
the application of the technique. Duda and Hart[6] preferred the normal
parameterization as illustrated in Fig. 1. A straight line is specified by
the angle θ of its normal and its algebraic distance ρ from the origin.
The equation of a line using these parameters is

$$\rho = x \cos \theta + y \sin \theta , \quad 0 \leq \theta \leq \pi .$$

If θ is restricted to the range between 0 and π, then the normal
parameters for a line are unique.

Suppose that we have a set $\{(x_1,y_1),(x_2,y_2),...,(x_n,y_n)\}$ of n figure
points and we want to find a set of straight lines that fit them. We
transform the points (x_i,y_i) into the sinusoidal curves in the θ-ρ plane
defined by

$$\rho = x_i \cos \theta + y_i \sin \theta. \tag{1}$$

It is easy to show that the curves corresponding to colinear image points
have a common point of intersection, say (θ_o,ρ_o). This point in the θ-ρ
plane defines the line passing through the colinear points. Thus the
problem of detecting colinear points can be converted to the problem of
finding concurrent curves.

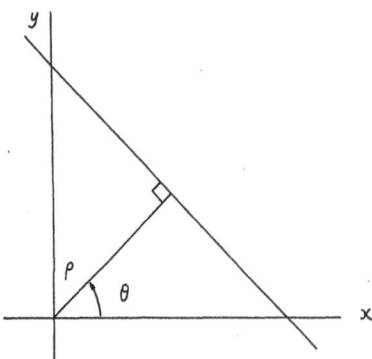

Fig. 1. The normal parameters for a line.

The Hough transform is generally implemented using an accumulator array. The parameter space is quantized into cells whose size is governed by the error that can be tolerated in θ and ρ. Each cell in parameter space is assigned an accumulator in a two-dimensional array. For each point (x_i, y_i) in the image space, the corresponding curve given by (1) is entered in the array by incrementing the count in each cell along the curve. After all figure points have been treated, the array is inspected to find cells having high counts. If the count in a given cell (θ_i, ρ_j) is k, then precisely k figure points lie (to within quantization error) along the line whose normal parameters are (θ_i, ρ_j).

Although the Hough transform was intended to detect lines, extensions of this technique have been described for the detection of circles[7], parabolas[8], ellipses[9,10]. The successful implementation of these extensions is dependent upon the selection of a set of parameters to characterize the type of curve to be detected. Attention has to be given in selecting lower dimensional parameters spaces for their computational efficiency and accumulator array storage reduction.

What is more interesting for our application is generalizing the Hough transform to non-analytic curves. The key to generalizing the Hough algorithm to arbitrary shapes is the use of directional information. Ballard[2] shows how the boundary of an arbitrary non-analytic shape can be used to construct a mapping between image space and Hough transform space. Such a mapping can be exploited to detect instances of that particular shape in an image. Again, the application of this technique depends on the ability to parameterize the shapes of interest, and the derivation of the mapping from edge-element information to shape parameters. Sloan and Ballard[11] say that their experience on the generalized Hough transform indicates that the technique is robust, given that the edge-element operator used to generate local evidence for the shape can provide reliable information about edge-element direction. Furthermore, they show that in some cases is possible to detect the desired shape even if it is partially obscured by another.

The generalized Hough transform is used for template pattern recognition[1]. Consider an image containing a target pattern of some kind that needs to be detected. One way of finding it is to apply a template of the pattern to every position of the image and measure its degree of agreement at each location. But the major problem with using templates is that the target pattern is usually a considerably distorted version of the template, it could be rotated and/or scaled in size and/or translated in position and so on. The Hough transform presents a way of coping with this kind of distorsions effectively and economically in many circumstances.

For this purpose the first important step is the description of the pattern. It takes a variety of forms depending on the task in hand. Then, characteristics of the pattern are listed explicitly in the so-called "R-table"[2]. Features of the type that is listed in the R-table are considered in the image and compared with those ones described in the R-table. The results of these comparisons indicate some cells in a suitable accumulator array and those elements are incremented. When all the image features have been used to access the R-table, the accumulator is inspected for maxima. If the features combine to form an example of the template, they will all increment the same cell in the accumulator, leading to an easily identifiable maximum showing the parameters of the transformation that occurred in the template. In the next section we will describe in details the instance of the previous algorithm used in our procedure. This will make clear the algorithm itself.

The detection of corresponding segments of shape boundary lines belonging to successive frames of a sequence is a problem we examined in previous papers [3,4]. The primitive segments we considered for the correspondence process were the result of a segmentation of the boundary. Using the generalized Hough transform as we do in this paper we don't have to segment the boundaries. Primitive segments are the edges of the polygonal approximating the boundary. We examine pairs of successive frames and we consider the shape on frame i as our pattern and that on frame i+1 as our image.

In this work the experiments are made using artificial data. An example of shapes represented in two successive frames of a sequence is shown in Fig. 2. The parts of the boundaries marked by dotted lines indicate modified parts. Furthermore, in this example the shape shows a rotation of about 30 degrees clockwise passing from frame i to frame i+1. Frequently, there are also variations in scale between contiguous frames (the shape is dilated or contracted).

As we said in the previous section, the key to generalizing the Hough algorithm to arbitrary shapes is the use of directional information. Because we want to examine the rotation and scaling of our pattern we use as pattern primitives straight-line segments described by length L and orientation θ, namely the edges of the polygonal approximating the boundary. The accumulator array is a two-dimensional array with rotation degrees along the columns and size scaling along the rows (rotations are counterclockwise). The Hough algorithm is implemented by using the following steps:
1. Form the R-table of the pattern (shape on frame i), namely form a list of length and orientation of all primitives of the pattern (Fig. 3).
2. Consider a primitive in the image (shape on frame i+1) with length L' and orientation θ'.
3. Consider each entry in the R-table; let L and θ be length and orientation. Compute $s=L'/L$ and $r=\theta'-\theta$.
4. Increment the accumulator cell (s,r).
5. When all the image primitives have been considered, the accumulator is inspected for maxima.

The previous algorithm provides a scale factor and a rotation factor

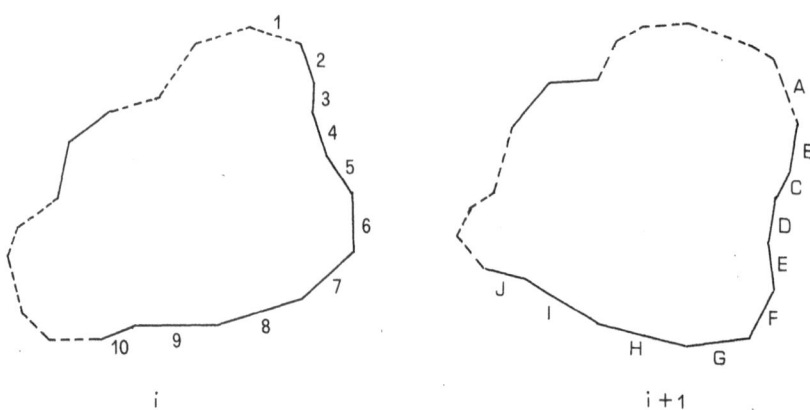

Fig. 2. Shapes on two successive frames of a sequence. Numbers and letters indicate some segments. Segments marked by dotted lines show modified parts.

Segment	Length	Orientation
1	4.12	345.97
2	3.16	288.43
3	2.0	270.0
⋮	⋮	⋮
⋮	⋮	⋮

Fig. 3. R-table for example in Fig. 2. It is
a list of length and orientation of
the primitive segments of frame i.

for a given shape located in two contiguous frames of a sequence. This means that the shape should be rotated and scaled of these values when passing from frame i to i+1. Frequently this is not true for every edge of the polygonal; in fact, portions of the polygonal in frame i couldn't have a correspondent in frame i+1 because modifications took place in that region. We call correspondence a pair formed by a segment of a frame and a segment of the successive frame so that the two segments indicate the same part of the shape. The previous algorithm is useful for establishing the correspondences between two contiguous frames; in order to do this we have to add something to the algorithm. In fact, when computing the Hough transform, we store the lists of the segment pairs incrementing the accumulator cells, grouping in the same list the pairs incrementing the same cell. Once we find the maximum of the accumulator, the list corresponding to the location of the maximum, i.e. the list of segment pairs which incremented that location, is already available; among these pairs we choose as correspondences those ones forming the longest sequence of correspondences which couple contiguous segments of the first frame with contiguous segments of the successive frame. Parts on the two shapes where

	20					
Rotation / Scaling	0°	18°	36°	...	...	342°
0.5						
⋮						
⋮						
⋮						
⋮						

Fig. 4. Accumulator array used in the experiments.

correspondences cannot be established identify modified parts and we will quantize these modifications by comparing their attributes. Examples are given in the next section.

EXPERIMENTS

The accumulator array we used in our experiments is a two-dimensional array with rotation factors along the columns and size scaling along the rows (see Fig. 4). Because it happens very often that, even the part of the curve without big modifications is not exactly the same on the two frames (see Fig. 5), we introduce a tolerance in the evaluation of rotation and scaling. More precisely, considering only the case of rotation, we say that there is no rotation if the difference of the segment orientations is less than the tolerance. In our experiments we used a tolerance T = 18 and an accumulator with 20 columns (see Fig. 4). Values in the first column are incremented when the comparisons of the orientation between two segments give a rotation less than T, namely between 0 and 17 degrees; the values in the second column are incremented if the rotation is between 18 and 35 degrees and so on. Then, if we locate a maximum in the second column, we can say that the pattern has been rotated from 18 to 35 degrees. Scaling values have also been quantized appropriately and the accumulator array contains 5 rows.

After we find the maximum of the accumulator in a location (i,j), we will look for the correspondences in the list corresponding to this location and in the two lists corresponding to the location (i,j-1) and (i,j+1) (if j=1, column j-1 will be the last column, if j indicates the last column, j+1 wil be equal to 1). This is a consequence of the rotation quantization. In fact, consider again T=18 and suppose that the accumulator maximum is in the first column and, actually, no rotation has occurred in the two frames. The list of segment pairs which incremented the accumulator cell where we found the maximum could include a pair with a rotation angle of 17 degrees, but will not include a pair with a rotation angle of -5 degrees, even if the last value is closer to the actual rotation angle. The segment pair with rotation angle of -5 degrees increments the accumulator cell on the same row but on column 20. Analogous situation happens if the actual rotation angle is 17 degrees and there is a segment pair with a rotation angle of 19 degrees; this pair will increment the cell in the same row but in the second column.

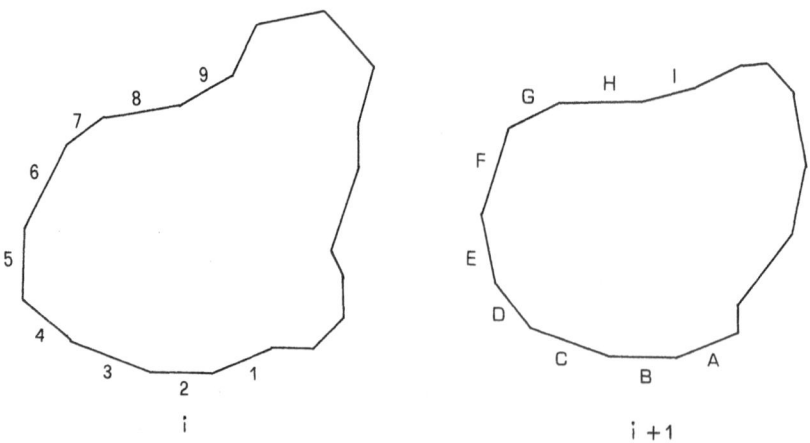

Fig. 5. Shapes on two successive frames of a different sequence.

This inconvenience of discarding useful segment pairs is overcome if we look for the correspondences in the three lists corresponding to the location of the maximum and to the locations preceding and following, on the same row, that one of the maximum. To better explain consider the frames in Fig. 2. There is only an absolute maximum in the accumulator array at cell (3,19) with value 21. This means that we detected a rotation of the pattern counterclockwise from 324 to 341 degrees and no variation in scale. The result is correct; in fact, the shape was rotated of about 30 degrees clockwise. The value of the accumulator cell (3,18) is 4 and that one on the cell (3,20) is 12. It follows that the three lists of segment pairs have a total of 37 elements. The longest sequence of correspondences of contiguous segments of the first frame with contiguous segments of the following frame will indicate the candidate correspondences; in this case we find (we indicate with numbers the segments on frame i and with letters those ones on frame i+1, see Fig. 2): 1 → A, 2 → B, 3 → C, 4 → D, 5 → E, 6 → F, 7 → G, 8 → H, 9 → I, 10 → J.

The correspondence 1 → A is discarded for the following reason. We compute the average of the rotation angle of the candidate correspondences and we choose as final correspondences those pairs whose rotation angle differs from the average less than T degrees. In our example the average rotation angle is 327 degrees and the correspondence 1 → A has rotation angle 307 degrees that differs from the average more than T, then it is discarded. The other candidate correspondences have a rotation angle that differs from the average less than T and they are the final correspondences for the frames in Fig. 2.

For the frames in Fig. 5 the absolute maximum is in cell (3,1) with value 12. This means neither rotation nor variation in scale of the pattern, that is the correct result. The candidate correspondences are: 1 → A, 2 → B, 3 → C, 4 → D, 5 → E, 6 → F, 7 → G, 8 → H, 9 → I. None of these is discarded because they have all rotation angle differing from the average less than T; consequently, they are the final correspondences for the frames in Fig. 5.

CONCLUSION

A technique has been presented for detecting corresponding segments of shape boundary lines belonging to successive frames of a sequence. This technique is based upon a generalization of the Hough transform, that was originally a method for detecting curves in digitized images, but it can be generalized for detecting instances of an arbitrary non-analytic shape in an image. The method is reliable even in case we have in the image a distorted version of the template; this suggested using it for analyzing sequences of frames describing the modifications that occurred on the boundary of a shape. Sequences of this kind are frequent in biomedical problems which deal with the analysis of the modifications of the boundary of a two-dimensional representation of an organ. The experiments described in the paper, even if they are made with artificial data, show the effectiveness of the method.

REFERENCES

1. T. O'Shea and M. Eisenstadt, "Artificial Intelligence: Tools, Techniques, Applications," Harper and Row, New York (1984).
2. D.H. Ballard, Generalizing the Hough transform to detect arbitrary shapes, Pattern Recognition 13, 111:122 (1981).

3. M.F. Costabile, C. Guerra, and G.G. Pieroni, Matching shapes: a case study in map sequence analysis, Computer Vision Graphics and Image Processing 29, 296:310 (1985).

4. G.G. Pieroni and M.F.Costabile, A method for detecting correspondences in a sequence of modifying shapes, Pattern Recognition Letters, to appear.

5. P.V.C. Hough, Method and means for recognizing complex patterns, U.S. Patent 3069654, (1962).

6. R.O. Duda and P.E. Hart, Use of the Hough transformation to detect lines and curves in pictures, Commun. ACM 15, 11:15 (1972).

7. C. Kimme, D.H. Ballard, and J. Sklansky, Finding circles by an array of accumulators, Commun. ACM 18, 120:122 (1975).

8. H. Wechsler and J. Sklansky, Automatic detection of ribs in chest radiographs, Pattern Recognition 9, 21:30 (1977).

9. S. Tsuji and F. Matsumoto, Detection of ellipses by a modified Hough transformation, IEEE Trans. Comput. C-27, 777:781 (1981).

10. G.G. Pieroni and O.G. Johnson, Methodology to simulate visual recognition of waves in a wave field, Proc. COMPINT 85, Montreal, September 8-12, 774:777 (1985).

11. K.R. Sloan, Jr. and D.H. Ballard, Experience with the generalized Hough transform, Proc. Fifth International Conference on Pattern Recognition, Miami Beach, Florida, December 1-4, 174:179 (1980).

A PROCEDURE FOR KNOWLEDGE ELICITATION

IN IMAGE INTERPRETATION EXPERIMENTS

U. Cugini (1), P. Mauri (2), P. Mussio(3), and M. Protti(3)

(1) Politecnico di Milano, P.zza L. da Vinci 32, Milano, Italy
(2) S.G.S. Laboratorio di Affidabilita'
(3) Universita' degli Studi di Milano
     Dipartimento di Fisica via Viotti 5, Milano, Italy

1. Introduction

ISIID (Interactive System for Image Interpretation Design [1] is a software environment designed to help an expert-in-some-field-not-aware-in-computer-science toghether with an information analyst to create a procedure for the interpretation of images from a given class. The use of ISIID in the design of different image interpretation experiments [2] [3] [4] [5] was performed following an empirical methodology outlined in [1].

These experiences have suggest an unified, structured procedure for the definition, design and implementation of interactive tools. The developed tools are designed to help the user in his activity of interpretation of digital images. They are therefore called Automatic Assistant (AA). This procedure is here described following the SADT techniques [6].

Two aspects seem to be peculiar to our methodology.

The first is that a representative of the users is always a member of the interdisciplinary team which designs the required tool. He owns the knowledge to be translated into the AA, it is therefore called the 'expert'. The expert has to guaranty the quality of this AA by:

1) partecipating at its design by specifying his requirements, testing the proposed tools and certifying their meaning to his discipline.

2) validating AA by confirmating its results.

The second peculiar aspect of our experience seems to be the study of user and AA discrepancies in classification of the same set of data.

The study of this discrepancies allows the refinement of the AA and/or the rationalization of the user's non-automatic procedure of data interpretation.

Partially supported by Consiglio Nazionale delle Ricerche
grant nr. 84.02610.58

That is, we admit that on a set of data never examined before, both AA and user may make a mistake. The AA because the elicited knowledge in not sufficient for new cases or because it was improperly elicited or it was improperly coded into rules.

The user because he sometimes contractdicts himself by not following the rules he stated in previous cases. Moreover the expert is often used to work with analog and not digital images and data are often gathered from unusual platforms [3] [4]. That is, beeing expert in the discipline, he is not expert on this particular data analysis. Therefore the word 'expert' denotes here a role in the design of AA, which seems not present in other current expert system design experiences [7] [8].

By this activity the expert rationalize his own description of the interpretation activity. For this reason, the result of the interdisciplinary work for the definition of an AA and for image interpretation gives as a result the explicit elicited knowledge. In other words, at the beginning of the design of an AA not only the algorithms related to the procedure which can be informally described by the expert are often opaque [9], but even features and structures to be identified are not clearly defined. In this case, knowledge elicitation requires an extensive data exploration [10]. The algorithmic aspects of this elicited knowledge result translated into rules of AA [11] [12] (fig.1).

2. Digital image interpretation

Image interpretation is the activity by which an expert associates structures present in an image with objects present in a scene, from which the image was drawn [13].

The main idea underlying the approach adopted in our experiments is that the interpretation of a digital image may be performed by the total or partial recognition of set of relevant properties of its structures.

Digital pictures or images are two dimensional arrays, whose elements (pixels) are integer numbers in a finite range.

A structure in a digital image is a set of pixels, which satisfies some relations, [13]. A named structure or named part of a structure is called feature. Description of a structure is a set of values (properties) assumed by a set of variables (attributes) associated to some features of the structure.

Properties are not only numerical, their values may also be logical, each value being associated to a different degree of plausibility of the examined feature.

The properties computed for a given structure are hints for its classification. These hints, combined together, allow a candidate interpretation of the structure itself.

Due to the different scales, used in the evaluation of the properties, only equivalence and order relations are always valid for the measures define below.

Therefore mutivalued logical trees (MVLT) [14] are used to combine the hints derived by each feature into the evaluation score of the whole structure, in that way interpreting the digital image.

3. System definition, knowledge elicitation, confirmation

3.1 Digital images interpretation context A-0 (fig 1)

In the following three levels of expression regarding the system definition are presented. SADT conventions are outlined in the caption of fig. 1. The three levels are described in the following paragraphs, by the description of input, output mechanism, control and activity. Each one of those is defined only the first time it is referred.

The first SADT diagram "Digital image interpretation context" (Fig.1) shows the digital image interpretation activity as a whole.

3.1.1 Digital image interpretation A0

This node describes the interactions and constraints from the environment to the bounded context which represents the whole activity of digital images interpretation.

INPUT <u>Images:</u> Images to be interpreted must belong to the same class; that is they must be sensed and digitized with the same techniques, must be interpreted for the same purpose within the same experiment.

CONTROL <u>A priori criteria:</u> used by the expert community when the images are interpreted before the starting of this whole activity. These criteria are generally not formally defined in the sense of computer science.

MECHANISM <u>Human interaction:</u> In the different phases of activity different kinds of people are involved: the expert, the information analyst and the user.

<u>Tools:</u> Interactive tools provided by the information analyst and traditional tools provided by the expert.

OUTPUT <u>Interpreted images:</u> the automatically interpreted images following the new criteria (part of elicited knowledge).

<u>Elicited knowledge:</u> It is expressed by a set of rules driving the decision about the strategy to be followed in the automatic interpretation. Most of them are codified both for the computer execution as programs and for person to person communications following suitable notations (e.g.α-ω form of APL notation) [15].

<u>Automatic assistant:</u> A software system which helps the user in interpreting his images. It is driven by the formalized part of the elicited knowledge.

3.2 Digital image interpretation (fig 2)

At present, to 'use' an AA the experimenter has before to define its 'system'.

3.2.1 System definition A1

Problem analisys is performed and (whenever it is possible) a formalized solution, tuned on a suitable sample of images, is proposed.

INPUT <u>Sample of images:</u> It is selected from the class to be studied and is used for the definition of the first tentative release of the AA.

MECHANISM <u>Exploration tools:</u> Allow the expert to find hints and clues about meaningful structures in the data [1].

<u>Confirmation tools:</u> Allow the expert to confirm that his interpretation matches with the one of the proposed AA.

<u>Expert:</u> He is the disciplinary expert who must act as a designer even if he does not necessarily know computer science.

<u>Information Analyst</u>: he is a data analyst aware of system analysis, who knows information structured methodologies (e.g. SADT), and must be able to sensibly try to apply them to the description of unformalized situations.

3.2.2 Use A2

In this phase users exploit the confirmed AA and elicited knowledge produced in the system definition phase (A1 node) to interprete new sample of images. Use of the system will be not more investigate in this paper because it is out of our present aims.

3.3 System definition (fig 3)

It is decomposed into two activities: "Knowledge Elicitation" and "Confirmation".

3.3.1 Knowledge elicitation A11

Expert's knowledge is elicited by observing his interpretation activity on analog and digitized images and thereafter formalized into rules. The characteristics of the exploration tools used in our approach allow the implementation of a first tentative AA. If the proposed AA is reiected in the confirmation phase, the knowledge elicitation activity will be repeated taking into account warnings and discrepancies focused by the confirmation activity.

INPUT First sample of images: Set of digitized images (of objects belonging to known types) from the same class.

Images from the last sample examined: Digital images used in a failed confirmation are added to the first sample of images because their interpretation is known while discrepances between AA and expert interpretations of this sample are estabilished and warnings derived. See node A12 (confirmation output).

CONTROL A priori interpretation & acceptance criteria: Unformalized knowledge about the interpretation description and decision used by the expert on interpreting (analog) images. They are used before and indipendently of automatic tools application. These criteria are the same in the Knowledge elicitation and confirmation activities because in this phase they are intended as those informally expressed by a whole scientific community.

Warnings & discrepancies: Generated by a failed confirmation activity, they are used as a control in the redefinition and/or refinement of the system.

MECHANISM Exploration tools: Analog and digital devices used by experimenters in both traditional images interpretation and in definition of new procedures for digital image interpretation.

OUTPUT Proposed elicited knowledge (P.E.K.): Rules and procedures elicited by the analysis of the expert interpretation.

Proposed AA: It is tested as to programming correctness and coherence on the interpretation of the first sample of images.

3.3.2 Confirmation A12

The proposed AA is applied to a new sample of images never examined before by the expert or the AA. Its efficacy is evaluated comparing AA results with the results from human analysis. If the comparison is acceptable, both P.E.K. and AA are confirmed. If the comparison fails, warning and discrepancies between AA and expert interpretation are generated in order to be used in a system redefinition phase (see A11).

INPUT New sample of images This images belong to the same class of that used in the knowledge elicitaion phase, nevertheless they must have never been examined before, either by the expert, or by the AA.

CONTROL A priori confirmation criteria: These criteria are the same of knowledge elicitation activity while the experts should be different in the two steps.

MECHANISM Confirmation tools: Programs to manage and compare the results of the activity of proposed AA and expert on the same data.

OUTPUT Confirmed elicited knowledge and AA: If the confirmation is succesful, the proposed P.E.K. and AA are accepted and outputted to use.

Warning & discrepancies: If the confirmation fails, mismatchings are signed out and are used going through a redefinition or refinement of the system. Discrepancies between expert and AA interpretation of the same sample of images are pointed out and warnings derived (see A1 node).

Images from the last examined sample: Images used for confirmation phase are now interpreted and known by the expert and by the AA. Therefore they may only be used for the new exploration and not for a new confirmation.

3.4 - Knowledge elicitation (fig. 4)

It is decomposed into four activities: "Analysis of expert interpretation", "Translation into rules", "Test of AA" and "Acceptance".

3.4.1 - Analysis of expert interpretation A111

The expert interpretes a set of traditional images and with the information analyst collaboration defines explicitly the structures of interest and their features, attributes and properties in the corresponding digitized images.

CONTROL Warnings & discrepancies: A first kind of warnings and discrepancies may be generated by the last step of the knowledge elicitation activity itself. This happen when AA and P.E.K. have to be revised before any confirmation control. Similarly a second kind of warnings and discrepancies may be generated by a failed confirmatuion activity (see output of A12 node).

MECHANISM Traditional devices: Traditional tools provided by the expert.

OUTPUT Expert interpreted images: The first sample of images is interpreted by the expert and commented both by him and and by the information analyst. This comments and interpretation are used by them to define the AA and then to test and accept (or reject) it.

Explicit definition of structures, features, properties, attributes: The expert and the information analyst together characterize the subset of objects of interest in the experiment by finding out their descriptions (i.e. features, properties and attributes of the structures in the digital images).

3.4.2 - Translation into rules A112

Tentative explicit definitions of the descriptions are translated into rules which allow an automatic interpretation of the images by the information analyst, while the expert checks the proposed tools against the data at disposal.

CONTROL A priori interpretation criteria of the information analyst: In this phase information analyst knowledge about structured methodologies and computer science are required for the definition of rules and the design the AA which allows to manage them.

MECHANISM "ISIID and expert analyst interaction"
OUTPUT <u>Tentative elicited knowledge:</u> A tentative set of rules is defined.
It must be tested on the images already analyzed by the expert to get a
first validation. Information analyst and expert must be aware that this
set of rules is generally not complete nor congruent in the first
definition step.
   <u>Tentative AA:</u> It is validated only from the programming point of view.

3.4.3 - Test of AA A113

   The tentative tools are used to interprete the same sample of images
examined by the expert, to check the comprehension between the expert and
the information analyst.
CONTROL <u>Tentative elicited knowledge:</u> see output of A112 (translation into
rules). It is required because AA is an interactive tool.
MECHANISM <u>Tentative AA:</u> Output of A112 node (translation into rules).
Tools under development are tested against the same data used for their
definition, to check the correspondence of their interpretation with that
of the expert.
OUTPUT <u>Classified images:</u> Images classified by the AA.

3.4.4 - Acceptance A1114

   AA and expert interpretation of the same sample of images are
compared. If the comparison is negative, agreements and discrepancies
between the two interpretations are signaled and warnings derived, to drive
a revision of the expert analysis.
CONTROL <u>A priori acceptance criteria:</u> They are predefined specification of
the levels of concordance between expert and AA.
MECHANISM <u>Evaluation tools:</u> Defined to verify the a priori acceptance
criteria.
OUTPUT <u>Warning & discrepancies:</u> Discrepancies are the differences between
the interpretations of the AA and expert. They must be examined case by
case, and the reasons of different classification or strategy of
interpretation pointed out. Warnings are indications of malfunctions or
incoherences in the behaviour of the tentative tools.
   <u>Proposed elicited knowledge:</u> PEK is coherent with the expert. It is
proposed for the confirmation step.

4. Conclusions

   We have examined the problem of knowledge elicitation from the point
of view of the experimenters. We proposed that some refinements or
revisions of the tentative P.E.K. and AA occurs whenever some notable
discrepancies are observed between AA and expert behaviour. Similar
criteria are used to evaluate if a new knowledge elicitation is required
after a confirmation step.
   This methodology has been used in the implementation of different
experimental systems which are now under test of a more extensive use in
different fields of applications.
   A comparison analysis should be done from different points of view.
In any case the result of this work of generalization of our experience is
a protocol for the interdisciplinary design of an AA for image
interpretation. At the same time this description can be seen as a unique
framework to connect the different criteria to be used in the design of an
A.A. proposed for a discussion at last.

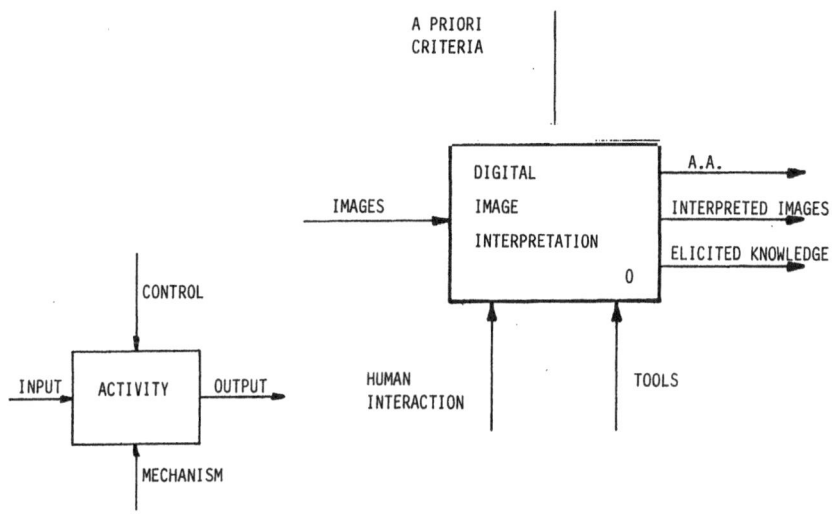

Fig. 1. Digital Image Interpretation Context

Digital image interpretation context: described by the SADT graphic technique [6] for purposeful description of activities.

In a SADT model a graphic representation of the hierarchical structure of an activity is presented, decomposed with a firm purpose in mind: the point of view of the analysis. In our case the analysis is done from the expert's point of view.

SADT is based on a graphic representation of activities and of their relations derived by a limited set of graphic primitives, just arrows and boxes.

BOXES represent parts of a whole in precise manner. ARROWS represent interfaces between parts. DIAGRAMS represent wholes and are composed of boxes, arrows, natural language names and certain other notations. Each diagram is identified by a node code which indicates the position in the overall tree.

The box is the functional building block of SADT notation which can be interfaced to other boxes by four modalities used to classify with respect to the activities data involved. These data can be related to the activity as: INPUT, CONTROL, OUTPUT and MECHANISM.

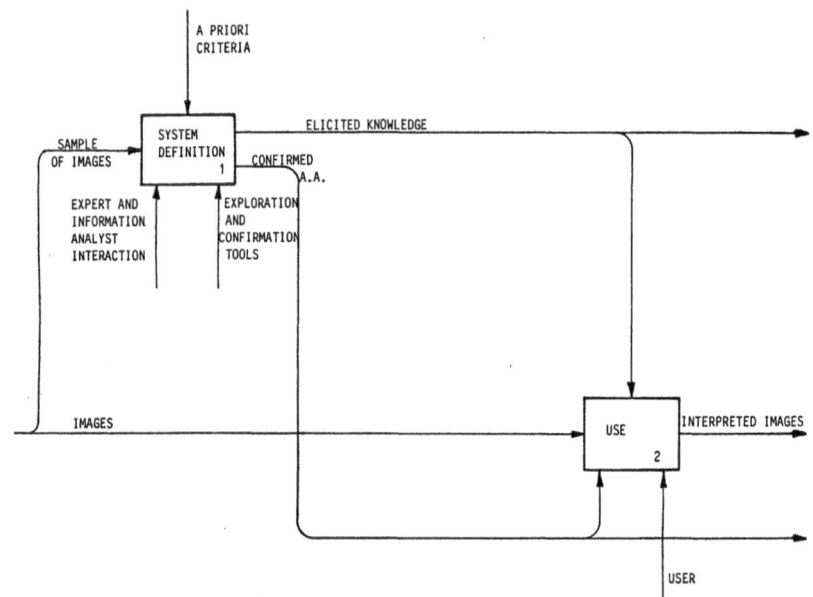

Fig. 2. Digital Image Interpretation

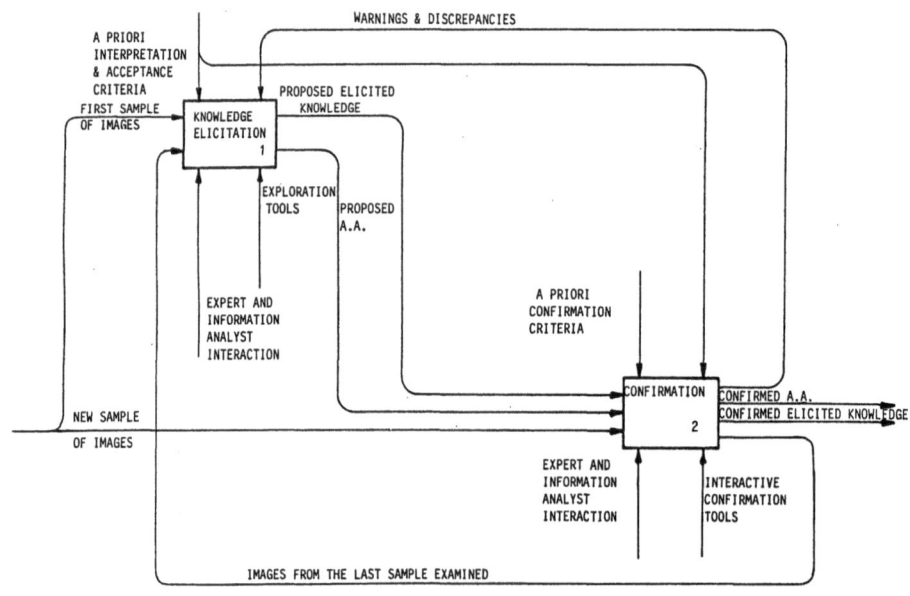

Fig. 3. System Definition

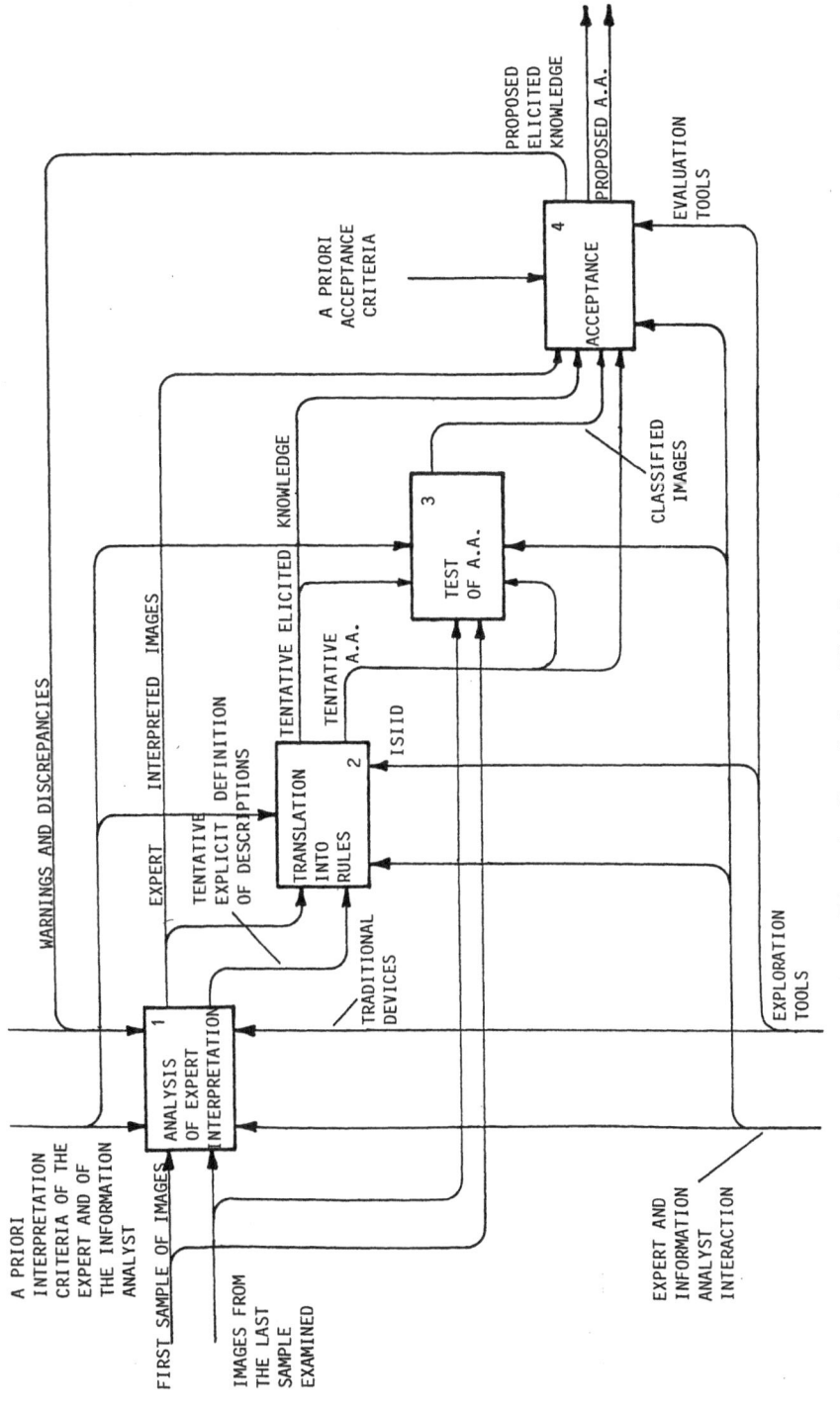

Fig. 4. Knowledge Elicitation

185

5. References

1. U.Cugini, M.Dell'Oca, D.Merelli, P.Mussio, A computer aided system for interactive definition of digital image interpretation, in DIGITAL IMAGE ANALYSIS,S. Levialdi ed., Pitman, London 1983.
2. U. Cugini, G. Ferri, P. Mussio and M. Protti Pattern directed restoration and vectorization of digitized engeneering drawings, COMPUTER & GRAPHICS, vol 8,nr 4, pg. 337-350, 1984.
3. A. Della Ventura, A. Maggioni, P. Mussio, A. Pawlina, Features detection and classification of rain patterns: knowledge acquisition for automatic interpretation of radar images, presented at 3rd ICIAP, Rapallo,1985.
4. A. Della Ventura, A. Rampini, R. Rabagliati and R. Serandrei Barbero. Glacier Monitoring by satellite, IL NUOVO CIMENTO, marzo-aprile 1983. Compositori ed.
5. P. Mussio, Design of A Pattern-Directed system for the interpretation of digitized astronomical images, in DATA ANALYSIS IN ASTRONOMY, V. di Gesu' ed., Plenum Press, 85.
6. D.T.Ross "Structured Analysis (SA): a language for communicating ideas", IEEE Transactions on software engineering vol. SE-3,N.1 Jan. 1977, pp. 16-34
7. L.Johson,E.T.Kerarnou, Expert System Technology:A Guide, Abacus Press, London, 1985.
8. B.G.Buchanan, D.Barstow, R.Bechtal, J.Bennet, W. Clancey, C. Kulikowschy, T.Mitchell, D.A. Waterman. Constructing an expert system,BUILDING EXPERT SYSTEMS, Hayes-Roth, Waterman, Lenat eds.
9. L.A.Zadeh, Fuzzy sets and their application to pattern classification and clustering analisys, CLASSIFICATION AND CLUSTERING, S. Van Rizing ed., Accademic Press, London 1976.
10. J. W. Tukey, Exploratory data analysis, Addison Wesley, 1977.
11. F. Haies-Roth, D.A. Waterman, Principles of pattern directed inference systems, PATTERN-DIRECTED INFERENCE SYSTEMS, Waterman and Haies-Roth eds., 1978.
12. R.S. Michalsky and R.L. Chilausky, Knowledge acquisition by encoding expert rules versus computer induction from examples: A case study involving soybean pathology. FUZZY REASONING AND ITS APPLICATIONS, Mamdani & Gaines eds., Academic Press, 1981.
13. D. Merelli, P. Mussio and M. Padula. An approach to the definition, description and extraction of structures in binary digital images. CVGIP. 31,19-41 (1985).
14. R.S.Michalsky, Variable-valued Logic and its applications to pattern recognition and Machine Learning, North Holland, 1976
15. K.E. Iverson, Elementary Analysis, APL press, Swartmore.

IMAGE PROCESSING
APPLICATIONS

KNOWLEDGE ACQUISITION FOR AUTOMATIC

INTERPRETATION OF RADAR IMAGES

Anna Della Ventura,[1] Alessandra Maggioni,[1] Piero Mussio[2] and
Alona Pawlina[3]

1 I.F.C.T.R. - C.N.R.
  via Bassini 15, Milano
2 Dipartimento di Fisica
  via Viotti 5, Milano
3 C.S.T.S. - C.N.R.
  Dipartimento di Elettronica
  piazza Leonardo da Vinci 32, Milano

ABSTRACT

The present study concerns the automatic interpretation of horizontal
digitized rain maps compiled from radar registrations.

The description and classification of rain patterns is pursued
following a more general approach to the DI interpretation based on the
definition of relevant image structures and their attributes meaningful
for the experiment.

The development of the specific tool, starting with the initial
knowledge base through several exploration-confirmation cycles and aiming
to the knowledge assessment, is described.

The performance of the prototype tool is then discussed.

INTRODUCTION

The main reasons of the growth in the field of automatic or computer
assisted interpretation of digital images are:
a-the continuous increase of imagery data from a multitude of environments
and sensors and
b-the necessity to develop unambiguous criteria for the segmentation, classification and, generally, image interpretation process.

Efficient interpretation methods can be however assessed only in the
context of real experiments.

The present study applies some techniques of what is now called
"knowledge based" image analysis to the identification and classification
of rain patterns observed on radar derived images.

The experience in processing of radar data achieved by the Propagation
Group of C.S.T.S. and the experience in image interpretation collected by
the Image Group (I.F.C.T.R. and Physics Department) met in developing (and
building the prototype of) a specific tool for the study of spatial structure of rain.

Original Data Set

Meteorological radars can supply the estimation of rainfall intensity for wide geographic regions allowing the studies of spatial structure of rain whose knowledge is required by a number of applications, such as the design of microwave communication systems (see International Radio Consultative Committee, 1981) or short term weather forecasting (Joss,1981).

The present study concerns the horizontal structure of rainfall based upon bidimensional Ground Rain Maps (GRMs) compiled from radar observations (see Pawlina,1981). A large collection of such maps was generated from the observations at the Spino d'Adda radar station in north Italy carried out in 1980 within the framework of the SIRIO Propagation Experiment (Centro Studi Telecomunicazioni Spaziali,1983).

Each rain map, already in digitized and thresholded form, refers to a short time interval in the region surrounding Milan, of almost 8000 Km^2, at the at the average height of 1.5 Km from the ground.

The complexity and variety of atmospheric precipitation systems (see for instance Houze,1981) makes not easy the task of (manual or automatic description and classification of rain patterns. Such classification, based only on the pictorial information contained in GRMs was approached in this study and involved two types of criteria: the morphological ones, relating to the pattern shape and the intrinsic ones relating to the variability of rain intensity (grey level) within the pattern.

The classification is oriented towards radio communication problems as it stresses the detection of "dangerous" rain formations, i.e. the ones which cause serious failures in the operation of microwave radio links. The rain patterns in this context are very extended rain patches with or without embedded regions of higher intensity as well as (usually smaller) nuclei of very intense rain and their organizations into larger structures.

An approach to DI interpretation

As regards the technique of interpretation of digital images, a quite general one, described in Cugini et al.,1983 and implemented as a series of facilities referred to as ISIID (Interactive System for Image Interpretation Definition) represented a solid basis for developing a specialized tool for radar imagery analysis here presented.

The main idea underlying this approach is that the interpretation of an image may be performed by the total, or partial, recognition of a set of relevant features of its structures.

The weighted combination of these features allows the decision about the nature of the real objects which originate the patterns in the image. In other words the image interpretation consists of:
a- identification of a set of features relevant to the classification.
b- assignment of a set of scores to each feature.
c- definition of a tool, which combines contextually the scores, gained by the recognized features, into the score of the whole pattern.

So, in our view, the DI interpretation is a two stage process, composed of:
1- collection of hints for total or partial DI description and
2- classification of DI by means of a proper decision process which evaluates and interprets the description.

The problem is that often the decision process itself is only partially defined by the human interpreters, thus making the interpretation process not transparent (in terms of Zadeh,1977). The two stage procedure (Cugini et al.,1983) takes into account this important reality. The procedure itself starts with the exploration stage where a set of DIs is examined by a human interpreter who:
1- describes and classifies the set by means of classes, features and attributes usually adopted by him in a non-automatic process ("a priori"interpretation)

2- performs preliminary analysis of the set by means of the ISIID tools
in order to define procedures for the interpretation
3- produces a set of descriptions and related interpretations which result
in package of programs (APL functions in ISIID environment)
4- tests the programs against the same data set used in the step 1 and
checks the correspondence between the computed results and those from the
"a priori" interpretation. If the comparison is unsatisfactory the whole
exploration process is repeated after necessary modifications until acceptable results are obtained.

The second stage - the confirmation process - involves a new set of
DIs not analyzed before (but from the same image collection) which is separately interpreted by both the automatic tool and the human interpreter
(who should ignore the specific strategy of the automatic one).

If the comparison between the results of the two interpretations is
satisfactory the tools which have been developed are accepted, otherwise
they are rejected and the experimenters try to refine or, if necessary,
redefine descriptions and decision criteria. By doing so a new exploration
cycle, involving the whole "known" set of images, with a deeper a priori
knowledge of the data, begins.

The basic concepts underlying the above "tool generation" process are
presented in the next section (and in more detail in Della Ventura et al.,
1985), while the following sections concern the development of the actual
tool for radar images and the discussion of the final (but still pioneer-
istic) results.

IMAGE DESCRIPTORS: CONCEPTS AND EVALUATION

Ground Rain Maps are digitized images (DI), that is two dimensional
arrays whose elements are integer numbers in a finite range. DIs are referred
to as "binary" (BDI) when their elements assume values in the range $\{0,1\}$
only, or "coloured" (CDI) otherwise.

A pixel (picture element) is described by a triple P: X, Y, C where
X and Y identify the position of the pixel in the array (DI) and C is the
associate integer number.

A "structure" is a set of pixels which satisfy some relations (Merelli
et al.,1985). So, for instance, a "blob" is a set of pixels connected to a
given one. Then an "object" is a structure composed of blobs, which satisfy
some relations.

A named structure or a named part of it is called a feature. "Description" of a structure is a set of values associated to some features of the
structure or to the structure itself.

Properties may be numerical or logical, their values spanning a set,
each value being associated to a different degree of plausibility of the
examined feature and denoted by a different symbol.

Properties of a given structure are hints for its classification.
These hints, combined together, allow the interpretation of the structure
itself, i.e. the identification of the class and type of real object present
in the digitized scene from which the structure in the DI was generated by
the observation process.

Due to different scales, used in the evaluation of the properties,
only equivalence and order relations are present in the measures defined
below. Therefore a multivalued logic is used to combine the observed properties. Let P be the partition induced by the relational operators on the
range of an attribute. We map each element of P into a score. In the interpretation procedure, each score denotes the weight that the expert assignes
to the presence (absence) of the observed property in the recognition process.

Scores are combined by multivalued operators, that is combinatorial
functions which map the input values (scores gained in the observation process by features) into an output value, the score gained by the combined
set of observed properties.

The first step was the observation, carried out together with the specialist, of a representative sample of images (32 GRM with 178 objects) for the definition of classes of rain patterns and the determination of their characteristic features.

GRMs, thresholded at the visibility value corresponding to the rain intensity of 5mm/hr, are composed of objects which don't show any directly perceptible regularity, their number varying from one to several tens per map, the area ranging from one pixel to about 30% of the whole image, the shape being extremely variable.

As regards the grey level distribution, i.e. the object shape in the tridimensional space, flat objects with all values close to the visibility threshold can be observed, as well as objects showing one or more nuclei, embedded in lower intensity regions.

These observations represented an initial knowledge base which was followed by the knowledge assessment resulting from the exploration-confirmation cycles described below.

The prototype system was built on the basis of the following assumptions:

1- three classes of objects related to typical rain formations were defined as:

    a-widespread structures of low intensity (Basic Rain(B))

    b-isolated intense structures generally not extended (Supercell(S))

    c-large structures constituted by an area of basic rain with several nuclei (Multicell(M))

2- the morphological object attribute "indentness", and the intrinsic one "presence of nuclei", chosen as discriminating characteristics.

The application of the tool to the analysis of a new data sample (13 images with 102 objects) and the comparison between the automatic and human interpretation showed 83 objects in agreement, 4 failures and 15 objects having characteristics which didn't match any defined class. These results showed first the major discriminant power of the grey level distribution compared to the indentness degree, and secondly the still insufficient (i.e. not diversified enough) nuclei description and class stratification.

According to these indications, the priority of the selected attributes was modified. The nuclei definition was corrected by introducing their extension attribute; the distinction was introduced between Residual Nuclei(R) and Nuclei(N), the former ones characterized by smaller area and corresponding to developing or dissolving intense rain regions.

As a result three new classes of objects were introduced:

    - Cell(C)

    - Supercell with Residual Nuclei(SR)

    - Multicell with Residual Nuclei(MR)

These classes, similar respectively to (B),(S),(M), are characterized by the presence of one or more residual nuclei at different intensity levels The formal definition of six classes is given in Fig.3.

New confirmation tests were thereafter carried out.
The results, shown and discussed in the next section, matched the previously defined acceptance criteria thus terminating the exploration-confirmation cycle.

Feature computing procedures and the decision-process

The evaluation of the object indentness gives a score to this attribute from Very Indented (VI) to Very Compact (VC) through the intermediate Indented (I) and Compact (C) ones. Objects of uncertain classification are also accounted for:to such objects the score Doubt (D) is given.

The indentness score is assigned to the object by computing a set of morphometric or morphological attributes which are indentness indicators.

```
                           PERIMETER
         -------- ---- ---- ---- ----
        | AP OP.1   25   60   80   |
        |------1|----|----|----|----|
        |       | D  | VI | /  | /  |
        |-----30|----|----|----|----|
        |       | C  | D  | /  | /  |
 AREA   |-----60|----|----|----|----|
        |       | VC | C  | D  | VI |
        |----100|----|----|----|----|
        |       | /  | D  | I  | I  |
        |----200|----|----|----|----|
        |       | /  | VC | D  | D  |
         -------- ---- ---- ---- ----
```

Fig. 1. The AP operator maps the area
and perimeter values into an
indentness score: Very Indented
(VI),Indented (I),Compact (C),
Very Compact (VC),Doubt (D).

The combined values (subdivided into ranges) of the perimeter (P) and area
(A) give the object the first temporary indentness score.
This is the task of the operator AP shown in Fig. 1.

Other operators similar to this one are the nodes of a logical decision
tree shown in Fig. 2. Each operator accepts two inputs:
1- the temporary indentness evaluation from the preceding stage
2- one of the following:
   -n. of internal holes
   -n. of adjacent connected objects
   -n. of bridge or triangle pixels (subsets of branch points)
   -n. of filaments
An example of the procedure operation is given in Fig. 2.

Information on the presence of nuclei and on their intensity is obtained by slicing the object at two rain intensity values (20 mm/hr and
40 mm/hr). At each level the number of the nuclei and their area are evaluated. Each nucleus is then classified as Residual Nucleus (R) or Nucleus
(N) according to its area (A) attribute ($2 \le A \le 4$ for (R) and $5 \le A$ for (N)).

The procedure labels each object with its "nuclei" feature description,
which summarizes, by means of a suitable string of characters, the number
and type of the nuclei at the two intensity levels. In the string:
   -the number of nuclei is represented by: 1(one), n(one or more),
   m(at least two)
   -the type of nuclei by: N(Nucleus), R(Residual Nucleus)
   -the intensity level by: F(First), S(Second).
Different sets of nuclei are separated by the character: + .
For example: 1NF+nNS+mR   means:
one nucleus at first level, one or more nucleus at the second level, at
least two residual nucleus at either level.

Fig. 2 shows an example of nuclei evaluation.

The results of the attributes evaluation procedures are the inputs
for the operator NI shown in Fig. 3 which provides the final object classification while Fig. 4 examplifies its operation.

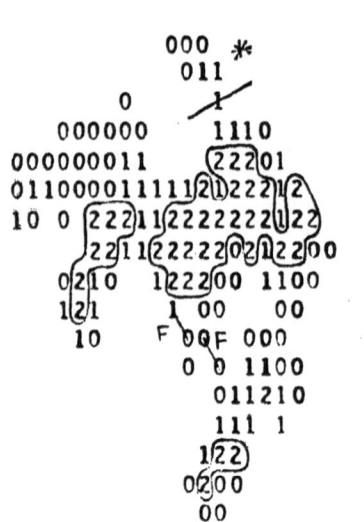
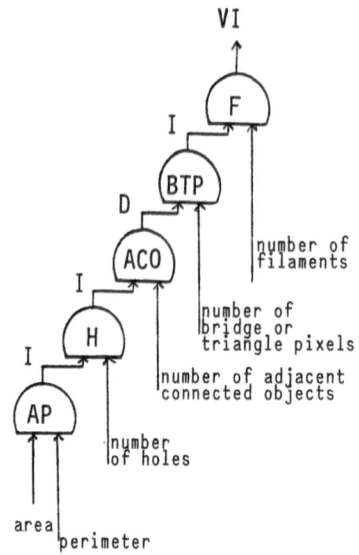

NUCLEI EVALUATION

	NUCLEI	RES.NUCLEI
FIRST LEVEL	2	1
SECOND LEVEL	0	0

THE OBJECT IS CLASSIFIED AS mNF

INDENTNESS EVALUATION

AREA=135   AND   PERIMETER=75
NUMBER OF HOLES=0
N. OF ADJACENT CONNECTED OBJECTS=1(*)
N. OF BRIDGE AND TRIANGLE POINTS=6
N. OF FILAMENTS=2 (F)
THE OBJECT IS CLASSIFIED AS VI

Fig. 2. Example of nuclei and indentness evaluation

NI OPERATOR	VC	C	I	VI
	B	B	B	B
1RF	C	B	B	B
mRF	C	C	C	B
1NF	SR	C	C	C
1NF + nR	SR	SR	C	C
1NF + nNS	S	S	S	S
1NF+nNS+nR	S	S	MR	MR
mNF	MR	MR	MR	MR
mNF + nNS	M	M	M	M

Fig. 3. Object classifier (NI operator): the "Nuclei" scores combine
with "Indentness" scores into the final object classification:
Basic rain (B), Multicell (M), Supercell (S), Cell (C),
Residual Multicell (MR), Residual Supercell (SR).

In the confirmation process 25 images (118 objects) were examined; the results of the automatic interpretation were then compared with those of the human interpreter.

This comparison is shown in the confusion matrix of Fig. 5. Rows represent the result of the automatic procedure, while columns contains the result obtained by the human interpreter.

The number of objects in agreement, (110), is on the diagonal of the matrix, whereas the numbers which are elsewhere in the matrix, (8), stand for objects whose interpretation was different in the two processes.

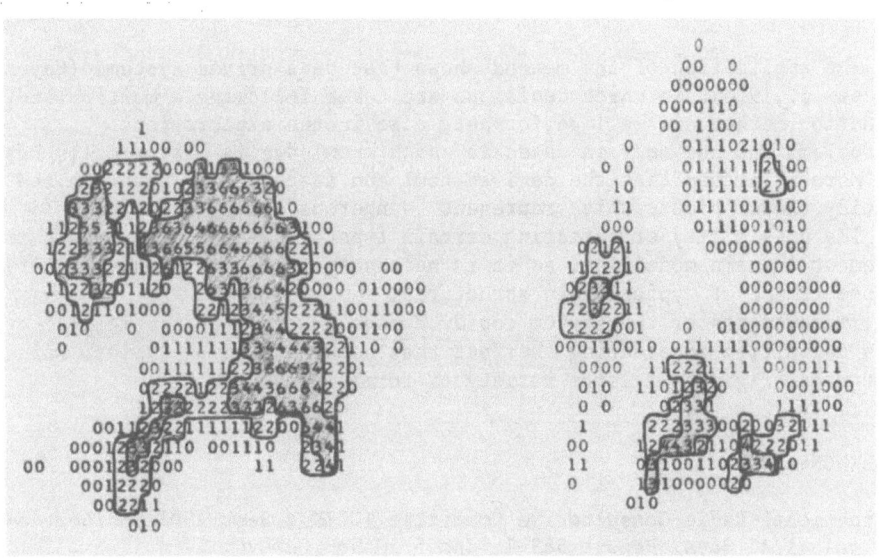

Fig. 4. Example of classification of objects contained in a portion of GRM. The indentness evaluation classifies as I (Indented) the object on the left and VI (Very Indented) the object on the right. The nuclei description shows 1 nucleus at the first level and 3 at the second one (1NF+nNS), for the first object, and 3 nuclei and 1 residual nucleus at the first level plus 1 nucleus and 2 residual nuclei at the second level (mNF+nNS) for the second object. Combining the indentness and nuclei evaluation the objects are classified respectively as Supercell (S) and Multicell (M).

Bottom row and far right column show the total number of objects in each class for both interpretations.

The figure of 92% of objects in agreement, was considered satisfactory. In particular the results showed that no other changes in the class definition were necessary, as every object has been classified, by the human interpreter too, as member of one of the 6 classes of rain formations, defined in the exploratory process.

Moreover it was confirmed that the contour indentness is in relation to the evolution of rain formation, as growing or estinguishing formations were found more indented than those in their mature stage of activity.

	B	C	SR	S	MR	M	TOT
B	65	2					67
C		13			1		14
SR		3	10				13
S				10			10
MR				1	6		7
M					1	6	7
TOT	65	18	10	11	8	6	118

AUTOMATIC INTERPRETATION

Fig. 5. Confusion matrix showing the results of the interpretation performed by the human interpreter and the automatic one.

The application of the method shows that data driven systems (Hayes Roth et al.,1978), in which decisions are taken following a multivalued evaluation method are well performant also in the exploration of problems and not only in cases in which knowledge is historically based.

More it proved that the derived tool can successfully describe and identify those objects which represent "dangerous" rain formations.

The possibility of detecting certain type of patterns is a basic requirement in rain modelling, as it is necessary to identify and quantify the occurrence of typical rain structures.

Improvements of the system could be made towards still more realistic class definition considering the fact that combinations of typical rain structures originate a large variety of formations.

REFERENCES

International Radio Consultative Committee (CCIR), Sept.1981,Radiometeorological data, Report 563-1, doc.5/5049-E,Geneve.

Joss,J.,Nov.1981,Digital radar information in the Swiss Meteorological Institute, 20-th Conf. on Radar Meteorology, Boston, Preprints AMS.

Houze,R. A., 1981, Structures of atmospheric precipitation systems: a global survey, Radio Science, vol.16, n.5, pp. 671-589.

Pawlina,A., May 1984, Some features of ground rain patterns measured by radar in north Italy, Radio Science, vol.19, n.3, pp. 855-861.

Centro di Studi per le Telecomunicazioni Spaziali, 1983, Programma Sirio, vol. 1-3, Consiglio Nazionale delle Ricerche, Rome.

Cugini,U., Dell'Oca, M., Merelli, D., Mussio, P., 1983, A computer aided system for interactive definition of digital image interpretation,in "Digital Image Analysis", S.Levialdi ed.,Pitman, London.

Merelli, D., Mussio, P., Padula, M.,1985, An approch to the definition, description and extraction of structures in binary digitized images, CVGIP,31,19-49.

Zadeh, L., A., 1977, Fuzzy sets and their application to pattern classification and clustering analysis, in:"Classification and clustering", J.Van Ryzin ed., Academic Press.

Della Ventura, A., Maggioni, A., Mussio, P., Pawlina, A., 1985, Features detection and classification of rain patterns: knowledge acquisition for automatic interpretation of radar images, Report E.I. 1,IFCTR,CNR.

Hayes Roth, D., A., Waterman, B., Lenat, J., 1978, Principles of pattern directed inference systems, in "Pattern directed inference systems" Waterman,D., Hayes Roth, F., ed., Academic Press.

A SYSTEM FOR MORPHOLOGICAL ANALYSIS AND CLASSIFICATION

OF ASTRONOMICAL OBJECTS

Fabio Pasian, Mauro Pucillo and Paolo Santin

Osservatorio Astronomico

Trieste, Italy

ABSTRACT

A flexible system for the analysis and the classification of astronomical objects is described. The system consists in a set of utilities allowing object segmentation (standard and 'fuzzy'), basic and specialized preprocessing (filtering, grey-level thinning, calibration, curve tracking, etc), various feature extraction methods depending on the particular application, clustering and classification algorithms. The system features efficient data handling, allowing easy managing of very large images, and a flexible catalogue structure, where information on analyzed objects and classification parameters is kept.

INTRODUCTION

Morphological analysis is of great interest in the field of astronomical research, both for quantitative analysis and classification purposes. Anyway, the problem of shape analysis is not a simple one in the case of astronomical imagery. As a matter of fact, objects of astronomical interest are difficult to deal with, due to the almost total absence of edges and to the very low signal-to-noise ratio, thus making the segmentation phase of the data processing chain a very complicated task.

In the following, a system designed for morphological analysis is described, with particular reference to the methodologies used to deal with the particular and specific problems connected to the processing of astronomical images.

The problems being analyzed are the shape analysis of a single astronomical object at different levels of luminosity and the shape analysis and classification of a large number of objects identified on photographic plate. The morphological analysis system proposed can be divided into the three classical phases of any pattern recognition system: image preprocessing, feature extraction and feature analysis and classification. Each single step will be discussed in detail in the following.

DATA STRUCTURE

The heart of the processing system is the catalogue, a very flexible and effective data structure where data coming from the feature extraction phase are inserted (figure 1). The catalogue structure is defined once for all via an initialization phase, which allows the user to define (in number and contents) the fields the catalogue is divided into: the logical structure is then stored in a definition table. For each application program, either system-defined or user-written, access to the catalogue is made through an interface which reads the definition table and, accordingly, accesses the actual stored data. The interface not only performs the catalogue data management, but also contains modules referring to data presentation, statistics, and the like (figure 2).

The catalogue furthermore offers a very effective way of handling large images (the size of a standard astronomical image is commonly 10000x10000 pixels): the whole image can be safely divided into subparts and the relative positions are saved in the catalogue so to correctly perform such operations as rotation, stretching, etc. This feature is particularly useful in the case of large data cubes (images of the same astronomical objects at different wavelength bands).

PREPROCESSING

The preprocessing phase of the system refers to the operations that might be performed on the raw image in order to allow an easier segmentation step. The problems concerned with astronomical imagery stated in the introduction, make preprocessing a very desirable step to be taken before object identification and extraction is performed. In particular, the system contains filtering algorithms (both linear and non-linear), edge detection and template matching, besides arithmetics on images.

Particular care has been taken in order to overcome problems arising from non-stationary backgrounds: two different preprocessing approaches have been studied. The first one exploits the concept of information transform (Chang 1984; Santin 1984): each pixel of the original image is mapped into conjugate pixel, whose value represents the local content of information in a predefined neighbourhood of the pixel itself. In the conjugate domain, the object features are enhanced and the background features are smoothed out with invariance of the object barycenters positions thus allowing much easier object identification.

An alternate approach is the use of RNM non-linear filters (Nodes,Gallagher 1982, Malagnini et al 1985a), which allow the computation of a background estimate, to be subtracted from the original unfiltered image.

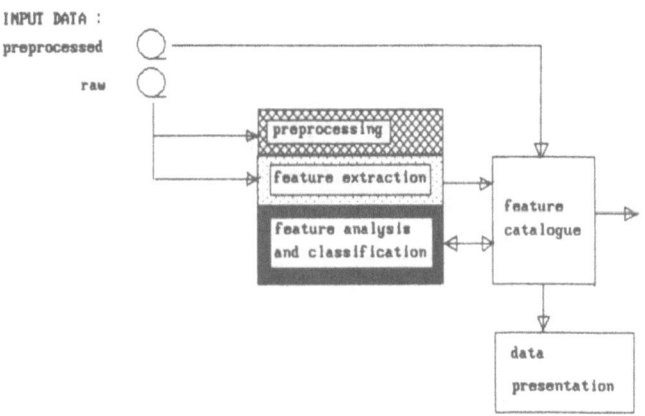

Fig.1. Logical structure of the system and data flow.

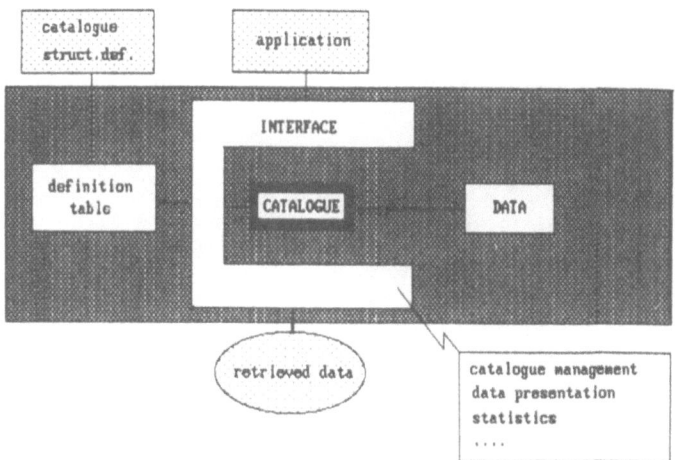

Fig.2. Structure of the catalogue and data handling.

FEATURE EXTRACTION

Segmentation of the raw or of the preprocessed image to extract the object whose morphologies are to be studied, is probably the most hard task, due, as previously stated, to the usually low signal-to-noise ratio of the astronomical images and to the nature of the objects themselves.

Since the morphological analysis in our case is performed on pixels possessing the same level of luminosity, the characteristics of the astronomical objects often lead, from an image analysis point of view, to have noisy or non-connected isolevel curves to track. The approach used to solve this problem is to extract from the image the feature to be analyzed by means of a fuzzy segmentation algorithm and then to perform a grey-scale thinning operation on the fuzzy image obtained (Pasian, Vuerli 1985 - figure 3). The core lines of the fuzzy image are then tracked and costitute the features on which morphological analysis is performed. Of course, when the signal-to-noise ratio is sufficiently good, the isolevel curves may be tracked with no particular preprocessing.

Each branch of the curve is saved separately: further segmentation is then to be performed so as to make a distinction between curve branches to be analyzed and curve branches to be disregarded as possibly spurious information due to noise. Data referring to the extracted features are then fed into the catalogue.

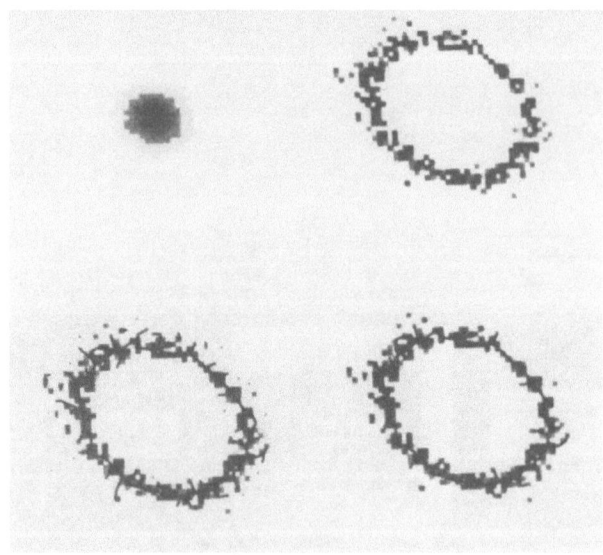

Fig.3. Example of fuzzy segmentation: upper left, original object (density range 0.6-2.6); upper right, fuzzy set corresponding to the probability of pixels to have a 0.8 density; lower left, extracted core line; lower right, filtered core line.

The segmented curve is transformed into a (x(l), y(l)) parametrized form in order to be analyzed by the feature analysis phase.

FEATURE ANALYSIS AND CLASSIFICATION

Once the curves are written in parametrized form, they are analyzed by the well known Fourier Descriptors technique (Zahn,Roskies 1972; Pasian,Santin 1985).

The x(l), y(l) representation of the curve is transformed into a normalized curvature cumulative function φ^* (NCCF), which can be expanded into Fourier series:

$$\varphi^*(t) = \varphi\left(\frac{Lt}{2\pi}\right) + t = \mu_o + \sum_{1}^{\infty} {}_k A_k \cos(kt - \alpha_k)$$

$$t = \frac{2\pi \ell}{L}$$

(1)

The A_k and α_k (amplitude and phase of the Fourier series) are called the Fourier Descriptors of the curve. The extracted curve is uniquely represented by a point in an N-dimensional space, where N depends on where the Fourier series (1) is decided to be truncated.

Fourier Descriptors have interesting properties, such as invariance to scaling, rotation and traslation; futhermore simple curves of astronomical interest, such as circles and ellipses, have peculiar values for certain particular A_k and α_k .

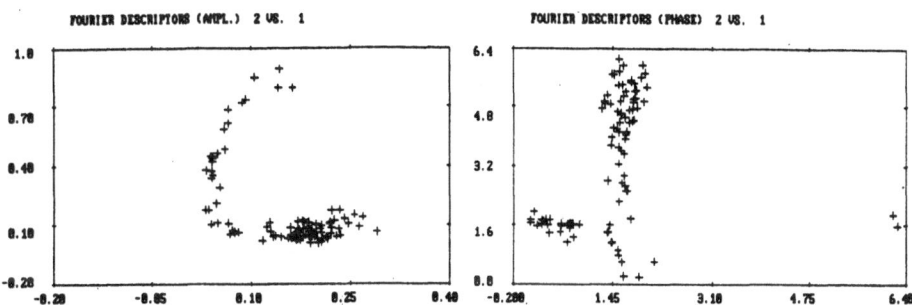

Fig.4. Positions of extracted isolevel curves, corresponding to stars, in two of the possible Fourier Descriptors planes: (a) first two even amplitudes; (b) first two even phases.

Once the extracted curve is described in the N-dimensional Fourier space, classification is desirable. Two ways can be followed for this purpose: comparison with the positions of a set of models in the N-dimensional space, or comparison with the positions of centroids corresponding to clusters of points equivalent to curves extracted from various training sets.

Models and centroids may constitute an enlargeable data base of known shapes with whom each new extracted curve can be compared.

APPLICATIONS

In the following, an example of application of the techniques described to shape recognition in astronomy is given. A set of objects identified on a photographic plate and classified by the FODS system (Malagnini et al 1985b) as "stars" has been analyzed. Figure 4 shows the positions of the points corresponding to isolevel curves extracted at different luminosity levels, plotted on planes defined by two couples of Fourier Descriptors. Even in two dimensions, instead of the 28 dimensions of the selected Fourier space, the presence of two different clusters is clear. The curves reconstructed from the centroids of the two clusters found in the 28-dimensional space are shown in figure 5. Figure 5a represents the isolevel shape of an ideal star, while figure 5b represents the isolevel shape of a bright star, the deformation due to the diffraction caused by the structure holding the plate on the focus of the telescope mirror.

Another example is given in figure 6, where isolevel curves extracted from two different galaxies at various luminosity levels are compared to an elliptical model. In the graph, abscissa values correspond to the axes ratio of the model ellipses, while ordinate values correspond to a parameter defining the "resemblance" of the extracted curve to the noiseless elliptical model. Lower "resemblance parameter" values correspond to curves extracted at lower signal-to-noise ratios.

ACKNOWLEDGEMENTS

This work was partially supported by a CNR-GNA grant. Data were processed at the ASTRONET pole of Trieste. Albino Lanza, Claudio Vuerli and Rosanna Savonitti wrote some software modules used in the system and referring to fuzzy segmentation, grey-scale core line tracing and clustering, respectively. The authors wish to thank Giorgio Sedmak for useful discussions on problems related to shape analysis in astronomy.

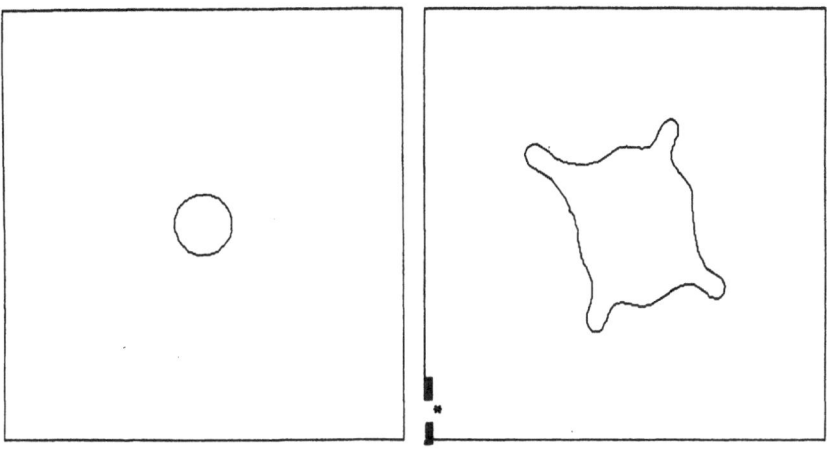

Fig.5. Curves reconstructed from the positions of the two centroids found in the 28-dimensional Fourier Descriptor space.

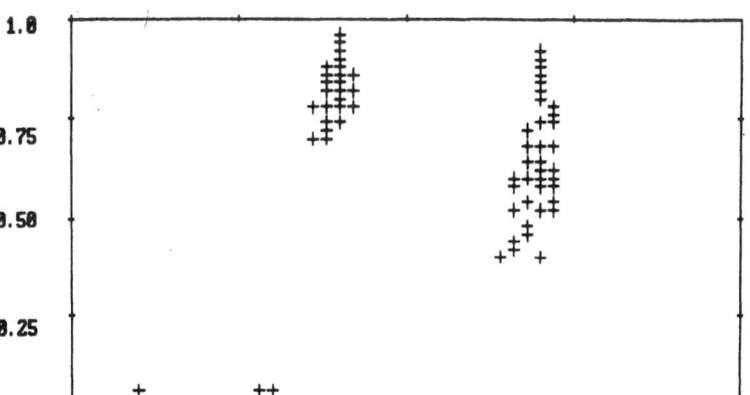

Fig.6. "Resemblance parameter" of curves extracted from two different astronomical objects VS. axes ratio of elliptical model.

REFERENCES

Chang S.K., 1984, Image information measure and encoding techniques, in: "Digital Image Analysis", S.Levialdi ed., Pitman, London.

Malagnini M.L., Pasian F., Pucillo M., Santin P., 1985a, Faint objects in crowded fields: discrimination and counting, in: "Data Analysis in Astronomy", L.Scarsi, V.Di Gesu` eds., Plenum Press, New York.

Malagnini M.L., Pasian F., Pucillo M., Santin P., 1985b, FODS: a system for faint object detection and discrimination in astronomy, Astron. Astrophys. 144, 49:56.

Nodes T.A., Gallagher N.C.Jr., 1982, Median filters: some modifications and their properties, IEEE Trans. ASSP 30, 739:746.

Pasian F., Santin P., 1985, Morphological analysis of extended objects, in: "Data Analysis in Astronomy", L.Scarsi, V.Di Gesu` eds., Plenum Press, New York.

Pasian F., Vuerli C., 1985, Core line tracing of fuzzy image subsets, Pattern Recognition Letters, (in press).

Santin P., 1984, Object detection with the information transform, in: ASTRONET 1983, G.Sedmak ed., S.A.It.

Zahn C.T., Roskies R.Z., 1972, Fourier descriptors for plane closed curves, IEEE Trans. C 21, 269:281.

PRELIMINARY RESULTS ON STRESS INSPECTION BY IMAGE PROCESSING

R. A. Fiorini,* P. Coppa and O Salvatore

*Dipartimento di Energetica, Politecnico di Milano
Milano, Italy
Centro Ricerche FIAT, Torino, Italy

ABSTRACT

A digital image processing computer facility was used to compare sequences of images to investigate the dynamic behavior of the temperature differences due to the thermoelastic effect on the external surface of a test specimen. The specimen consists of two car body metal sheets joined together by three welding spots in the middle. It was first modeled by Finite Element Technique and then tested on an MTS unit monitored by an infrared camera. Theoretical and experimental results are compared.

INTRODUCTION

In the mechanical manufacturing process both quality inspection and laboratory testing are well known procedures to assure the fitting of components to the design. In both cases thermography can properly be used. In fact, its capability to non destructively evaluating defects and to map applied stresses on the specimen surface by means of the thermoelastic effect allows a saving of a considerable amount of resources.

In a lifetime of a vehicle, the car body plays an important role and, in addition, the complexity of the structure makes thermographic analysis as a competitive test method. At this early stage, we have examined fatigue test samples, consisting of two car body sheets joined together by three welding spots in the middle as depicted in Figure 1 (strained structure).

This kind of specimen can be considered the representative model for the whole car body and it is one of the fatigue specimens usually tested in order to characterize car body sheets.

Usually experimental structural analysis methods are based on strain gauges, photoelasticity, holography and stress lacquers, while theoretical ones use the finite element approach. The application of strain gauges on the surface of the specimen is a well established method to measure the strain and the associated stress. This method allows high sensitivity to be achieved and to obtain absolute measurements even directionally. Unfortunately, it gives information from a localized area; it is a time consuming procedure and cannot be used for small components.

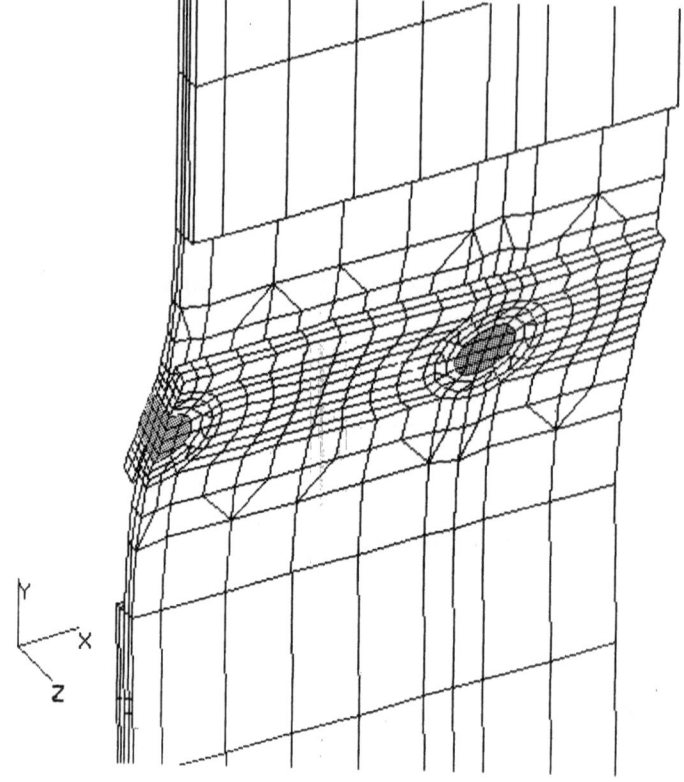

Fig. 1. Specimen model (strained structure).

DISCUSSION

The thermoelastic effect is well-known for gases (adiabatic compression or expansion); for solid materials it still exists, but in much less extent due to the different value of the thermal expansion coefficient. The thermoelastic regime is characterized by an adiabatic cooling of the sample (Kelvin, 1851) due to the conversion of a small fraction of the energy in the thermal bath of the crystal into mechanical work assisting the stress reacting to the imposed deformation: the deformation produces an increase of volume and the sample resists to this change by lowering its temperature and shrinking accordingly. Therefore, if elastic regime holds, when a body is subjected to a stress history, a thermal difference ΔT during the time can be measured. In that case the following formula holds[1,2]:

$$\Delta T = \frac{a\ T}{r\ C_S}\ \Delta s \qquad (1)$$

where Δs is the difference in the sum of the principal stresses, T is the mean temperature of the sample, a, is the linear thermal coefficient, r, the density of the material and C_S, the specific heat at constant stress. From relation (1), in the case of steel at ambient temperature (300 K), as an example we obtain $\Delta T = 0.001$ K for a stress difference Δs of about 1.1 MPa. A theoretical calculation was performed to evaluate the expected stress map on the surface of the fatigue test sample with three weld spots as previously described. The model was developed by the PATRAN-G pre-post processing package and the computations were performed by the NASTRAN program.

206

In Figure 2 the resulting s_{yy} stress map on the surface between the two metal sheets is shown: that is the surface where the most intensive stress concentration appears; scale is N/mm^2. On the external surface, see Figure 3, the stress values are about 10% of the innermost ones. Experimentally, during the fatigue test, the fracture originates just from the internal surface, where the F.E. analysis evaluates the maximum stress concentration factor; the concentration factor is about 15 times the average stress on the whole specimen cross section. Usually, the real stress concentration factor is lower than the computed one, because the modeling does not take into account the plastic relaxation effect, occurring in fatigue tests, which results in decreasing the value.

To select a suitable instrument for evaluating surface temperature on structures, we must select its required performance. Several major factors should be considered:

1) temperature range;
2) absolute accuracy;
3) temperature sensitivity;
4) spatial resolution;
5) channel capacity;
6) output requirements;
7) spectral considerations.

In particular we wish to focus your attention on the seventh parameter, spectral considerations. In fact, infrared radiation does not move through the atmosphere as easily as visible light. There are two practical IR bands: from 3 to 5 microns and from 8 to 14 microns. At room temperature (300 K), objects emit about 15 times more energy in the long wave than in the short wave range according to blackbody Planck's law[3]. Unfortunately, blackbodies do not exist in nature because "real surfaces"

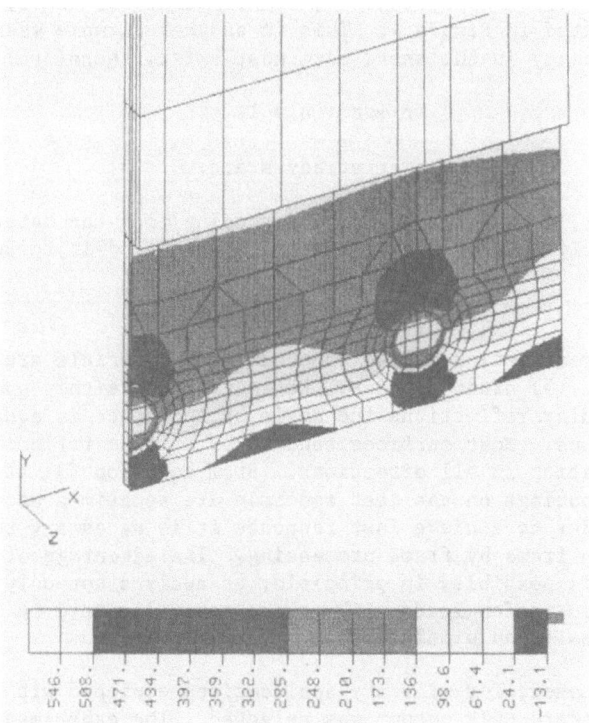

Fig. 2. S_{yy} internal surface stress mag.

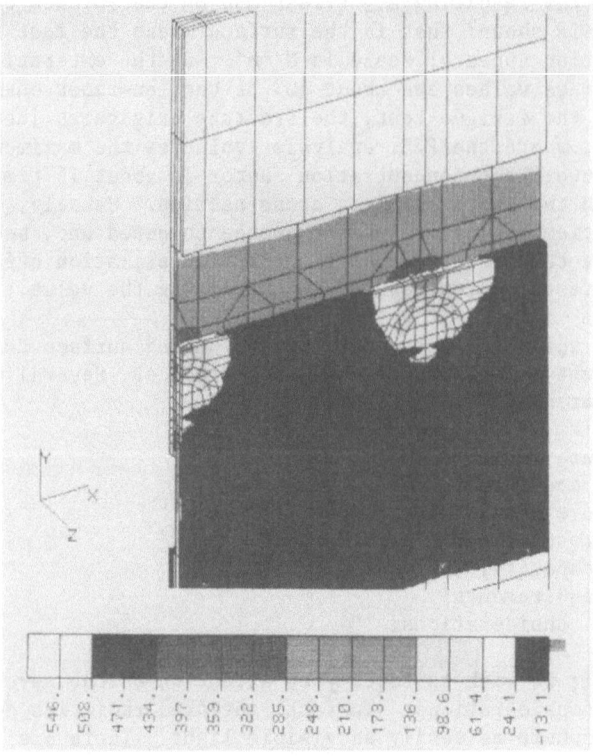

Fig. 3. S_{yy} external surface stress map.

are not perfect absorbers or emitters. They also have some reflectance.
The relationship between reflectance r, transmittance t, absorbance a and
emittance e is stated in Figure 4. This is another example where the
conservation of energy in the short term must exist, therefore:

$$r + t + a = 1$$

$$e = a \text{ at steady state.} \qquad (2)$$

The values of a, r, t range from 0 to 1 depending upon the material and the
configuration involved. For opaque materials t = 0 and it follows that:

$$e = 1 - r. \qquad (3)$$

In the infrared portion of the spectrum most materials are opaque and
therefore Equation (3) often applies. Reflectance is either specular or
diffuse. In specular reflections the angle of incidence is equal to the
angle of reflectance. Most surfaces tend to be diffuse reflectors in that
they reflect radiation in all directions. From Equation (3) it is clear
because special coatings on the test specimen are sometimes used as
enhancers. In order to achieve fast response it is necessary to use an
approach, based on frame by frame processing. The advantage of this technique is that it is possible, in principle, to analyze not only cyclic load
histories, but also random loads, like those generally used in fatigue
tests on car bodies (road simulation).

An infrared camera for military applications equipped with a refractor
telescope and standard CCIR output was selected. The experimental set up
was designed to achieve a temperature sensitivity of about 0.04 C at 300 K
and a spatial resolution of about 0.30 mm using 512 × 512 pixels per frame.

The digital image processing system architecture was already described in literature[4] and the image processing program library VIPS (Viable Image Processing Software)[5] offers full support to researchers and technicians. The test specimen, in the shape and size like the F.E. model previously described, was clamped on a MTS mod. 810 fatigue test machne with a 100 KN maximum load capability. Tests were performed using a constant amplitude sinusoidal load history, with a stress ratio R = 0.1 and a maximum load ranging from 8 to 29 KN. The load frequency range was from 1 to 6 Hz in order to see directly, on the monitor, the oscillating behavior of the surface temperature distribution due to the thermoelastic effect. As an example Figure 5 is the CRF 928 recording used as a reference.

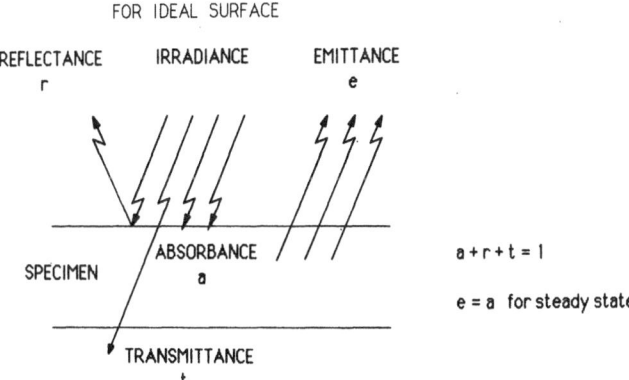

Fig. 4. Basic radiometric relations.

In this case the load was 24 KN at 2 Hz and the temperature difference range $\Delta T = 2°C$ was discretized into 256 levels mapped by seven colors: cyan, red, green, magenta, yellow, blue and white.

Cyan, on the low left side of the picture, represents the warmest points and white, on the low right side, the coldest ones. The CRF 930 recording, see Figure 6, corresponds to the sinusoidal peak compressive stress causing an increasing temperature around the weld spots. In order to enhance these temperature changes, point by point temperature difference using CRF 930 and CRF 928 images and a redistribution of color intervals are performed, see Figure 7. Now we have eight colors, the previous seven ones plus black that maps the warmest points; each color maps a temperature difference $\Delta T = 0.125°C$. You can see from Figure 8 that we use a 95 × 95 pixel squared window in order to perform a statistical analysis. The squared window named "R" is used as a reference. We obtain:

Color Percentage Window	Red	Green	Mag	Yell
Ref.	0.56	53.91	45.12	0.41
1	5.66	69.17	25.07	0.09
2	7.70	69.07	23.13	0.09
3	8.77	74.64	16.53	0.04

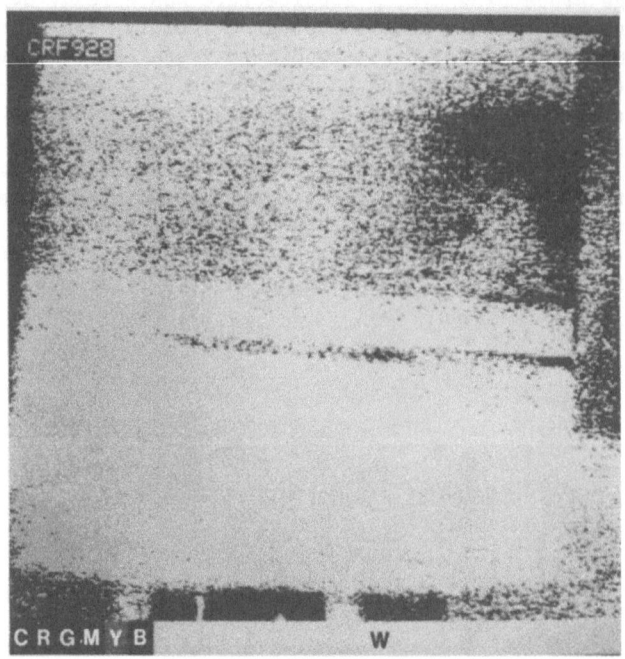

Fig. 5. Test load = 24 KN at 2 Hz reference recording.

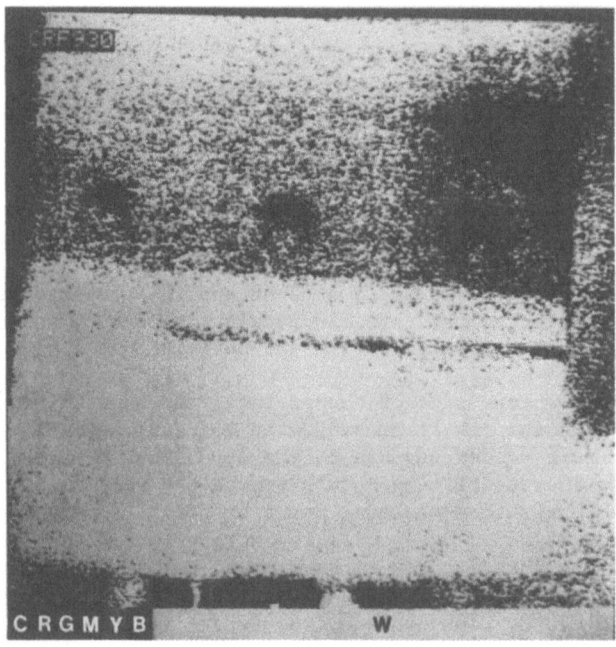

Fig. 6. Test loss = 24 KN at 2 Hz peak compressive stress recording.

Now you can see that there is a thermal asymmetry, probably due to the asymmetric application of the test load to the specimen, but the surface temperature distribution is in good agreement with the s_{yy} external surface stress distribution computed by F.E. modeling (see Figure 3). Using the same color scale and therefore the same temperature sensitivity, the CRF 101 recording in Figure 9 reports the temperature distribution after a test

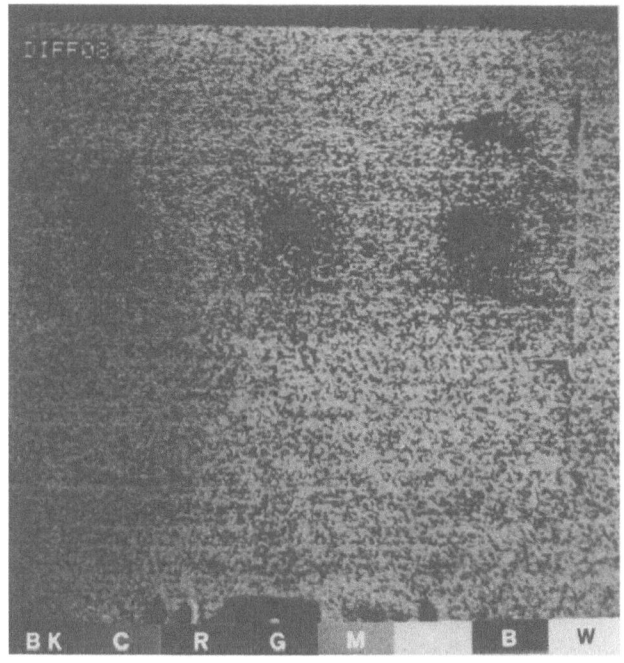

Fig. 7. CRF930 and CRF928 point by point difference.

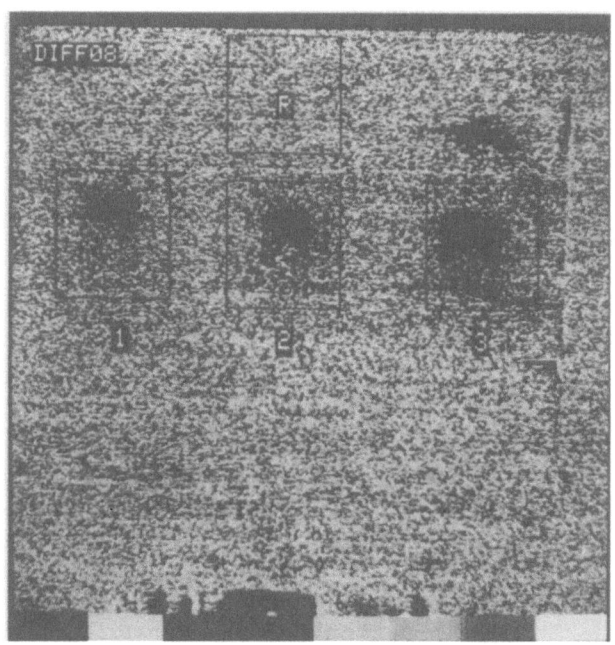

Fig. 8. Statistical analysis using squared windows.

load increase up to 29 KN just an instant before the separation of the test specimen into two parts showed in Figure 10. The specimen heats up violently as soon as the kinks and the initially sessile dislocation loops inside it start moving in a more and more organized fashion, and multiply.

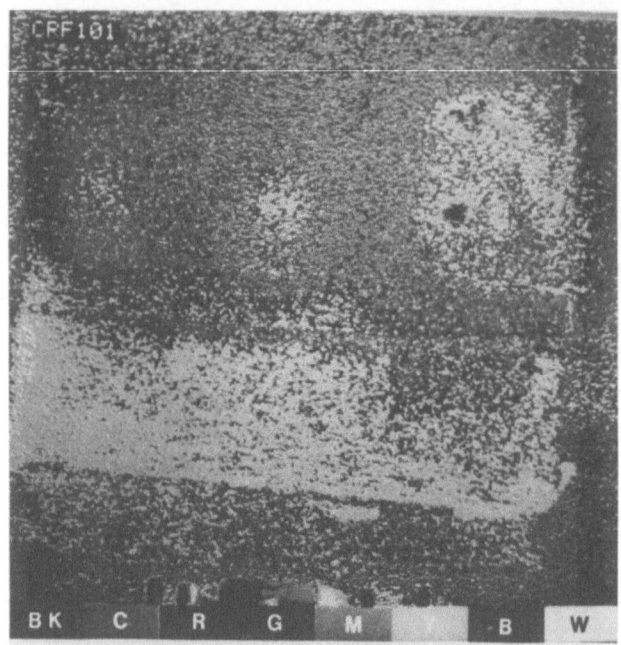

Fig. 9.   Test load = 29 KN at 2 Hz.

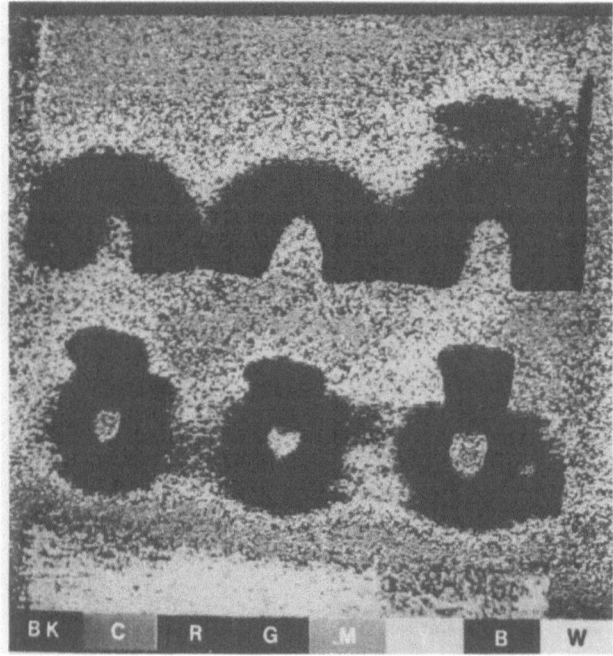

Fig. 10.   Separation of the test specimen into two parts.

CONCLUSION

The comparison of the F.E. model results with the I.R. camera recordings clearly shows a good agreement in the stress and temperature surface
distribution, if elastic behavior holds. Although the stress concentration
zones are well enhanced with both methods, the F.E. modeling presents more

enhanced stress values on the external surface than those reconstructed from the experimental temperature distribution recordings.

This fact is due both to the theoretical modelling method (greater values than real ones) and to the experimental method (smaller values than real ones). The latter effect is mainly due to the thermal wave propagation from the high stress concentration internal zones to the external surface, to the thermal lens and optical interference effects particularly during the elastoplastic transition.

The syncronization of I.R. recordings with the programed load history available from the fatigue test machine can allow the reconstruction of temperature propagation from the high stress concentration internal zones to the external surface. Therefore, when the highest stress concentration zones are in the interior of a body, it is necessary to include in the model the thermal lens, optical and nonlinear effects in order to obtain a quantitative tool. In that way it could be possible to solve the so-called INVERSE THERMAL PROBLEM for 3D structures and to monitor quantitatively the elastoplastic transition of the material, but a lot of computing power would be required. This thermal wave imaging technique is still in early stages of development, but it holds great promise, particularly in quality inspection, laboratory testing and mechanical manufacturing process.

Acknowledgements

The present work was sponsored by FIAT AUTO, IVECO ENGINEERING, the C.N.P.M. Research Center of the Italian National Research Council and the Department of Energetics, Politecnica di Milano. The authors wish to thank the above mentioned organizations for permission to present this paper, the Department of Electronics, Politecnico di Milano, and Mr Stefano Sensolo, C.N.P.M., C.N.R., for their cooperation.

REFERENCES

1. D. E. Oliver, P. Stanley, and J.M.B. Webber, The use of sensitive transducers to produce maps of cyclically loaded structures, Proceedings of the SESA Annual Conference, Cleveland, Ohio (1983).
2. M. H. Belgen, Structural stress measurement with an infrared radiometer, ISA Transactions, 6:49-53 (1967).
3. E. M. Sparrow, and R. D. Cess, "Radiation Heat Transfer", Brooks Cole, Belmont, California (1966).
4. R. A. Fiorini, R. Fumero, and R. Marchesi, Cardio-surgical thermography, Proceedings of SPIE., 359:249-256 (1982).
5. VIPS Reference Manual V.4.03, Dipartimento di Energetica, Politechnico di Milano (1985).

CLUSTER ANALYSIS AND REPRESENTATION FOR

TYPOLOGY OF MECHANICALLY WORKED SURFACES

A. Bruzzone[*], P.M. Lonardo[*] and G. Vernazza[+]

*Istituto di Tecnologie e Impianti Meccanici
 Università di Genova
+Dipartimento di Ingegneria Biofisica ed Elettronica
 Università di Genova

INTRODUCTION

In production engineering an important area of research concerns the typology of surfaces machined with different cutting processes in order to define relationships between the generation variables, the surface finish parameters and the functional properties[1,2,3].

Cluster analysis can offer a useful relief to resolve the problems regarding classification and recognition of surface microgeometry.

The parameters introduced for surface microgeometrical description are becoming increasingly numerous, including both statistical and geometrical characteristics.

Typically, the statistical characteristics are related to the profile amplitude and slope as well as to the moments of the different orders. The geometrical characteristics are defined taking into account the functional behaviour of the workpiece. Consequently each parameter considers a specific aspect of the surface, while an overall synthetic description does not exist at present.

The purpose of this paper is to supply an objective approach to classify and identify "natural" surface clusters, by adopting the most typical and used parameters.

To achieve this result a cluster analysis has been conducted based on the M.S.T. (Minimal Spanning Tree) algorithm[4].

The adoption of the M.S.T. method is justified by the assumption that a high correlation among some features can exist.

As in a previous work[5], we have considered some different and representative machining processes: turning, milling, grinding (surface and plunge), honing, E.D.M. (Electric Discharge Machining), shot peening. Two of these are single point cutting processes and produce nearly periodic profiles (turning and milling), the others produce nearly random profiles.

Although each process is mechanically different from each other, the surfaces obtained cannot be distinguished automatically by simply observing individual parameters. This is due to the fact that the ranges covered by such parameters are often overlapping by varying the process.

The use of cluster analysis has demonstrated instead that it is possible in some way to recognize distinct classes of machining processes.

A cooperative work developed by the CIRP Scientific and Technical Committee, "Surfaces"[6] has supplied the reference data employed in this analysis.

Aim of the CIRP research was to assess which of the surface parameters could be used to characterize a machining process.

Samples accurately machined in different laboratories were collected and examined by means of a roughness measuring instrument. The data corresponding to the profile ordinates were processed in order to obtain the required parameters.

Table 1 reports the typical roughness parameters and other statistical functions referred to the symbols given in Fig.1.

Table 1.

$Rt = y_{max} - y_{min}$

$Rp = y_{max}$

$Rq = \sqrt{(\int y^2 \, dx)/L}$

$Ra = (\int |y| \, dx)/L$

SkewO = skewness of ordinate distribution
KurtO = kurtosis of ordinate distribution
Da = arithmetic average slope
Dp = geometric average slope
SkewS = skewness of slope distribution
KurtS = kurtosis of slope distribution
Max = maximum density of slope distribution

Furthermore, the ratios Rp/Rt and Rq/Ra have been proposed.

In addition to the parameters considered in the CIRP report, the m and n coefficients of the Beta function have been computed and introduced as features. Therefore, in all, 15 features have been examined.

The surface samples tested are 79, divided according to 8 physical classes, corresponding to the machining processes specified in Table 2.

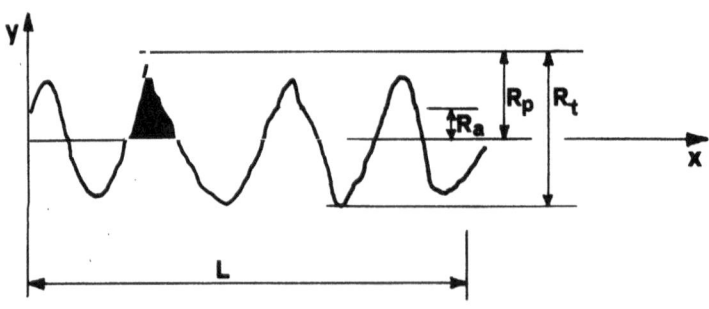

Fig. 1. Roughness profile

Table 2.

Specimen No		Working Process
From	To	
1	10	Surface Grinding
11	19	Turning
20	31	Milling
32	41	Plunge Grinding
42	51	Honing-Soft
52	61	Honing-Hard
62	72	E.D.M.
73	79	Shot-Peening

Due to the low number of samples as compared to the number of classes and available features, and considering the correlation between some of them, the analysis has been developed by adopting sets of features with different numerosity.

For the clustering analysis the MST method has been applied adopting the Euclidean distance as weight factor of the edge. To evaluate the appropriate threshold distance d_0 on the edges, and consequently the number of "natural" clusters, different curves have been considered.

Among these, particular relevance is assumed by the following:
- number of clusters c as a function of $K = d_0/\bar{d}$, where $\bar{d}$ is the mean edge lenght of MST;
- minimal and maximal cardinal numbers of clusters;
- meaningful clusters, i.e. the clusters with cardinality greater or equal to a given value n^*, versus K; this curve is useful to avoid the effect of the singleton or poor clusters.

An overall description of the clustering process can be achieved by representing the complete sequence of partitions. For this purpose a diagram reporting the progressive clustering process of each sample versus c has been developed.

In this way it is possible to observe how and when the clusters coalesce in greater ones: vertical lines define the value where the grouping occurs. Each area of the same pattern represents the machined surfaces belonging to the same cluster.

Moreover, in order to examine the results of cluster analysis two methods of linear displays have been used.

The possibility of presenting and analysing high-dimensional data in two dimensional space, in an appropriate way, is very interessting for human presentation. However, a number of errors are obviously introduced in every procedure[7].

For this presentation we have considered two methods.

The first one (simple ordination), is based on the research, in the original space, of the two farthest points. The straight line passing through these two points is assumed as the first axis; the second axis is the straight line, perpendicular to the first axis, drawn from the point which is the farthest from the first axis.

The new 2D display is obtained by projecting all the points from the original space on this new plane.

The second method for 2D presentation is based on the classical method of principal components, considering the two first eigenvectors of the scatter matrix of the original points as the axes of the new 2D plane. Different factors have been introduced to evaluate the 2D mapping results. Since the MST method is based on distance evaluation, the following error function has been considered:

$$e = \sqrt{\frac{\sum\limits_i \sum\limits_j (d^*_{ij} - d_{ij})^2}{n(n-1)}}$$

where n is the sample size, d_{ij} is the distance between the samples i and j in the original feature space, while d^*_{ij} is the corresponding distance in the transformed plane. For the principal component method a further coefficient is introduced:

$$r = \frac{\lambda_1 + \lambda_2}{\sum\limits_i^d \lambda_i}$$

where d is the features number, λ_i is the generical eigenvalue of the scattering matrix, λ_1 and λ_2 are the highest eigenvalues. The approaching of r to 1 means a strong correlation among the features; consequently the space reduction in this situation can be obtained with minimal informmation loss.

RESULTS

The analysis here developed has considered different sets of features, evaluating both the efficiency of the method in view of an automatical recognition of machining processes, and the performance of the 2D presentation.

In particular we have selected the following sets of features:
- the complete set   (15 features);
- Rt, Rp, Rq, Ra, Skew0, Kurt0, Da, Dq, Skews, Kurts, Max   (11 features);
- Skew0, Kurt0, Dq, Max, Rq/Ra   (5 features);
- Rt, Rp, Skew0, Dq   (4 features);
- Rq, mBeta, nBeta   (3 features).

This progressive space reduction has evidentiated that the higher numbers of features are less useful and create some spread effect. On the contrary, too few features are not sufficient to discriminate every working process.

Anyway a detailed investigation about the discriminating power of each feature has not been carried out. As an intermediate space dimensionality appears more attractive, in the following the analysis referred to the set of 4 features is reported in detail.

The curves of Fig. 2 and Fig. 3 show respectively c(K) and c*(K), drawn assuming n* = 3. These curves display an interesting value of K near 1.2, where the maximal value of clusters (8) appears, and the first plateau of curve c(K) is present.

Fig. 4 shows the clustering process with the complete sequence of partitions. The samples are sorted according to the machining process. As it can be seen, the greatest cluster is mainly built up by the points belonging to surface grinding, turning and plunge grinding. Continuing the process, the same cluster incorporates well defined groups corresponding respectively to EDM, shot peening, honing soft and honing hard. Particular evidence assumes the behaviour of EDM which is the last to collapse into the overall cluster. This behaviour has been observed also by adopting different sets of features, and can be explained considering that the physical principle of EDM is completely different from the other machining processes. Similarly, shot peening presents an early cluster covering a wide range of K. It is remarkable the merging, which occurs at an intermediate step, of plunge grinding into surface grinding, to which it is physically similar.

Fig. 5 reports the behaviour of the error function e for different

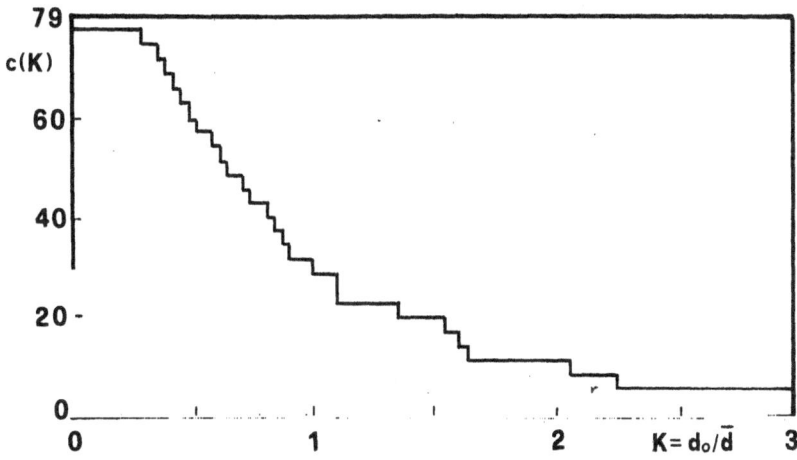

Fig. 2. Number of clusters c versus K

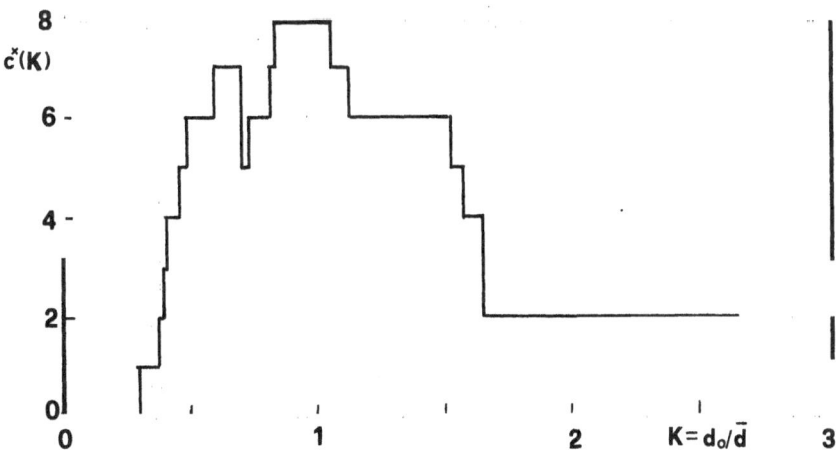

Fig. 3. Number of meaningful clusters c*, for n* = 3, versus K

features groups, referred (a) to the simple ordination method and (b) to the principal components transformation. As it can be seen by increasing the cardinality of the feature groups, a pseudo-regular trend is shown in the latter diagram, while in the former diagram a discontinuity appears above the 8 features group, according to the particular sequence of the feature sets selected. Consequently, for simple ordination the 2D display can be considered acceptable up to near 8 parameters.

In the y axes the errors are given in percent, while in absolute values the maximal error associated to the principal components method is about 2.5 greater than the simple ordination method.

Fig. 6 reports the behaviour of the r coefficient. It can be seen that the discontinuity around the 8 features group shows a relevant information loss for the 2D mapping, which confirms the above observations.

The next figures show the 2D display of the points belonging to the original space of 4 features. The simple ordination method and the principal components transformation have been examined. The points

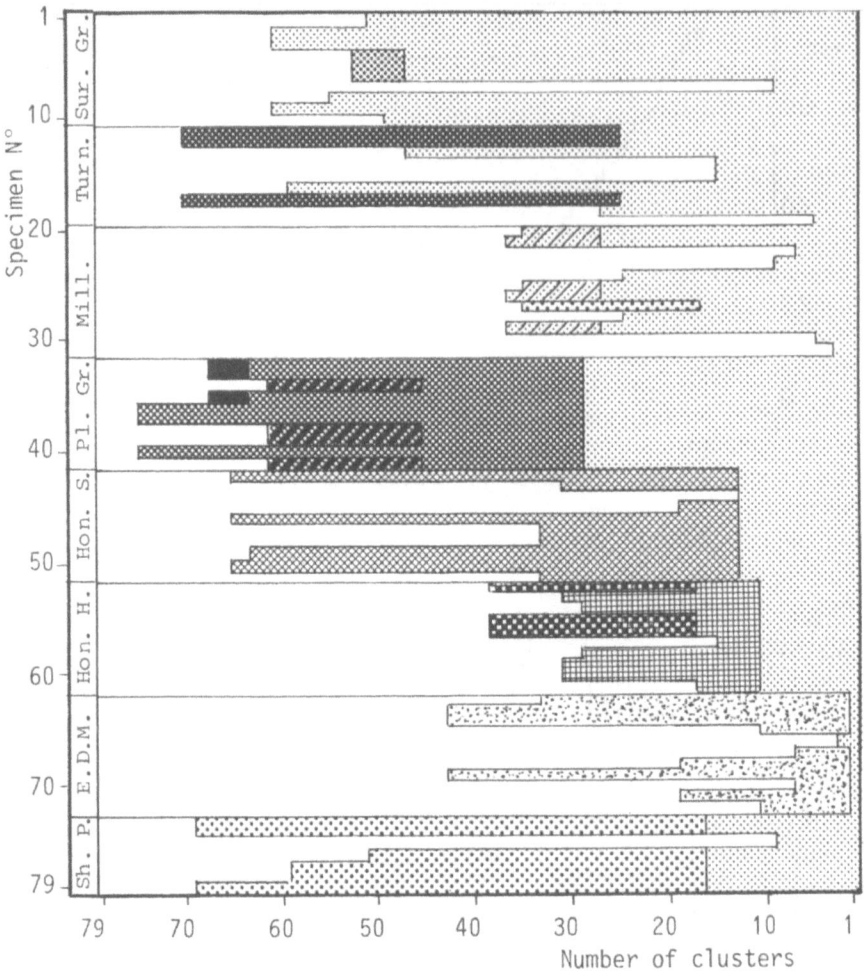

Fig. 4. Clustering process

classification has been made by adopting both the physical grouping, tantamount to the working process, and the "natural" clusters selected by the MST algorithm.

Fig. 7 displays the projection through the simple ordination method with the physical classification. The 2D observation allows two distinct groups to be recognized ((bigger + and bigger*) corresponding respectively to EDM and honing-hard. All the remaining surfaces are nearly mixed in a central group.

Fig. 8 displays on the same plane the projection of the points classified through MST at c = 29 and with $n^* = 3$: at least 5 of the "natural" clusters result visually distinct after the projection. The clusters appearing mixed up correspond to surface grinding and milling, which are nearly joining together, as it can be observed in Fig. 4.

In Fig. 9 the projection is shown having adopted the principal components method, with the physical classification. Only the EDM processing (bigger +) appears to be very distinct. Partially recognizable are honing hard (bigger *) and turning (.).

In Fig. 10 the projection in the same plane is shown with points classified through MST. In this case one "natural" cluster associable to EDM (bigger +) is clearly visible. Two other clusters are visually recognizable to a certain extent.

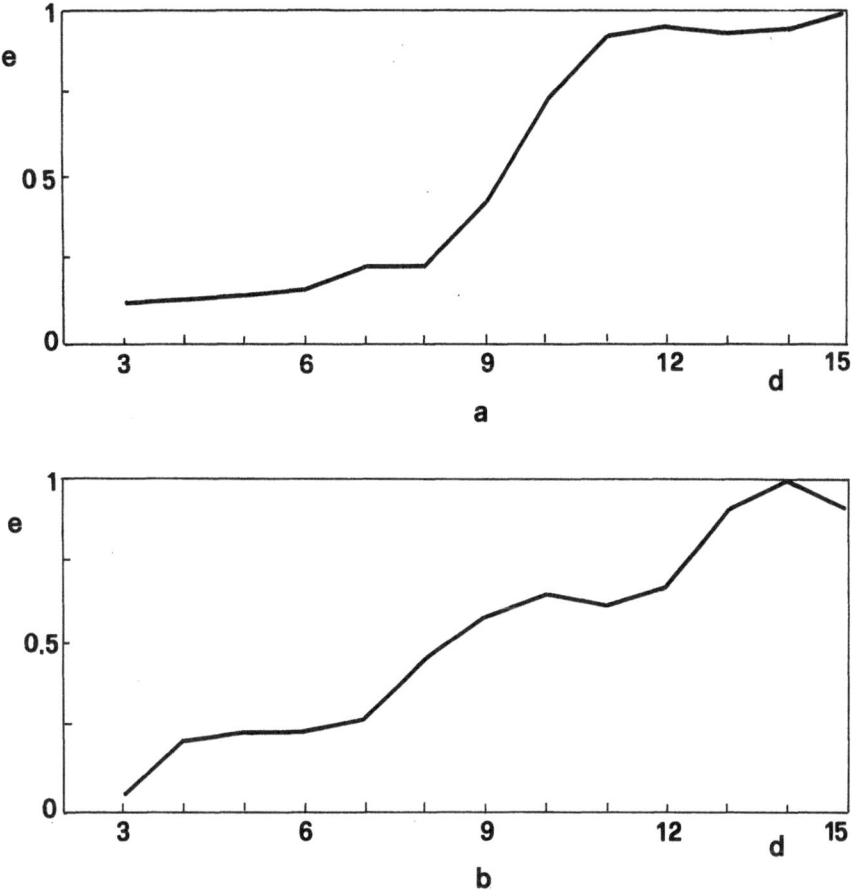

Fig. 5. Error function e versus the cardinality of feature groups:
(a) for the principal components transformation
(b) for the simple ordination method

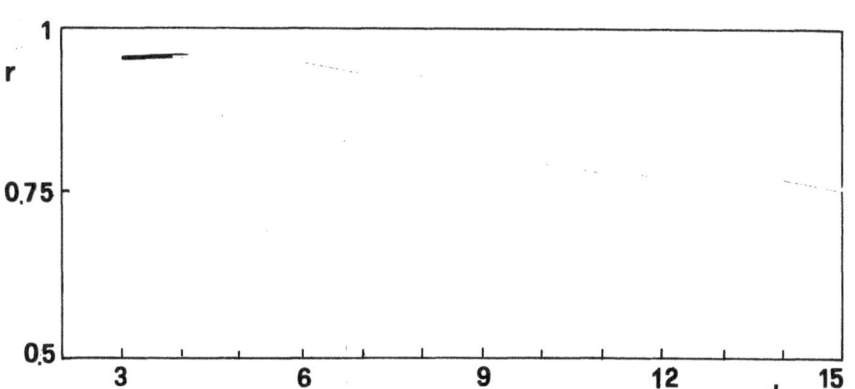

Fig. 6. Coefficient r versus the cardinality of feature groups.

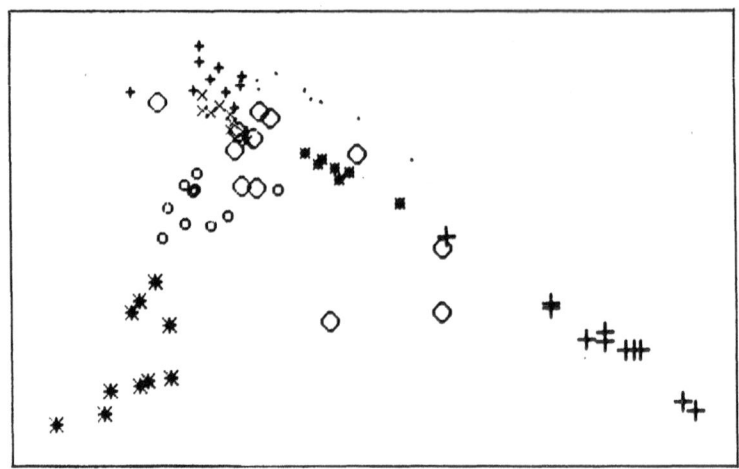

Fig. 7. 2D display of the projection, through the simple ordination
method, from 4 features space; data points classified
according to the physical classification

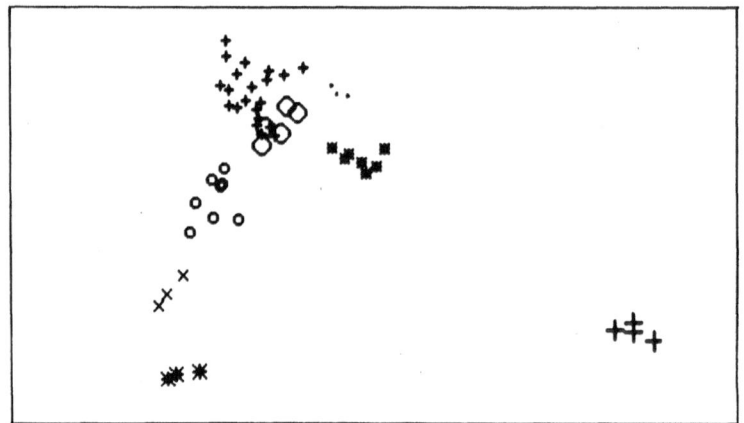

Fig. 8 2D display as Fig. 7; data points classified according
to MST (c = 29, n* = 3)

DISCUSSION

The application of the MST method to analyse the microgeometrical
characteristics of machined surfaces has demonstrated to be a promising
approach to face problems in profile classification.

Generally a better 2D representation has been observed employing the
simple ordination method in comparison with the principal components
method. However the 2D mapping using the examined features is not
sufficient to supply a clear clustering, since a strong everlapping is
observed. Therefore the clustering analysis adopting the human approach
(2D) is not exploitable and higher space dimensionality should be
considered for an automatic and more resolving classification.

Moreover other powerful discriminating parameters should be
researched, i.e. features related to the spectral properties of profile,
in order to obtain easier clusters detections.

It must be outlined that the small size of the sample set, often

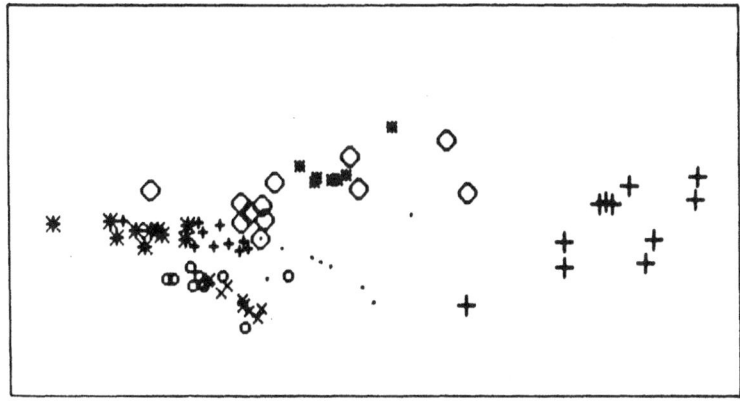

Fig. 9. 2D display of the projection, through the principal
components method, from 4 features space; data points
classified according to the physical classification

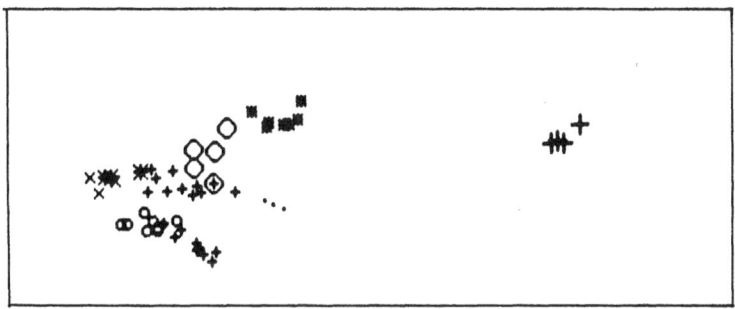

Fig. 10. 2D display as Fig. 9; data points classified according
to MST (c = 29, n* = 3)

reduced by the cardinality threshold keeping out the less numerous groups,
may introduce certain statistical errors. Consequently the obtained
results are to be considered only as preliminary and should be validated
by a new wider measurement set.

Nevertheless the present results are conforting for their physical
meaning. Indeed the clustering algorithm has allowed the profiles
corresponding to typical working processes, mainly EDM and shot peening,
to be retrived from a sample set. The employed techniques are suitable to
be used in further analysis involving other aspects of the subject, such
as the functional behaviour of the machined surfaces, in order to optimize
the production process.

REFERENCES

1. D.J.Whitehouse, Typology of manufactured surfaces, <u>Annals of the CIRP</u>,
      vol.18 (1970).
2. M.Santochi, M.Vignale, A study on the functional properties of a honed

surface, <u>Annals of the CIRP</u>, vol.31/1 (1982).

3. A.Villa,   S.Rossetto, R.Levi, Surface texture and machining conditions, <u>ASME Journ. of Eng. for Industry</u>, vol.105 (1983).

4. R.O.Duda,   P.E.Hart, "Pattern classification and scene analysis", J.Wiley & Sons, N.Y. (1973).

5. P.M.Lonardo,   A.Bruzzone, Pattern recognition approach to surface classification, <u>Annals of the CIRP</u>, vol.34/1 (1985).

6. J.Peters,   P.Vanherck, M.Sastrodinoto, Assessment of surface typology analysis techniques, <u>Annals of the CIRP</u>, vol.28/2 (1979).

7. Yi-tzuu Chien, "Interactive pattern recognition", M. Dekker, N.Y. (1978).

A COMPUTER VISION MODEL FOR THE ANALYSIS

OF CLASSES OF HAND-WRITTEN PLANE CURVES

S. Impedovo* and M. Castellano**

* Istituto di Scienze dell'Informazione
Università degli Studi di Bari
Via Amendola 173, 70126 Bari, Italy
** Istituto Nazionale di Fisica Nucleare
Via Amendola 173, 70126 Bari, Italy

ABSTRACT

The objective of this paper is to research the properties
that allow the characterization of classes of hand-written plane
curves. To this purpose the change in shape among plane curves
which belong to the same class is considered as a dynamic
phenomenon where shape deformation is assumed as arising from a
motion consistent with the perception of the human visual
system. A preliminary investigation to select the physical laws
these deformations are linked to is developed by using
the velocity fields, obtained through the well known
computer vision motion-techniques.

INTRODUCTION

It is well known that the problem of plane curve discrimination
arises in several fields of pattern recognition [1]. To solve
this problem many sophisticated data acquisition systems (see
the tablets designed and commercially divulgated in the last
years) [2], good preprocessing algorithms (see filters and data
compression algorithms) [3,4,5], perfect mathematical models for
plane curve description [6,7], very good set of features
[1,8,9], formally correct definition of similarity [10,11,12] and
a very large number of classification algorithms have
been proposed [13]. Notwithstanding all the progress made in
this field the investigation of what the human visual system
implements to discriminate plane curves is still of great
interest.

Fortunately, the studies of Wallach [14], Fennema and Thompson
[15], Marr and Ullman [16], Adelson and Movshon [17], Poggio

[18], Yuille [19] on the human visual system and those of Hildreth [20], Nagel [21], Horn and Schunk [22], Prager and Arbib [23] on motion give us tools to investigate the consistency between plane curve recognition algorithms and the recognition mechanism of the human visual system .

In this paper , the shape deformation among plane curves, representing hand-written numerals and belonging to the same class of style [10,11,12], is considered as a dynamic phenomenon and the computer vision motion-techniques are used to investigate class properties. To this purpose, some considerations on the velocity field consistence with the human visual system perception of shape deformation are presented.

COMPUTER VISION MODELS FOR HAND-WRITTEN NUMERAL CLASS CHARACTERIZATION

Let us consider the set of continuous finite length plane curves which, as known, is a Hilbert space [24]. This space can be represented using the complete orthonormal system of the Fourier trigonometric vectors [7]. In many practical cases only Fourier spaces with finite dimension are taken into account. For instance, it has been shown that to represent hand-written numerals only the first four Fourier coefficients are needed [1]. To avoid the dependence of the features on position, size and orientation of the shape, in many applications, Fourier descriptors derived by Fourier coefficients are used [1,8,9]. In the example of hand-written numerals presented in ref.1, the descriptors $d(2)$, $d(3)$ and $d(4)$ were utilized and a tri-dimensional complex space $\underline{C}^3$ was investigated. If the polar coordinates are used and both modules and phases of each Fourier descriptor are quantized, this space can be represented as a tri-dimensional array of cubes each consisting of QxQxQ plane curves ($2\pi/Q$ is the quantum step of the descriptor phases) [25].

In general, if a Fourier descriptor space of (N-2)-dimension is considered, the two (N-2)-tuple

$$(d(2),\ldots,d(N-1)) \tag{1}$$

and

$$(d(2)+k(2)\,\Delta d(2),\ldots,d(N-1)+k(N-1)\,\Delta d(N-1)) \tag{2}$$

(Where $(k(2),\ldots,k(N-1)) \neq 0$ is a boolean (n-2)-tuple, and $\Delta d(k)= \Delta|d(k)|\ \exp(j\Delta \measuredangle d(k))$, $\forall k=2,\ldots,N-1$, is the quantum step of the k-th Fourier descriptor .)

represent adjacent plane curves.

If the values of quanta steps are duly defined so that the shape deformation takes place in a spatial window of 10÷15 prime of the visual angle, then the shape distortion between the plane curves in (1) and (2) can be investigated using the short-range theory of human visual system perception.

If c_1 and c_2 are two plane curves (fig. 1) and $\mathbf{v}(s) = v^\top(s)\,\mathbf{u}^\top(s) + v^\perp(s)\,\mathbf{u}^\perp(s)$ (where $\mathbf{u}^\perp(s)$ and $\mathbf{u}^\top(s)$ are unit direction vectors) denotes the displacement vector of the arc "ds" of curve c_1 on curve c_2, then some measures of the local deformation can be given by $\mathbf{v}(s)$, $d\mathbf{v}(s)/ds$ and $d^2\mathbf{v}(s)/ds^2$.

If the space of $(N-2)$-dimensions of the Fourier descriptors $d(k) = c(k)/c(1)$ (where k ranges from 2 to $N-1$, and $c(k)$ is the k-th Fourier coefficient) is investigated, it is easy to show that the square root of the functional:

$$\Theta : \mathcal{U} \to \underset{=}{\mathbb{R}} \left| \forall \mathbf{V}_{c_1} \in \mathcal{U} : \Theta(\mathbf{V}_{c_1}) = \int_{c_1} \left| \partial \mathbf{v}(s)/\partial s \right|^2 ds \right.$$

defined on the $\mathcal{U}$ space of all the deformation-fields $\mathbf{V}_{c1}$ of c_1,is a norm and also that the $\mathcal{U}$ space is a Banach space [20]. This follows from the hypothesis that when using Fourier descriptors the subspace of all pure translation (null space of the functionals) is empty [26]. Hildreth by using a theorem from the Rudin [27] , shows that under the "aperture problem " constraints of the human visual system , there exists a unique velocity field which has a minimal norm and is congruent with the shape deformation observed by the human visual system [20,28]. Consequently the velocity field which satisfies these constraints is the measure of the shape deformation of the plane curve c_1 that becomes c_2.

A question that now arises is what characterizes the velocity fields of shapes belonging to the same class of style. To answer this question some parameters defined on the velocity field corresponding to the Θ minimal were measured. Some of the parameters considered are:

1) The average of the vectors composing the estimated velocity field (e.v.f.):

$$\overline{\mathbf{v}} = \frac{1}{c_{1L}} \int_{c_1} \mathbf{v}(s)\,ds \quad ; \text{ where } c_{1L} = c_1 \text{ Length}$$

2) The standard deviation of the vectors in the e.v.f.:

$$\sigma = \frac{1}{c_{1L}} \left(\int_{c_1} \left| \mathbf{v}(s) - \overline{\mathbf{v}} \right|^2 ds \right)^{1/2}$$

3) The average of the first and second order derivative of the vectors in the e.v.f.:

$$\mathbf{d}^1 = \frac{1}{c_{1L}} \int_{c_1} \frac{\partial \mathbf{v}}{\partial s}\,ds \quad ; \quad \mathbf{d}^2 = \frac{1}{c_{1L}} \int_{c_1} \frac{\partial^2 \mathbf{v}}{\partial s^2}\,ds$$

4) The standard deviation of the first and second order derivative of the vectors in the e.v.f.:

$$\sigma_{\mathbf{d^1}} = \frac{1}{c_{1L}} \left(\int_{c_1} \left| \frac{\partial \mathbf{v}}{\partial s} - \mathbf{d^1} \right|^2 ds \right)^{1/2}; \quad \sigma_{\mathbf{d^2}} = \frac{1}{c_{1L}} \left(\int_{c_1} \left| \frac{\partial^2 \mathbf{v}}{\partial s^2} - \mathbf{d^2} \right|^2 ds \right)^{1/2}$$

as well as all the averages and standard deviations of the modules and the arguments, with their first and second order derivatives, of the vectors composing the estimated velocity field, for their definition see symbol table.

EXPERIMENTAL RESULTS

Some velocity fields have been computed by taking into account the Fourier descriptors cyclic sub-space of the plane curves which were obtained by changing the phase of the second and third Fourier descriptors of a hand-written numeral. Fig 2 shows the samples of this sub-space (the size of the hand-written numerals was assumed to be smaller than a rectangle of 2x4 cm^2 and thus, quanta steps of $2\pi/16$ were used for the phases) obtained by the hand-written numeral three at the center of the map.

Tab.1 shows some values of the parameters defined in the previous section and computed along the main diagonal of the map in fig.2.

CONCLUSIONS

Experiments carried out up to now show that the features $\bar{\mathbf{v}}$, σ, $\mathbf{d^1}$, $\mathbf{d^2}$ and all the others defined above are not sufficient to solve the problem of characterizing hand-written numeral classes since they give only global information on the shape distortion.

To solve this problem other features must be take into account. Some observations can help to select them. For instance by looking at fig.3 the type of forces which determine the deformations among plane curves in the same class, can be discovered by means of a study of the dynamic of the points composing the plane curves. In order to do this, not only the behaviour of the vectors which belong to the same velocity field, but also the relationship among different frames must be investigated. To this purpose two approaches can be developed. One concerns the study of the dynamic point by point; the other takes advantage of the observation that the deformation of the shapes can be considered as the effect of forces applied to the arc of the plane curve(exactly those limited between zero-crossing points of the velocity field vectors, see fig.3), and concerns the uses of the cord vibration model.

228

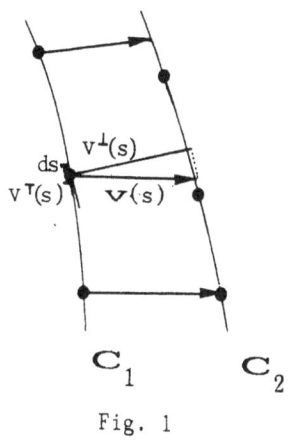

Fig. 1

Fig. 2   Plane curves obtained by the hand-written numeral three
at the center of the map changing the phases of the first
and second Fourier descriptor.

Table 1

	h	g	f	c	d	c	b	a	q*	p	o	n	m	l	k	j
Θ/c_{1L}	0.2570	0.2085	0.0652	0.1797	0.1097	0.0720	0.0685	0.0941	0.2932	0.2264	0.2844	0.0916	0.0948	0.1527	0.1070	0.1212
$d_{|\cdot|}$	1.9818	1.7388	2.1728	2.1290	1.8233	1.6171	1.8897	1.9562	1.6680	1.3826	1.6466	2.1399	2.2714	2.1511	2.0858	2.1363
$d_{\sphericalangle}$	-0.2776	-0.4878	-0.1597	0.0036	0.1094	-0.1568	-0.0808	-0.1112	-0.1421	-0.2541	-0.1254	-0.0025	-0.1644	-0.4605	-0.4239	-0.2693
$\sigma_{|\cdot|}$	0.1195	-0.1570	0.1255	0.1144	0.1228	0.1411	0.1261	0.1116	0.1187	0.1425	0.1330	0.1076	0.1157	0.1563	0.1502	0.1154
$\sigma_{\sphericalangle}$	0.1521	0.1469	0.1684	0.1808	0.1901	0.1709	0.0663	0.0651	0.1439	0.1418	0.1395	0.1343	0.1210	0.0982	0.1229	0.1439
$\bar{v}_x$	-0.5995	-0.8472	-0.8590	-1.0024	-0.9885	-0.7285	-0.4860	-2.2967	-0.1424	0.0668	0.3211	0.7171	0.8174	0.6927	0.3813	-0.1128
$\bar{v}_y$	0.4050	0.4083	0.4678	0.3847	0.0264	-0.3203	-0.5863	-0.6734	-0.5625	-0.6054	-0.5924	-0.3358	-0.1305	-0.1935	0.0350	0.2765
$d^{1}_{|\cdot|}$	0.2759	0.2222	0.2031	0.2641	0.2391	0.2061	0.1935	0.1953	0.2395	0.2105	0.2419	0.2465	0.2240	0.2353	0.2343	0.2401

$$d_{|\cdot|} = \overline{|\mathbf{v}(s)|} = \frac{1}{c_{1L}}\int_{C_1} |\mathbf{v}(s)|\,ds;$$

$$d^{1}_{|\cdot|} = \overline{\left|\frac{\partial \mathbf{v}(s)}{\partial s}\right|} = \frac{1}{c_{1L}}\int_{C_1}\left|\frac{\partial \mathbf{v}(s)}{\partial s}\right|ds;$$

$$d^{2}_{|\cdot|} = \overline{\left|\frac{\partial^2 \mathbf{v}(s)}{\partial s^2}\right|} = \frac{1}{c_{1L}}\int_{C_1}\left|\frac{\partial^2 \mathbf{v}(s)}{\partial s^2}\right|ds;$$

$$d_{\sphericalangle} = \overline{\sphericalangle \mathbf{v}(s)} = \frac{1}{c_{1L}}\int_{C_1}\sphericalangle \mathbf{v}(s)\,ds;$$

$$d^{1}_{\sphericalangle} = \overline{\sphericalangle \frac{\partial \mathbf{v}(s)}{\partial s}} = \frac{1}{c_{1L}}\int_{C_1}\sphericalangle \frac{\partial \mathbf{v}(s)}{\partial s}\,ds;$$

$$d^{2}_{\sphericalangle} = \overline{\sphericalangle \frac{\partial^2 \mathbf{v}(s)}{\partial s^2}} = \frac{1}{c_{1L}}\int_{C_1}\left(\sphericalangle \frac{\partial^2 \mathbf{v}(s)}{\partial s^2}\right)ds;$$

$$\sigma_{|\cdot|} = \frac{1}{c_{1L}}\left(\int_{C_1}\left||\mathbf{v}(s)| - \overline{|\mathbf{v}(s)|}\right|^2 ds\right)^{1/2}$$

$$\sigma_{d^{1}_{|\cdot|}} = \frac{1}{c_{1L}}\left(\int_{C_1}\left|\left|\frac{\partial \mathbf{v}(s)}{\partial s}\right| - d^{1}_{|\cdot|}\right|^2 ds\right)^{1/2}$$

$$\sigma_{d^{2}_{|\cdot|}} = \frac{1}{c_{1L}}\left(\int_{C_1}\left|\left|\frac{\partial^2 \mathbf{v}(s)}{\partial s^2}\right| - d^{2}_{|\cdot|}\right|^2 ds\right)^{1/2}$$

$$\sigma_{\sphericalangle} = \frac{1}{c_{1L}}\left(\int_{C_1}\left|\sphericalangle \mathbf{v}(s) - d_{\sphericalangle}\right|^2 ds\right)^{1/2}$$

$$\sigma_{d^{1}_{\sphericalangle}} = \frac{1}{c_{1L}}\left(\int_{C_1}\left|\sphericalangle \frac{\partial \mathbf{v}(s)}{\partial s} - d^{1}_{\sphericalangle}\right|^2 ds\right)^{1/2}$$

$$\sigma_{d^{2}_{\sphericalangle}} = \frac{1}{c_{1L}}\left(\int_{C_1}\left|\sphericalangle \frac{\partial^2 \mathbf{v}(s)}{\partial s^2} - d^{2}_{\sphericalangle}\right|^2 ds\right)^{1/2}$$

$$\bar{v}_x = \frac{1}{c_{1L}}\int_{C_1} v_x(s)\,ds$$

$$\bar{v}_y = \frac{1}{c_{1L}}\int_{C_1} v_y(s)\,ds$$

$$\sigma_{\bar{v}_x} = \frac{1}{c_{1L}}\left(\int_{C_1}\left|v_x(s) - \bar{v}_x\right|^2 ds\right)^{1/2}$$

$$\sigma_{\bar{v}_y} = \frac{1}{c_{1L}}\left(\int_{C_1}\left|v_y(s) - \bar{v}_y\right|^2 ds\right)^{1/2}$$

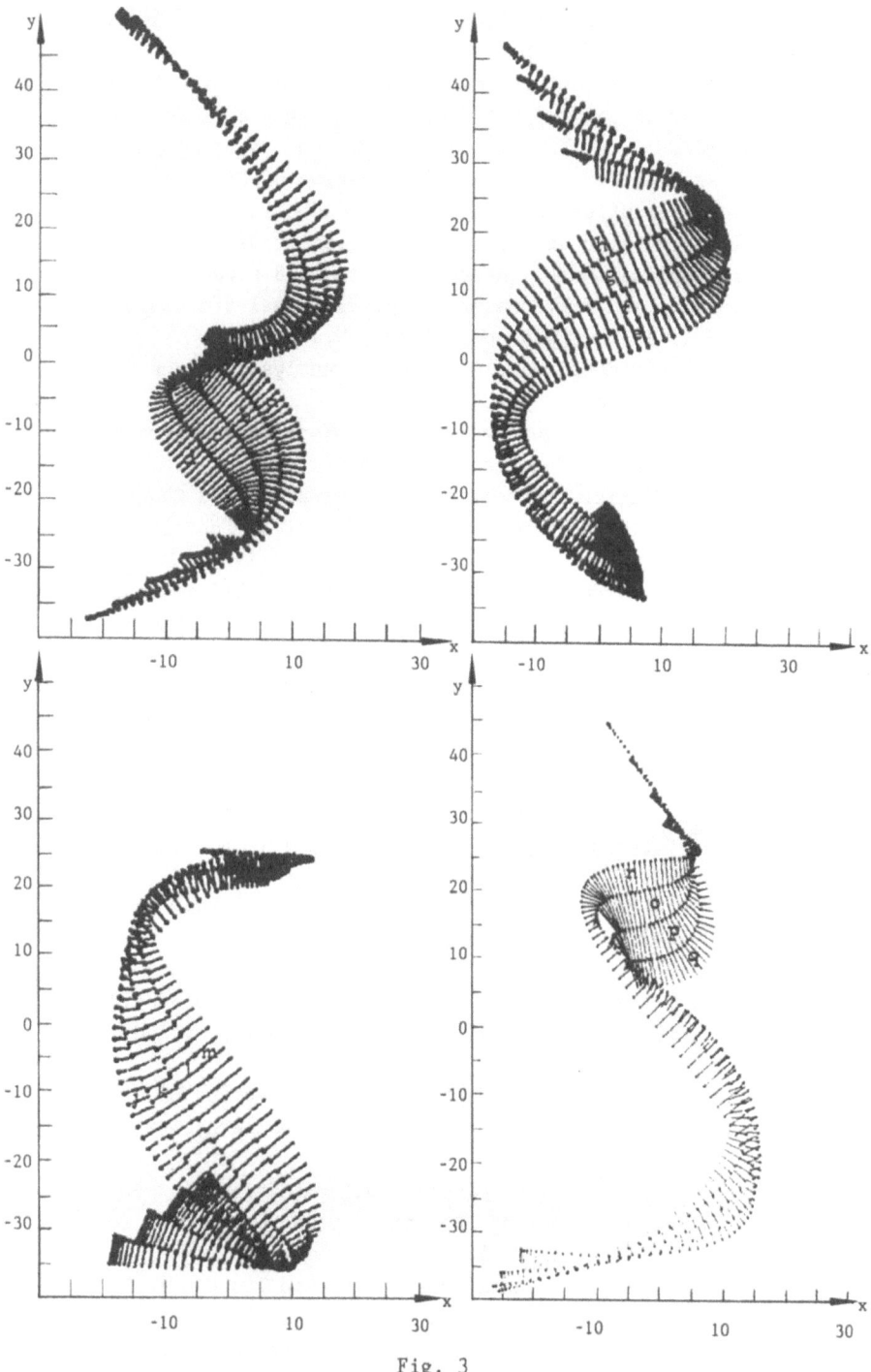

Fig. 3

REFERENCES

[1] S.Impedovo et al.;" A Fourier Descriptor Set for Non-stylized Numerals .", IEEE Transaction on System Man and Cybernetics, Vol. SMC-8, Aug. 1978, pp.640-645 .

[2] S.Impedovo;" Power Pattern Resolution in Human Vision ",Proc. SPIE 85, Application of Artificial Intelligence II,Vol. 548, pp. 263-268 .

[3] L.R.Rabiner,B.Gold;" Theory and Application of Digital Signal Processing.",Prentice Hall Inc. Englewood Cliffs, N.J.1975.

[4] V.Cappellini, A.G.Constantinides,P.Emiliani;" Digital Filters and their Applications ." Academic Press 1978 London.

[5] A.V.Oppenheim and R.W.Schafer;" Digital Signal Processing ", Prentice-Hall Inc. ,Englewood Cliffs , N.J. 1975.

[6] A.E.Taylor;"Introduction to Functional Analysis", John-Wiley and Sons inc., London.

[7] L.Schwartz;" Analyse-Deuxième Partie. Topologie Generale et Analyse Fonctionnelle",Hermann 1970 Paris.

[8] G.Granlund;" Fourier Preprocessing for Hand-Printed Character Recognition." ,IEEE Trans. Comp., Vol. C.21-3, pp. 195-201, Feb. 1972.

[9] E.Person and K.S.Fu;" Shape Discrimination Using Fourier Descriptors." ,IEEE Trans. Syst., Man, Cybern.,Vol. SMC-7,n.3 pp. 170-179, Mar. 1977 .

[10]S.Impedovo et al.;" Interactive System for Hand-Written Numerals Classification Based on Fourier Descriptors ". Proc. of the International Conference on " Image Analysis and Processing ". PAVIA 22-24 Oct. 1980 pp. 135-139.

[11]S.K. Parui,D.Dutta Majumder;" A New Definition of Shape Similarity."Pattern Recognition Letters, Vol.1, n. 1, pp. 37-42 , 1982.

[12]S.K. Parui,D.Dutta Majumder;" Some Similarity Measures for Open Curves."Pattern Recognition Letters,Vol.1,n.3,pp.129-134 1983 .

[13]J.Sklansky;"Pattern Recognition.Introduction and Foundations" Dowden, Hatchinson and Ross Inc. 1973, John Wiley and Sons inc.-London.

[14]H.Wallach;" On Preceived Identity:1. the direction of motion of straight lines." In On perseption(ed. H.Wallach).New York: Quadrangle 1976.

[15]C.I.Fennema,W.B.Thompson;"Velocity Determination in Scenes Containing Several Moving Objects." Comp. Graph. and Image Processing 9, 1979 ,pp.301-315.

[16]D.Marr,S.Ullman;"Directional Selectivity and Its Use in Early Visual Processing.",Proc. R. Soc.Lond.B 211, 1981, pp.151-180

[17]E.H.Adelson, & J.A.Movshon;" Phenomenal Coherence of Moving Visual Patterns ." Nature,Lond. 300, 1982, pp. 523-525.

[18]T.Poggio;" Visual Algorithms." In Physical and Biological Processing of Images", (ed. O.J.Braddick & A. C. Sleigh) Berlin : Springer - Verlag , 1983.

[19]A.L.Yuille;" The Smoothest Velocity Field and Taken Matching Schemes.", M.I.T. Artif.Intell.Lab.Memo 724, 1983.

[20]E.C.Hildreth;" The Computation of the Velocity Field .",
    Proc. R. Soc. Lond. B 221, 1984, pp. 189-220.

[21]H.H.Nagel;" Recent Advances in Image Sequence Analysis"
    Premier Colloque Image - Traitment, Synthèse, Technologie
    et Application; Biarritz - Mai 1984.

[22]R.K.P.Horn and B.G.Schunck; " Determining Optical Flow " ,
    Artificial Intelligence 17, 1981, pp. 185-203 .

[23]J.M.Prager,M.A.Arbib;" Computing the Optical Flow: The Match
    Algorithm and Prediction ", Computer Vision, Graphics and
    Image Processing n.24, 1983, pp. 271-304.

[24]S.Impedovo; " Plane Curve Classification Through Fourier
    Descriptors. An Application to Arabic Hand-Written Numeral
    Recognition ",IEEE Computer Society Press. Proc. of the 7-th
    Int.Conf.on PATTER RECOGNITION Vol.2, Aug.1984,pp.1069-1072.

[25]S.Impedovo et al.;"Surface Detection Algorithm in Three-
    Dimensional Complex-Space." Cybernetic System:Recognition,
    Learning, Self-Organization. Edit by E.R.Caianello and G.
    Musso.Research Studies Press LTD.J.W.and S.Inc. 1984,pp 157-
    168 .

[26]A.N.Kolmogorov and S.V.Fomin;" Elementy Teorii Funktsij i
    Funktsional' Nogo Analiza ", Copyright by Nauka, Moskov
    U.R.S.S. Cap. VII Sec.1.

[27]W.Rudin;" Functional Analysis ",New York : McGraw-Hill,1973

[28]E.C.Hildreth;" The Measurement of Visual Motion",A.C.M.
    distinguished dissertation series ,Cambridge , Massachusetts:
    M.I.T. Press.

EXTENDING PROLOG FOR A ROBOTIC ENVIRONMENT

A. De Santis *, A. Guercio*, S. Levialdi* and G. Tortora*

* Dipartimento di Informatica ed Applicazioni, Università di
Salerno
* Dipartimento di Matematica, Università di Roma

INTRODUCTION

Within a robotic environment where both a mechanical manipulator
and an artificial eye must cooperate in order to perform a well specified task
(perhaps a changing one in time) the software environment and
programming language play a crucial role in the design and
implementation of the control strategies. For this reason both from the area
of PR and AI many suggestions have been proposed in order to have
convenient software tools to help in writing, testing and debugging
programs that must operate within a robotic environment.

In a preliminary paper[1], a suggestion was made to extend the Prolog
interpreter in order to cope both with the input from a vision sensor (e.g. a
telecamera) and a controlled manipulator (e.g. a mechanical eye) so as to
build up experimentally a database originated from the sensory inputs and,
next, a conceptual framework, deduced from the previous data base. The first
database was named Perceptual Data Base whilst the second one was called
Conceptual Data Base and may be considered as equivalent to the knowledge
base currently used in expert systems technology.

In many practical applications the informations collected from the
sensors are not sufficient for the full planning and execution of the task so
that it might be necessary to retrieve and infer new data from the
Conceptual Data Base. Moreover new data may also be collected from the
environment if a particular situation demands it; in this case the sensors
will be oriented towards the acquisition of information to achieve
completeness. In order to achieve the expected facilities we have extended
the existing Prolog by means of a built-in predicate which will be tested for
contextual compatibility (i.e. for the particular scenario which is present
during the activity) and also by another predicate which is designed for the
practical execution of the allowed and useful actions.

In the next section we will describe such extensions and also, in the end, include a practical example of their utilization.

INFORMATION ACQUISITION

For each particular task to be achieved by the arm-eye system a number of hierarchical actions on objects may be considered, recursively until a basic one, which is performed on primary inputs called atoms. This chain of events may be represented as follows:

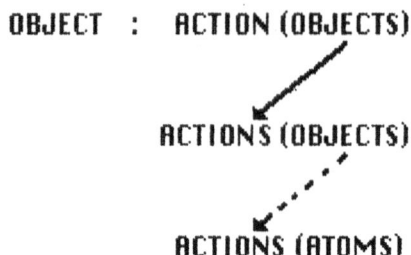

and is obtained by an analysis of the task according to the actual situation as observed by the sensors. Should this situation change, then the chain of events may be modified accordingly.

Referring to figure 1 we may see that artificial sensors will provide signals which are a sampled version of the natural scene via tactile and visual inputs. Such signals must be connected into useful and usable information so translating them into the Prolog facts framework [2,3]. In order to do this, every detected feature will be transformed into Prolog facts by means of a special program; the set of all registered facts is the basis of the perceptual information as directly acquired by the artificial sensors.

An external natural scene may be described by a human skilled operator in terms of basic concepts which both model and describe the underlying principles and mechanisms involved in the task performance. The contribution of such conceptual knowledge is reflected in the build-up of the Conceptual Data Base that will evolve by two mechanisms: 1) by new situations to be solved and 2) by human conceptual inferences.
The second mechanism may, in the future, be substituted by an expert system.

Since this software environment is Prolog oriented, the data base will be written as a Prolog-like program. Finally the synergism between the Perceptual and the Conceptual Data Bases will produce those control signals which will enable the system to execute the task according to the last input signals received and the updated conceptual inference as suggested by man. Should the scene change, another mechanism may be provided that may either stop the current execution or, in a more sophisticated version, acknowledge the differences and devise a new strategy.

THE PROLOG EXTENSIONS

The suggested extensions arise from the needs to: a) comply with the

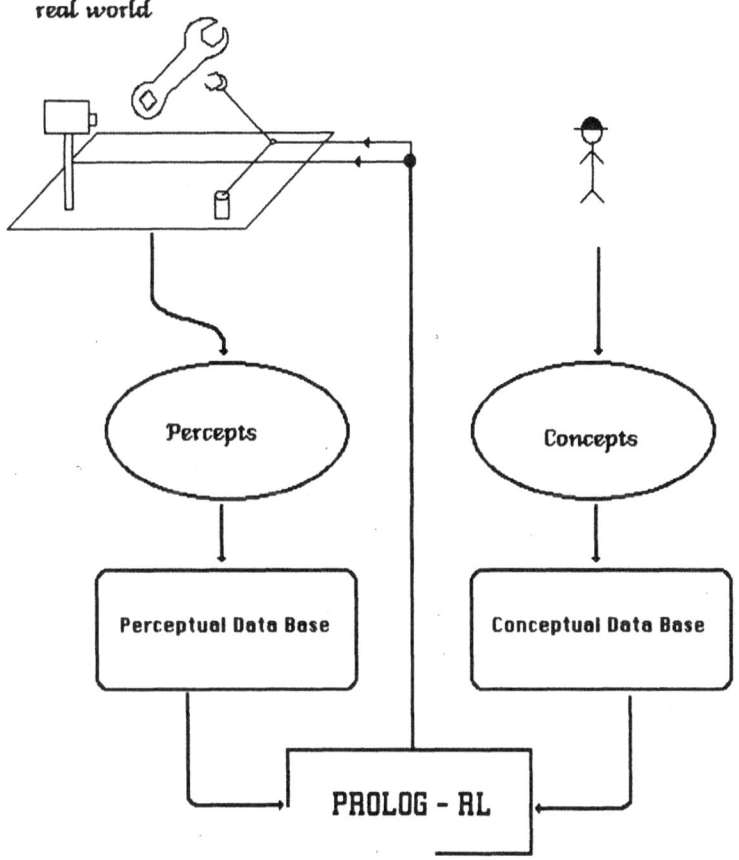

real world

Percepts

Concepts

Perceptual Data Base

Conceptual Data Base

PROLOG - RL

fig . 1 . Artificial sensors will provide signals which are a sampled
version of the natural scene .

robotic environment and therefore enrich the language with the natural operations for such tasks, i. e. actions; b) use and capitalize on the inference mechanism to validate only compatible actions; c) enable execution of those actions which are both compatible and derive from the last "snapshot" taken from the scene. We will now describe each one of those suggested extensions in order to enable a full understanding of our approach.

So as to introduce the operator actions we will firstly note that such actions may either be an elementary operation or a sequence of operations also included within an expression. The following recursive definition may be used:

1. (A_1)
2. $A_1 \, \hat{} \, A_2$
3. $A_1 \, , \, A_2$

1, 2 and 3 are actions, where A_1 and A_2 are elementary actions, " $\hat{}$ " is a logical parallel-AND and " , " is a logical sequential-AND. Finally, any combination of 1, 2 and 3 is also an action.

A rule in Prolog-RL has two components, a head followed by a body, separated by the symbol :- . The head will contain either a fact or an action and the body, as in standard Prolog, a sequence of facts. Whenever an action is present in the head of a statement, Prolog-RL will try to satisfy the subgoals contained in the body backtracking until all subgoals have been analyzed. As a simple example we will consider the implementation of the actions **ROTATE** and **MOVE_FAST** (in the head) for the circumstances in which an animal (an elephant) is close to the robot (in the body).

ROTATE(180°) , **MOVE_FAST** :- **elephant** (X) , **range** (X,close).

which stands for the combined actions of rotation and movement whenever both an elephant exists and its distance from the robot is under a threshold (close).

The second extension is the addition of a built-in predicate **next_action**(L) where L is the list of expressions which represents the next executable action (not necessarily to be executed).
Prolog-RL will search for the first satisfied clause in the Conceptual Data Base and the its head will be returned and assigned to L.
One of the fallouts of the introduction of the **next_action** predicate is its use as convenient testing and debugging tool in large programs.

The third and final extension consists in a second built-in predicate **"activate "** which will allow the execution of the next possible action on the basis of the previous action evaluation and contemporary scene status.
An action will be triggered by answering to the question mark (system prompt) with the **activate** predicate, which is totally equivalent to the invocation of the lastly computed executable action.
In fact,

? - activate

is equivalent to

238

? – b

where **b** is the output from the **next_action** predicate.

EXAMPLE

So as to clarify the mechanics of Prolog-RL a scenario will be given (similar to the one given by Maletz[4]) and should be considered not for its realistic value but merely for its pedagogical purpose.

Let us start by describing the natural scene which contains the following objects: humans, ducks, rats and an elephant which will be observed by a telecamera and followed (or not) by a mechanical arm.
The tasks to be accomplished are the following ones:
to ignore humans and ducks, escape from the elephant (if it is too near) and follow the rats.
By means of the acquisition devices the following features may be extracted and logically combined in a Prolog fact.
The object (X) size, which may be written **size** (X,K) where K may be large or small, the object legs number, **legs** (X,L) with L a number that may be 2 or 4, the object distance to the centre of the scene, **range** (X,Y) with Y being close or far.
All the above data constitutes the Perceptual Data Base to which the conceptual knowledge must be integrated.

> **human** (X) :– **legs** (X, 2) , **size** (X, large).
> **duck** (X) :– **legs** (X, 2) , **size** (X, small).
> **rat** (X) :– **legs** (X, 4) , **size** (X, small).
> **elephant** (X) :– **legs** (X, 4) , **size** (X, large).

According to the wanted behaviour of the manipulator we will request the following actions:

HALT   will stop the arm movement
ROTATE (30˚)   will swing around the camera position by a specified angle
MOVE_FAST   will rapidly shift the arm position towards the centre of the scene or away from it (note that the centre of the scene is the target of the telecamera)
ZOOM_IN (X)   will position the arm in correspondence to the object seen by the telecamera at a given time.

The Prolog-RL program containing and satisfying the above requirements will be the one given below.

a)   **ROTATE** (alfa) :– **human** (X) ; **duck** (X).
    (If the telecamera is pointed towards a human or a duck, rotate it by alfa degrees)
b)   **HALT ˆ ROTATE** (alfa) :– **elephant** (X) , **range** (X, far).
    (If an elephant is seen by the telecamera and its position is far then the arm is stopped and the telecamera is rotated)
c)   **ROTATE** (180˚) , **MOVE_FAST** :– **elephant** (X) , **range** (X, close).
    (If an elephant exists and it is close the telecamera is rotated and the arm is moved rapidly towards the position pointed by the telecamera)

d) **ZOOM_IN** (X) . **MOVE_FAST** :- **rat** (X).

(If the found object is a rat then the arm will follow it).

For a given scenario, including an elephant and a rat the Perceptual Data Base (PDB) contains the following facts:

1) **range** (1, far).
2) **legs** (1, 4).
3) **size** (1, large).
4) **range** (2, far).
5) **legs** (2, 4).
6) **size** (2, small).

For an action request, the question mark prompt will be answered by the **next_action** predicate. Only rules having an action in the head will be examined and the first clause in the Conceptual Data Base (CDB) will be analyzed. If the match is successfull, Prolog-RL will build up a list containing all the elementary commands required for the execution of the action. The first found clause is a) which fails (no match is obtained since neither a human nor a duck is present in the scene, (each subgoal calls its specification in the CDB to test for the presence of the object human or duck). The next, b) clause, will now be analyzed and this time a match will be found so validating the action contained in the head. The execution of such an action will be triggered only by the **activate** predicate. Moreover the c) clause when analyzed will not be satisfied whilst the d) clause is successfull.

As we have seen, Prolog was extended having in mind the new constraints and requirements imposed by a robotic environment, interactive dialogue and easy updating of new evidence that may affect the choice of future actions or movements in the scene.

REFERENCES

1. M. De Blasi, A. Guercio, S. Levialdi, G. Tortora, "Prolog-RL: a Proposal for a Task-oriented Language", MIMI 84, Int. Conf. on Mini and Micro Computers and their Applications, Bari, 1984, pp. 56-58.
2. W. F. Clocksin, C. S. Mellish, "Programming in Prolog", Springer-Verlag, Berlin, 1981.
3. K. L. Clark, S.A. Tarnlund, edits. "Logic Programming", APIC Studies in Data Processing, Academic Press, New York, 1982.
4. M. C. Maletz, "An Introduction to Multi-Robot Control using Production Systems", Proc. IEEE Symp. on Languages for Automation, Chicago, 1983, pp. 22-27.

DENSITY CURVES OF PROMETAPHASE CHROMOSOMES BY

SEMI-AUTOMATIC IMAGE PROCESSING

R. Bolzani, P. Battaglia and A. Forabosco

Chair of Histology and General Embryology
Institute of Human Anatomy
University of Modena
41100 Modena, Italy

The cytogenetic test is well suited for diagnosing chromosome abnormalities and is currently an irreplaceable instrument in preventative medicine programs fighting congenital malformations. Moreover, it is an important means for diagnosing neoplastic forms and monitoring the biological effects of environmental mutagens. These ample possibilities have led to a large demand for cytogenetic testing, which however cannot be readily met owing to the lengthy analysis procedure

Two solutions have been proposed to reduce the times required to perform the test: flow cytophotometry and the automatic analysis of the metaphase preparations. Activity in this latter field, which began in the early seventies, now includes several commercially available instruments consisting of image processors and a group of computer programs used for the routine analysis of metaphase chromosome preparations.

Techniques have recently been perfected to obtain prometaphasic chromosome preparations, which notably increase the degree of resolution of the test. The study of metaphasic chromosomes, while enabling the easy identification of all chromosomes and their possible numerical aberations, makes a precise definition of structural abnormalities difficult. Furthermore, the more subtle changes are not seen.

High resolution testing with prometaphasic chromosomes is important owing to the recent discovery of microcytogenetic chromosome pathologies such as retinoblastoma or Wilm's aniridia-tremor syndrome. Duchenne's muscular distrophy has also been shown to result from a submicroscopic deletion.

Naturally, this type of testing is not a routine diagnostic procedure and does not require the study of the entire metaphase but only of specific chromosomes.

The automation of prometaphasic chromosome analysis presents certain problems which make it completely different from the automatic cariotypization of metaphases. These chromosomes are more elongated and are often notably bent and overlapping. Furthermore, the greater definition of chromosomic bands requires high resolution digital conversion of the image, with high pixel to micron ratio. In fact, the spatial frequency pattern along a prometaphasic chromosome is notably greater than that in metaphase.

Not possessing a system capable of examining the entire metaphase at high resolution, we designed a procedure for high resolution analysis of individual chromosomes starting from their photographic image.

HARDWARE CONFIGURATION

Our system consists of a Tesak VDC 501 connected to a PDP 11/23 with two floppy disk drives and 10 MB hard disk. Images are acquired by means of a B/W TV camera, digitized with 256 grey levels and stored in RAM as a 512 X 512 pixel matrix. The operator interacts with the system by drawing lines or dots on the monitor with a light pen.

SOFTWARE

The microphotographic image is taken by means of a B/W telecamera. The image is then digitized and displayed on the monitor. The operator adjusts framing and focus directly on the digitized video image. After the set-up operation the image is stored. We employed a semi-automatic technique that requires the operator to identify the data pertaining to the segments forming the central axis of the chromosome with a light pen; the computer then generates the entire polygon. The number of segments of the polygon depends on the curvature of the chromosome.

To calculate the density curve along the length of the chromosome, the straightened image must first be re-constructed. The average density can then be calculated for each point of the segment that crosses the longitudinal axis. Straightening is achieved by dividing the image into perpendicular strips along the medial axis and then re-setting the strips on a straight axis. The average densities of the various strips establish the density curve of the chromosome.

Strictly speaking, it is not necessary to re-construct the straightened image since the averge density for each strip is sufficient. In effect, our program shows the whole chromosome image only if requested by the operator and by default provides the chromosome density curve.

The density curve is used to identify the various bands on the chromosome. This is achieved by filtering the curve with a digital band-pass filter. The filter is realized by using a two-stage moving averages function. The first removes the high frequency component. Since the moving average function is a low pass filter, the second provides the low frequency component supplying the filter output when subtracted from the signal. The resulting formula is:

$$D_i = \frac{1}{2n+1} \sum_{-n}^{+n} D_{i+k} - \frac{1}{2n+1} \sum_{-m}^{+m} D_{i+j} \qquad \text{,with n=7 and m=17.}$$

To reduce phase error, each stage is applied twice. The resulting bandwith of the filter ranges from 21.7 to 52.6 pixels. Lastly, the maximum values, representing the position and height of the identified bands, are found from the filtered curve.

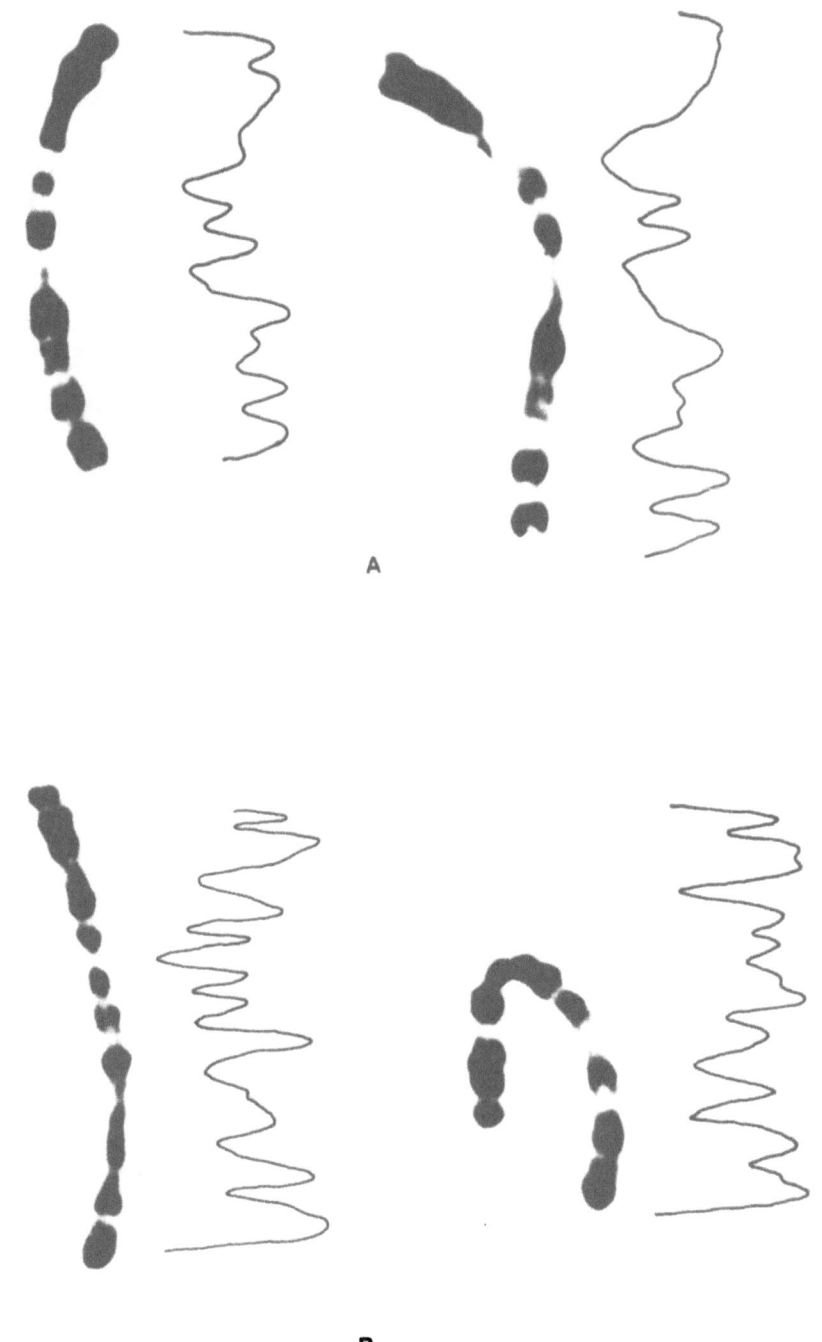

Fig.1. Chromosome number 1 (a) and 2 (b) and their density profiles.

CONCLUSIONS

The density curves of metaphasic chromosomes are used to identify the bands as density peaks, the presence and relative position of which can be utilized to compare homologous chromosomes. Experiments are currently being carried out on another type of comparison which, starting from the density curves of two homologous chromosomes, calculates their correlation coefficient. For this purpose the density profiles are normalized in length by linear interpolation.

This method has been applied with satisfactory results to the automatic cariotypization of metaphases and should be particularly useful for comparing two homologous chromosomes of the same metaphase.

REFERENCES
Piper J. Interactive image enhancement and analysis of prometaphase chromosomes and their band patterns. Anal. Quant. Cytology IV, 3:233-240, 1982.
Piper J. Image restoration and interactive processing for anylsis of high resolution banded chromosomes. In: Proc. 1st Int. Symp. Medical Imaging and Image Interpretation. Oct. 1982, pp 24-29, Berlin.

CLUSTER ANALYSIS OF NUCLEAR PORES IN MAMMALIAN CELLS

G.Vernazza and S.B.Serpico

Department of Biophysical and
Electronic Engineering
University of Genoa, Italy

INTRODUCTION

The number of classes included in a set of data and the distribution of these classes in a data structure constitute a great deal of information about the data structure. Having obtained clusters of sample points, one can derive statistical information on each cluster and interpret the qualitative features of the system represented by the data. The clustering approach becomes a very important tool when no a-priori knowledge is available [1]. If the data vectors form well structured clusters, i.e. compact and separate from each other, a simple clustering procedure can yield clear-cut and unique clusters. If the distribution of the pattern vectors is near uniform, the obtained clusters must be validated and analysed according to different classifications. Most practical cases lie between these two situations.

The purpose of this paper is to extend cluster analysis to nuclear pores in mammalian cells and to develop some euristic rules to prove the validity of the selected clusters. Pore complexes are generally assumed to be the sites of molecular and ionic exchanges between nucleus and cytoplasm [2]; they are not distributed at random, but located at some specific points. In fact, in different functional states, sudden changes in pore pattern and number have been detected.

In this paper the Minimal Spanning Tree method (MST) is applied to pore complex clustering in order to identify the related natural classes and to demonstrate that the distribution of these classes is strictly related to the cell activity and that their number is close to the chromosome one.

MATERIALS AND METHODS

Isolated rat liver nuclei were treated by the freeze-etching tecnique at Istituto di Anatomia (University of Bologna, Italy) and the electron micrographs of freeze-etched envelopes were acquired and analysed by the ACTA system, built and installed in the Dept. of Biophysical and Electronic Engineering, University of Genoa, Italy [3]. The ACTA system is based on a TV camera (Plumbicon tube) and a frame memory of 512x512x8 bits; the system is interfaced with an HP 1000 minicomputer for the control of the ACTA, and, through a serial link, with a DEC VAX750 computer for post-processing purposes. Four sub-images of each picture were acquired in order to achieve a sufficient spatial resolution; after the image segmentation phase, each pore corresponds to a black hole, while the background (membrane) is white.

For each electron micrographs two main hypotheses were used:
a) each picture is related to a hemisphere;
b) the unknown hemisphere is a mirror image of the measured one.
The former hypothesis allows one to simplify the distance computation and corresponds to a first approximation typically confirmed by biological measures; the latter hypothesis allows one to obtain the whole map without 'border effects'. The two assumptions were introduced to determine the total number of pores and the distribution on each nuclear membrane.

In order to evaluate the spatial distribution of the nuclear pores, a cluster analysis has been performed, in which the natural clusters are the spatial grouping of the pores on the membrane. According to this approach the 2D feature space corresponds directly to the nuclear surface and the features are the pore coordinates on this surface.

Many methods can be used for cluster analysis; we selected two different methods (ISODATA[4] and Minimal Spanning Tree[5]) to obtain independent results in order to compare them. While ISODATA seeks classical cluster configurations according to statistical properties, MST can also find laminar clusters. Some results obtained by the ISODATA method are reported in[6]; in this paper we only use the MST approach.

MST algorithm allows to identify the tree whose edge branches have the minimum lengths and connect all pores. Each edge length is the Euclidean distance between the two connected pores and it is calculated on the spherical surface.

By cutting all MST tree branches whose lengths are greater than, or equal to, a threshold length 'd_0', a partition of the original tree in Nc subtrees is obtained; according to this method each subtree is a cluster and Nc is the total number of clusters.

By decreasing the threshold value 'd_0' from the maximum branch length to zero, Nc ranges between 1 and the total number of pores. In this way a hierarchical clustering is obtained. Denoting by '$\overline{d}$' the mean length of MST edges and by 'k' the ratio $d_0/\overline{d}$, a curve of Nc versus k can be obtained.

Some specific procedures have been used in the calculation of the cluster centres and of the covariance matrices on the spherical surface to verify the point distribution for each cluster. The cluster centres, which can be regarded as the points that minimize the sum of the square distances from the related cluster points, were computed by means of an iterative algorithm based on the gradient function. To evaluate the covariance matrices, for each cluster a new 2D coordinate reference system was introduced on the equatorial plane parallel to the plane which is tangent to the spherical surface in the cluster centre. The coordinates of the projection of all the cluster points on the equatorial plane were used for the computation.

RESULTS

The pore distributions on the nuclear membranes of rat liver cells during different metabolic activities, after a freeze-etching process, are shown in Fig.1.

Possible changes in metabolic activity can modify the pore complex distribution and the pore number[7]. One stimulated nucleus (with phospholipid vesicles) and three unstimulated nuclei (controls) were analysed.

Fig.2 reports the number of clusters (Nc) versus the threshold 'k'.

Fig.3 shows the number of clusters Nc per unit k derivative, as a function of k.

The minimum and maximum numbers of pores versus the k value were

Table 1

Image	pore n.	k	n.clust.(>3pts)	n.clust.(>2pts)
n.1 (normal)	580	1.4550	14	28
n.2 (normal)	788	1.3295	22	24
n.3 (normal)	514	1.3500	22	24
n.4 (treated)	398	1.5650	22	24

computed for the clusters of each image (Fig.4).

This heuristic approach yields results easy to interpret whenever applied to a simple distribution of clusters, as verified on test images.

In such cases it is possible to find a wide range of k values for which the clustering results don't vary. The optimum k value is likely to be included in this range. When analysing more complex cluster distributions, as in our case, it is impossible to find a wide range of k values with the above mentioned property, so that it is advisable to look for discontinuity points.

(a)

(b)

Fig.1. Freeze-etch micrographs of a nuclear membrane: a) before stimulation; b) after stimulation

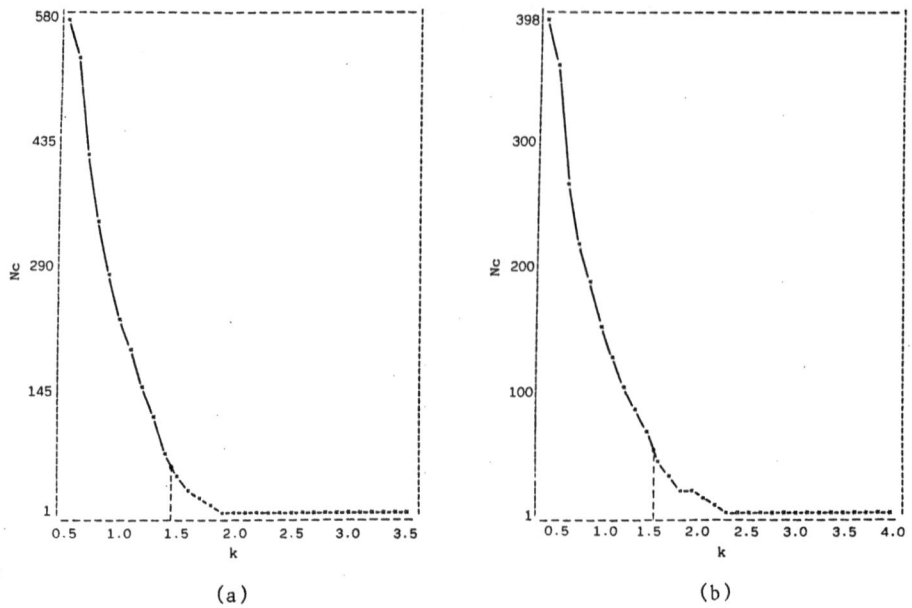

Fig.2. Number of clusters Nc versus the threshold k for two nuclei: a) normal; b) stimulated

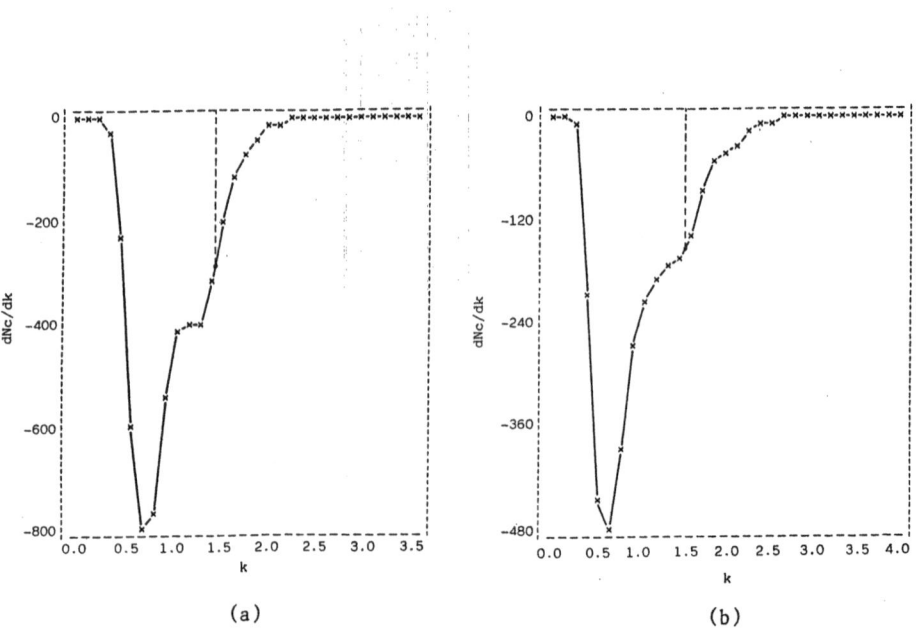

Fig.3. dNc/dk versus k for a normal nucleus (a) and a stimulated one (b)

The curve of the cluster number versus k (Nc(k)) presents a point of sudden change in the slope (Fig.2). It's easier to identify this point by considering the curve dNC/dk (Fig.3); for the same k value a sudden change in the maximum number of points per cluster is also detected (Fig.4). This situation occurs in each of the four images, and the k value obtained in this way gives about the same number of meaningful clusters (Table 1).

In the last two columns the number of clusters with more than 3 and 2 points are reported. The k value given in Table 1 are denoted by dotted lines in the figures.

This preliminary result shows that, unlike the numbers of pores, the number of clusters doesn't depend on the metabolic activity; it also demonstrates that the number of clusters is similar to the number of chromosomes. These results support a circumstantial linkage between the highly ordered structure of interphase chromatin DNA and the formation of individual metaphase chromosomes, possibly resulting from the collapse of localized rope-like chromatin fibres anchored to the nuclear envelope[6].
An additional analysis was performed on the clusters obtained by the k values given in Table 1. The calculation of the cluster centres allowed us to produce both the histograms of the distances between the cluster points and the cluster centre (Fig.5), and the histograms of the distances between all the couples of cluster centres (Fig.6). Unfortunately, lack of a sufficient number of images, due to the low efficiency and difficulties related to the freeze-etching technique, doesn't permit a reliable statistical investigation of these histograms. By examining the various covariance matrices and correlation coefficients, computed as described in the previous section, quite different values can be found for the clusters. The mean values of the correlation coefficients of the clusters ranges between 0.4 and 0.5 in the four images, showing no general tendency for laminar clusters (the absolute value of each correlation coefficient was considered).

DISCUSSION

This paper proves the usefulness of applying Pattern Recognition methods to the biological problem of the nuclear pore complexes. The results obtained are not conclusive because of the lack of a sufficient number of data to analyse. Nevertheless, they are quite interesting and involve many biological consequences. A larger amount of data would allow more statistical analyses, in particular, regarding the distance distributions.

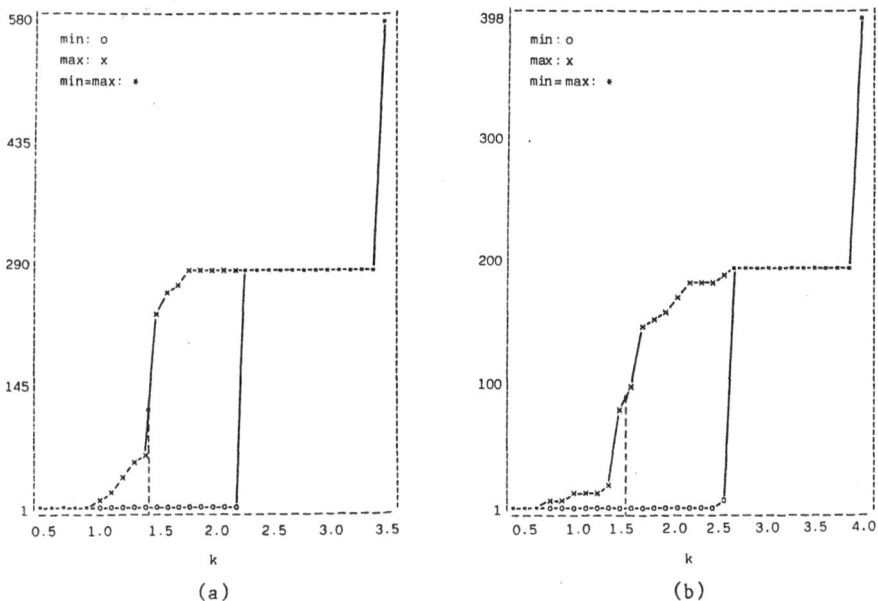

(a) (b)

Fig.4.Minimum and maximum numbers of points for the clusters of a normal nucleus (a) and a stimulated one (b).

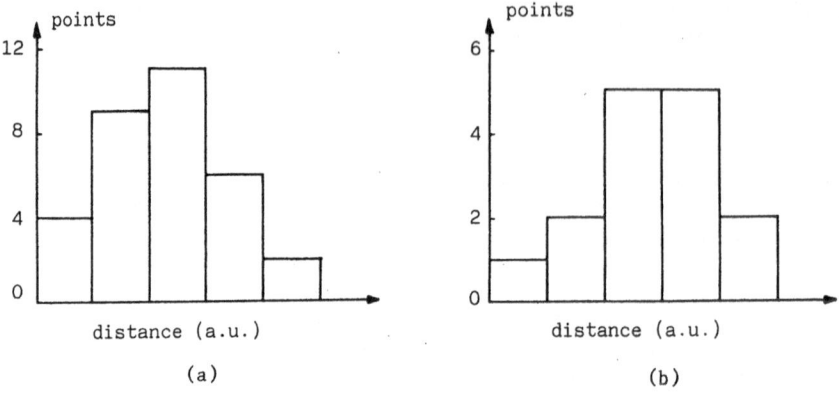

Fig.5. Distribution of the distances between the centre and the points of a typical cluster in a normal nucleus (a) and a stimulated one (b)

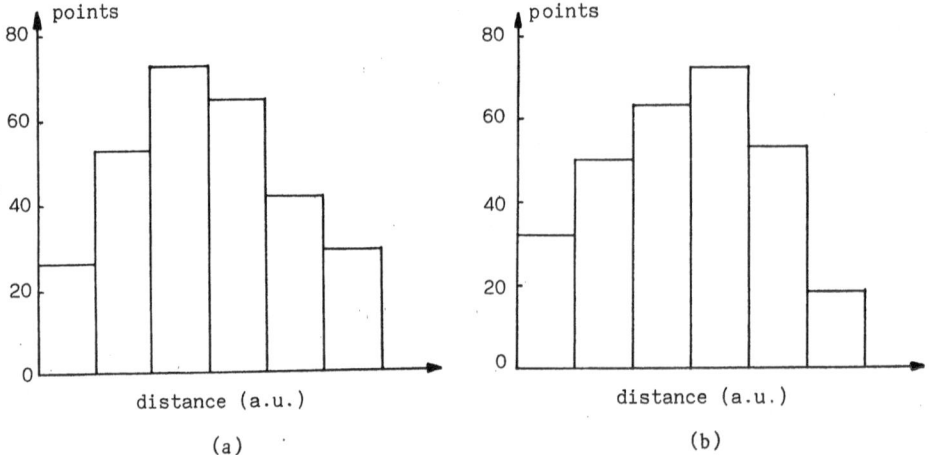

Fig.6. Distribution of the distances between all the couples of cluster centres in a normal nucleus (a) and a stimulated one (b)

REFERENCES

1. W. S. Meisel, "Computer-oriented approaches to pattern recognition," Academic Press, N.Y. (1972).
2. G. Maul, The nuclear and cytoplasmic pore complex: structure, dynamics, distribution and evolution., Int. Rev. Cytol. (suppl) 6:75 (1977).
3. F. Beltrame, A. Chiabrera, M. Grattarola, P. Guerrini, G. Parodi, D. Ponta, G. Vernazza and R. Viviani, ACTA: automated image analysis system for absorption fluorescence and phase contrast studies of cell images, 2nd ann. Conf. of the IEEE Eng. in Med. and Biol. Soc., Washington D.C. (1980).
4. J. T. Tou and R. C. Gonzalez, "Pattern recognition principles," Addison-Wesley Pub. Co., Reading, Massachussets (1974).
5. R. O. Duda and P. E. Hart, "Pattern classification and scene analysis," John Wiley, N.Y.(1973).
6. C. Nicolini, G. Vernazza, A. Chiabrera, I. N. Maraldi and S. Capitani, Nuclear pores and interphase chromatin: high resolution image analysis and freeze etching, J. Cell. Sci 72:75 (1984).
7. A. Manzoli, S. Capitani, et al., "Cell Growth," Ed. C. Nicolini, Plenum Press, N.Y. (1982).

INDUSTRIAL PARTS IDENTIFICATION BY MOMENT INVARIANTS

G. Biallo, L. Caponetti* and A. Distante**

* I.S.I. - Istituto di Scienza dell'Informazione - Bari
** I.E.S.I. - Istituto Elaborazione Segnali Immagini - Bari

ABSTRACT

This paper is concerned with automatic recognition of industrial parts from optical image. A method is described to recognize objects in a TV-image using moment invariants. Position and rotation of the object are derived from the first and second central moments.

This work has been supported by the National Research Council "Progetto Tecnologie Meccaniche".

INTRODUCTION

Some robot applications are in need of object manipulation and vision is very powerfull method of carrying information about these objects.

The most significant goal of a computer vision system is to identify the objects in a picture and to compute their position and orientation.

This paper is concerned with the recognition of objects such as complex mechanical parts using 2-D techniques.

The approach consists of image acquisition, preprocessing and object recognition. The most important problems of the image acquisition step are connected to the physical characteristics of the objects, the lighting conditions and the imaging system.

In fact image irradiance depends on the reflective properties of the object surfaces as well as on the illumination characteristics[1]. These reflective properties depend on its micro-structure and physical characteristics.

Object recognition is based on extraction of the intrinsic features. These features must be invariant with respect to traslation, rotation and size.

The features are generally descriptors that point out geometrical and regional characteristics of an image such as Fourier descriptors,

251

Hough descriptors, moment invariants and Topological descriptors (for example Eulero number).

This paper presents a system to recognize objects using geometrical features such as moment invariants and working under the following constraints:
- objects are two-dimensional and have similar microstructures;
- objects are stationary and no-overlapping;
- lighting conditions are controlled in order to have a reasonable contrast between objects and background;
- the TV-camera is fixed and its optic axis is perpendicular to the working plane.

VISION SYSTEM

The vision system consists of the following steps:
a) image acquisition;
b) image pre-processing;
c) object description using moments;
d) object recognition.

Image acquisition

The scene is observed from a standard direction of a Television Camera and converted into a grey-level image.

A Vidicon TV-Camera has been used to obtain a digitized picture (256x256 pixels of 256 grey-levels) of the observed object.

The object is placed on a working plane with dark surface and perpendicular to the optic axis of the TV-Camera. In this way the digitized image presents a reasonable contrast between the object and the background.

The lighting system consists of four lights placed in such manner that their axes form an angle of sixty degree with the working plane.

Image pre-processing

Image pre-processing consists of the following tasks:
1) The first task is to isolate object from background. A binary image is obtained by thresholding brightness values. Pixels are assigned one of the two possible values, 0 or 1, depending on whether the brightness is above or below some threshold value. This value is fixed if the lighting conditions are calibrated.
2) The second task is to extract boundary image using the gradient operator of Roberts and to detect the boundary coordinates using a border-following algorithm.

After this step contour boundaries of the object are labelled and coded in vectorial format. Number of the object borders and binary silhouette are also available.

Fig. 1 shows the results of the image pre-processing.

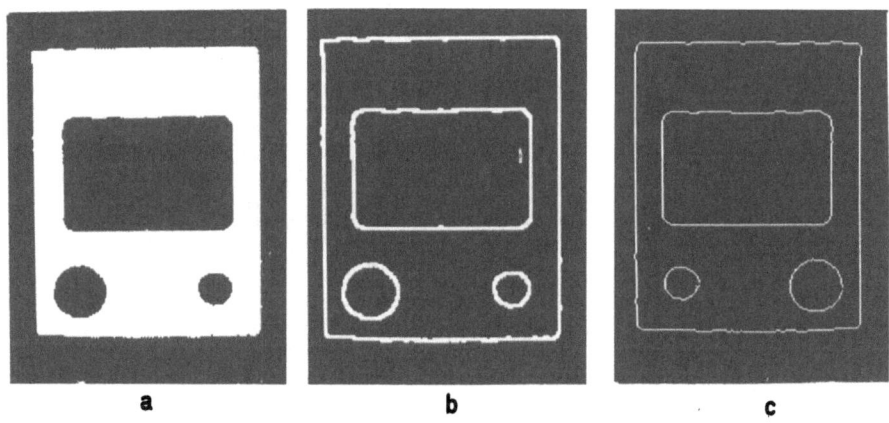

Fig. 1. a) Binary image; b) gradient image; c) contour image.

Object description using moments

In this step a geometrical description of the object is given using moment invariants[2].

Given a two-dimensional digital image $f(x,y)$ the moments of order $(p + q)$ can be expressed by the relation:

$$m_{pq} = \sum_x \sum_y (x-\overline{x})^p \ (y-\overline{y})^q \ f(x,y)$$

where x and y are the mean values of the image coordinates x and y. The point of coordinates equal to $\overline{x}$ and $\overline{y}$ is defined centroid of $f(x,y)$:

$$\overline{x} = \frac{m_{01}}{m_{00}} \qquad\qquad \overline{y} = \frac{m_{01}}{m_{00}}$$

The normalized central moments, denoted by n_{pq} are defined as

$$n_{pq} = \frac{m_{pq}}{m_{00}^{\gamma}} \qquad\qquad \gamma = \frac{(p+q)}{2} + 1$$

From the second and third moments a set of seven moment invariants can be derived. They are given by:

$$mi_1 = n_{20} + n_{02}$$

$$mi_2 = (n_{20} - n_{02})^2 + 4n_{11}^2$$

$$mi_3 = (n_{30} - 3n_{12})^2 + (3n_{21} - n_{03})^2$$

$$mi_4 = (n_{30} + n_{12})^2 + (n_{21} + n_{03})^2$$

$$mi_5 = (n_{30} - 3n_{12})(n_{30} + n_{12})[(n_{30} - n_{12})^2 - 3(n_{21} + n_{03})^2] +$$
$$(3n_{21} - n_{03})(n_{21} + n_{03})[3(n_{30} + n_{12})^2 - (n_{21} + n_{03})^2]$$

$$mi_6 = (n_{20} - n_{02})[(n_{30} + n_{12})^2 - (n_{21} + n_{03})^2] +$$
$$4n_{11}(n_{30} + n_{12})(n_{21} + n_{03})$$

$$mi_7 = (3n_{12} - n_{30})(n_{30} + n_{12})[n_{30} + n_{12})^2 - 3(n_{21} + n_{03})^2] +$$
$$(3n_{21} - n_{03})(n_{21} + n_{03})[3(n_{30} + n_{12})^2 - (n_{21} + n_{03})^2]$$

This set of moments has been shown to be invariant to translation, rotation and size[3, 5, 6].

The following parameters are also obtained in this step in order to give information about the object position and rotation:

- coordinates of the centroid to give information about the object translation;
- moment of inertia with respect to the origin given by the following relation:

$$m_0 = \sum_x \sum_y (x^2 + y^2) f(x, y)$$

The moment m_0 will be multiplied by a factor c^4 if the scale of the image $f(x, y)$ is changed by a factor c;

- principal axis of inertia given by the following relation:

$$tg^2\theta + \left(\frac{m_{20} - m_{02}}{m_{11}}\right) tg\theta - 1 = 0$$

The principal axis of inertia gives information about rotation of the object respect to a prototype[4].

The central moments of the image can be computed either from the image boundary or from the solid silhouette. The details of the image are better characterized by the moments computed from the boundary; the gross structural feature of the object can be characterized by those moments derived from the silhouette.

Object recognition

A data base of prototypes is build up in a learning phase. A prototype is created for each object to recognize using the steps previously described of image acquisition, pre-processing and object description.

Object recognition is performed by matching the description of observed object with the prototypes stored in the data set.

The position and rotation of the object is calculated using the first and second central moments. The position of the object is evaluated by the location of the centroid, while the rotation of the object in the image plane is defined by the axis of least inertia.

Centroid and axis of least inertia are derived from the solid silhouette.

RESULTS AND CONCLUSIONS

A set of fifty different industrial objects have been used to evaluate the methodology previously described.

Fig. 2 shows some industrial objects that have been acquired.

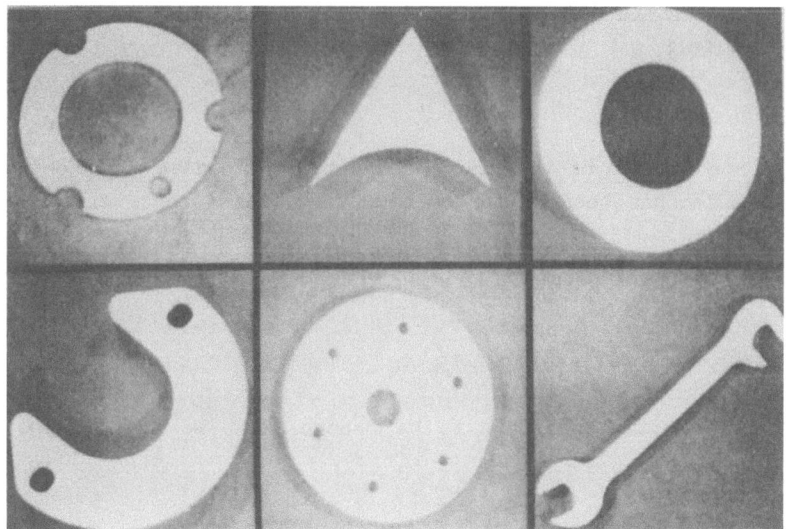

Fig. 2. Industrial objects

Each object to recognize has been acquired at different position and rotation.

A prototype has been created using the mean values of the features extracted from these images and has been inserted into a data base.

For example Tab. 1 shows the features of two different objects.

Table 1. Moment invariants

		Piece 9	Piece 15
track moments	mi_1	3.865876	3.935286
	mi_2	0.1151830	6.127955
	mi_3	0.2826739	7.382452
	mi_4	0.4449061	0.8440477
	mi_5	-4.0900752E-02	1.695131
	mi_6	0.1290046	1.871155
	mi_7	0.1523841	1.251279
silhouette moments	mi_1	0.2504621	0.3246374
	mi_2	1.3536486E-03	5.1612757E-02
	mi_3	3.2950287E-05	5.4551414E-03
	mi_4	1.2967376E-05	6.3744141E-04
	mi_5	1.5368047E-10	1.1372045E-06
	mi_6	-2.7659178E-07	1.4354692E-04
	mi_7	2.1961434E-10	3.4599998E-07

The recognition of the unknown object X, placed at a random position and orientation has been performed computing the distance from each data base prototype.

The objects which distance function $d(\bar{x},\bar{y})$ is internal in the interval

$$\left\{ \min\left[d(\bar{x},\bar{y})\right] \ , \ \min\left[d(\bar{x},\bar{y})+\delta\right] \right\}$$

are selected such as candidate to be recognized. Two different distance functions are used:
– mean square error

$$d_1(\bar{x},\bar{y}) = \sum_{i=1}^{n} (\bar{x}_i - \bar{y}_i)^2$$

– sum of absolute value differences

$$d_2(\bar{x},\bar{y}) = \sum_{i=1}^{n} (|\bar{x}_i - \bar{y}_i|)$$

For example, Fig. 3 shows the distance d_1 for boundary and silhouette moments of four objects acquired in random position. The value obtained from the silhouette appear to be less susceptible to the noise.

The function d_1 appear to be more discriminant and also is easier to implement that the function d_2.

The recognition process isn't influenced, in a considerable way, by the quantization noise of the image.

The classification ambiguity is less than 5% for the analysed objects.

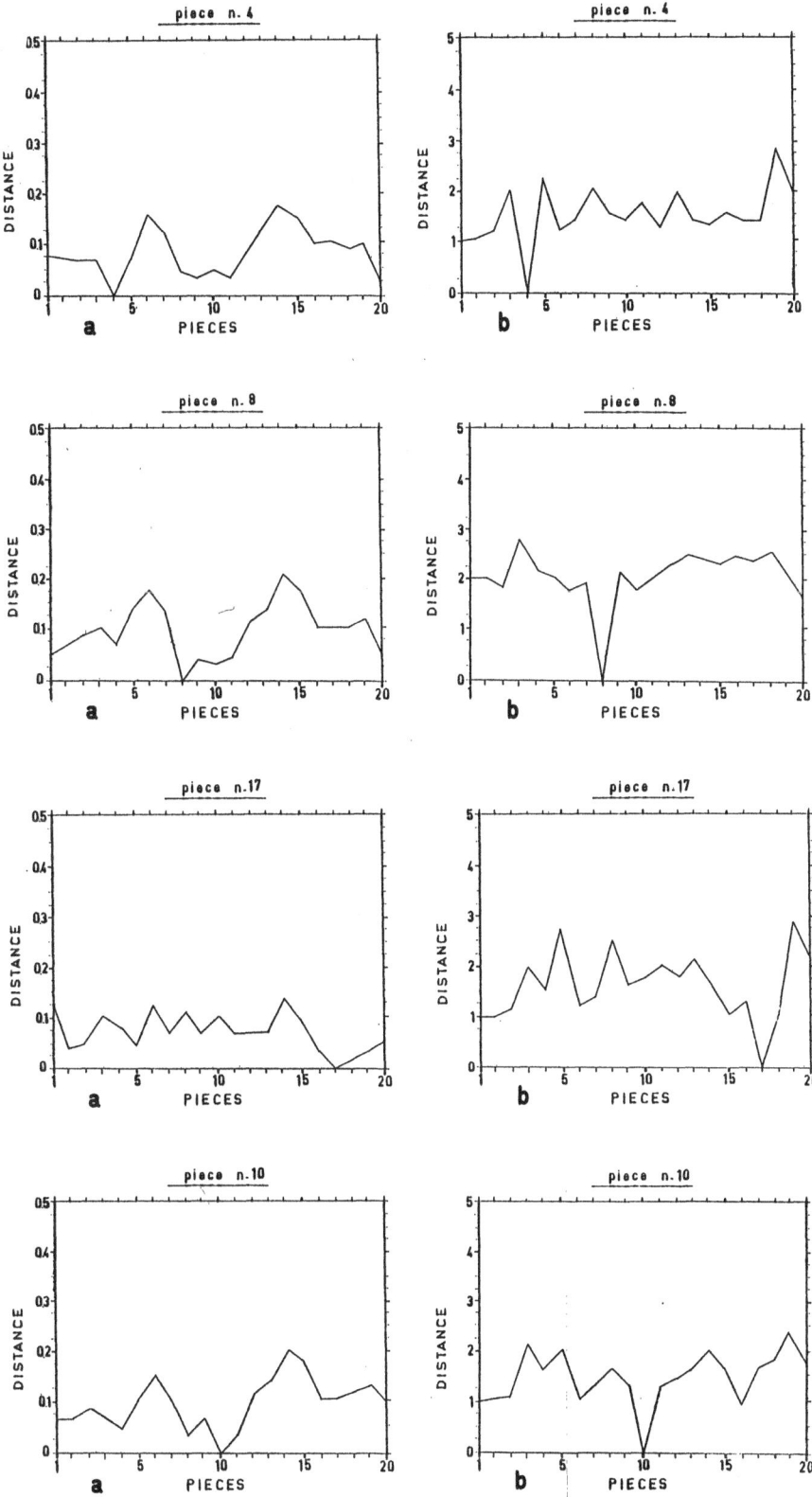

Fig. 3. Distance function d₁ calculated for boundary (a) and silhouette moments (b) of four unknown objects.

REFERENCES

1. D.A. Ballard, C.M. Brown, "Computer vision", Prentice Hall, (1982).
2. M.K. Hu, "Visual pattern recognition by moment invariants", IEEE Trans. Inform. Theory, vol. IT-8, Feb. (1962).
3. R.C. Gonzales, P. Wintz, "Digital image processing", Addison-Wesley Publishing Company (1977).
4. A. Rosenfeld, A.C. Kak, "Digital picture processing", Academic Press, (1982).
5. S.S. Reddi, "Radial and Angular Moment Invariants for Image Identification", IEEE Trans. on Pattern Analysis, vol. PAMI-3 n. 2, Mar. (1981).
6. S.H. Dudani, K.J. Breeding, R.B. Mc Ghee, "Aircraft Identification by Moment Invariants", IEEE Trans. on Computers, vol. C-26, n. 1, Jan. (1977).

IMAGE PROCESSING IN ITALY: A FIRST REPORT

Stefano Levialdi and Andrea G. Fabbri*

Dipartimento di Matematica
Universita' di Roma, Roma, Italy
*Istituto di Geologia Marina del C.N.R.
Bologna, Italy

ABSTRACT

Pattern recognition and image processing started in Italy from two
academic sources: the physicists from the Faculty of Sciences, and
engineers from the Department of Electronics, around the year 1960.
Although the motivations were different, they both considered some
theoretical problems concerning the possibility of designing machines that
would "recognize" shapes, and of solving practical problems such as
efficient OCR, biomedical image analysis, noise cleaning by filtering, as
well as some novel applications in the fields of archaeology, ecology and
landscape preservation.

About thirty active groups at Universities, National Research Council
Institutes and industrial companies can be counted. An Italian chapter of
IAPR is present with over one hundred members. Its current activities
range from satellite imagery to astronomical image processing. As in many
emerging fields, the geosciences have stimulated new methodologies and
applications to shape analysis, texture and automated map analysis.
Promising aspects are indicated.

This contribution initiates a systematic account of the image processing activity in Italy by proposing a yearly newsletter with classified
references to the published work and a report of the emerging developments.

INTRODUCTION: ITALIAN RESEARCH IN IMAGE PROCESSING

Two main philosophical schools were the basis for the expansion of the
research activity in image processing and pattern recognition: (i) the
School of Physics (lead by theoretical physicists) and (ii) the School of
Electrical Engineering (computer scientists). In the first group, the
motivation was directly related to the desire to model biological systems
(according to cybernetics and the pioneering work of McCulloch and Pitts,
see W. S. McCulloch and W. Pitts, A logical calculus of ideas immanent in
nervous activity, Bull.Math.Biophys., p.5, 1943). Neuron models, learning
algorithms, associative memories and experimental work on the vision
system, were some of the tracks which produced, as a by-product, some
results in pattern recognition (both machines and algorithms). In the

second area, firstly by network design and construction, and later by simulation on computers, some practical problems were tackled, such as: chromosome kariotyping, blood cell analysis, character recognition (both printed and handwritten), nuclear event classification, and fingerprint recognition.

As in many other areas, Italian work is characterized by good individual efforts, some connections to foreign work but small impact on the national reality and, above all, insecure and ephemeral funding.

About twenty years ago, the first association for automatic pattern recognition was born (GRAF: Gruppo per il Riconoscimento Automatico delle Forme) which organized small informal meetings to discuss the current state of local research, distribute preprints and try to coordinate the funding requests.

Yet, pattern recognition first and image processing next, had no academic status, which meant that no career nor promotion could be based on these subjects. The fast development of computer graphics, non numerical processing and the diffusion of high level programming languages promoted the field and stimulated many new workers.

Some national conferences in cybernetics (held every two years) started in 1965, and other international conferences on image analysis and processing (the first one, called International Conference on Image Analysis and Processing, was held in Pavia in 1980, and the second one in Selva di Fasano in 1982) have shown that the Italian community is active with about thirty groups, partly belonging to research institutions within the National Research Council (C.N.R.) and partly in the University as well as in the Private Industry.

. Many have said that both pattern recognition and image processing are made up of a clever set of tricks which only work satisfactorily in well defined cases and that the ability of the recognizer is not to choose the algorithm but to choose the correct problem, and in the definition of the significant features that one wants to extract from the patterns on one part and the other part is in doing it efficiently.

Both these methodogical aspects also belong to many other research areas and may therefore benefit from them. Artificial intelligence (with the problem state definition and its heuristic techniques), signal analysis (with the filtering tools), perception studies (showing the relevance of the Gestaltic approach), structured programming (using top-down analysis and coding), etc., all these areas have shed light on research work performed by the Italian community.

There exists an Italian chapter of the International Association of Pattern Recognition (I.A.P.R.) and there are about one hundred members in this chapter. It is difficult to avoid forgetting some groups (they are not coordinated nor interconnected in any way as yet due to the difficulties mentioned previously).

SCANNING THE COUNTRY FROM NORTH TO SOUTH

Let us now scan the country from North to South.

Trieste

The Faculty of Engineering hosts a group which originally worked in the analysis of signals of biological nature and gradually moved to images.

The Astronomical Observatory in Trieste also employs image processing for the analysis of astronomical data.

Milan

Being the industrial and economical capital of the country, Milan has many "islands" of activity:

(1) A group from the Istituto di Fisica Cosmica e Tecnologie Relative of the C.N.R., started research in this area many years ago in connection with the structural description of shapes (for geographical and geophysical applications). They have suggested an interesting coding scheme, made extensive use of the APL interpreter, and are present at international meetings with their work.

(2) Another group, of bio-mathematical nature, is active at the Istituto di Biometria e Statistica Medica of the Faculty of Medicine. Classification methods and statistical description of patterns within the chromosome area and in cytology have been their main working fields.

(3) At the Politecnico of Milan, Department of Mechanical Design, a group of researchers have started to work in CAD systems and in automatic recognition of mechanical blue prints.

(4) Some work on image processing and coding as well as shape description is also carried out at the Department of Electronics of the Politecnico.

Turin

At the C.S.E.L.T. of Turin, a group has worked on digital filtering for image transmission and coding. At the Faculty of Sciences of the University of Turin and at the Politecnico of Turin some researchers have worked on problems of speech analysis and recognition using special hardware and sophisticated techniques for signal segmentation.

Genoa

At the University of Genoa, Institute of Physics, a very ancient group (started at the end of the 50's) did some work on a perception-like machine for pattern recognition. A machine was built termed PAPA, and a number of experiments on guided and automatic learning were carried out. Later, at the Institute of Mathematics of the same University, a group became interested in problems of surface descritpion, polygonal approximation, and surface representation. At the E.L.S.A.G. factory, a machine known as EMMA (a multiprocessor associative memory machine) was designed and built for optical character recognition for mail sorting applications. At the same factory, a group of persons is conducting applied research in speech analysis and synthesis, image processing, and pattern recognition.

Savona

At the Ferrania factory in Savona, research is being conducted on computerized radiography.

Pavia

At the University of Pavia, Department of Informatics and System Sciences, many years ago a group of researchers studied and developed algorithms for improving computational efficiency when using the Fourier Transform for two-dimensional cases. Work in coding, restoration and feature extraction of patterns has been carried on. Some particular transforms, such as the Hough transform, have been studied in collaboration with the group at E.L.S.A.G. in Genoa.

Florence

At the University of Florence, Faculty of Engineering, an old group in digital filtering has worked for many years also in connection with the European Signal Processing community. Applications range from radar signals to works of art, where images must be restored in order to reduce their degradation by time or other agents.

Rome

At the University of Rome (La Sapienza), Institute of Physics, a group of astronomers have originated an Image Processing Center where techniques for image storing, display, and labeling are used. A programming environment to help the astronomer has been developed so as to facilitate interaction with astronomical data, provided histogramming facilities, etc. The I.B.M. Scientific Center in Rome is active in image processing since its foundation (1978); pollution problems and astronomical applications have been considered. A special hardware termed Acienda has been built for fast and efficient image processing.

Bari

At the University of Bari, Department of Physics, and Institute for Information Sciences, some groups have been active in handwritten character recognition, Landsat image processing, and biomedical applications. A number of important devices for data acquisition and plotting have been designed and built. C.S.A.T.A. (Consorzio per lo Studio ed Applicazioni di Tecnologie Avanzate) is another important institution made by a conglomeration of partners from the University and some governmental Agenices); it has a large group of persons working in image processing for land use and management. Both Landsat and photogrammatic images are processed and integrated into a regional data base for studying alternative strategies for land management. Problems of geometric correction, map generation and labelling, histogram equalization, etc., have been considered.

Naples

The Institute of Cybernetics of the C.N.R. (Italian National Research Council) in Naples had, since its foundation in 1968, a picture processing group that studied the properties of digital images. Algorithms for parallel processing of images, studies on shape descriptors and some applications to biomedical problems were analyzed. At the University of Naples, Department of Communications of the Faculty of Engineering, a group has studied problems of image compression and coding.

Palermo

At the University of Palermo, Faculty of Sciences, and at the Institute of Cosmic Rays and Informatic Applications of the C.N.R., some work has been done on convolution algorithms (and reconstruction), clustering and fuzzy set theory applied to classification.

In this scan, it is very likely that some groups have been omitted. For this reason it is deemed necessary to work at a complete inventory of the existing work being developed in Italy. In the following section some representative examples of applications developed by Italian researches are described in more detail.

Presently, research activity in Italy is directed in four main areas:

(1) digital image analysis and pattern recognition;

262

(2) parallelism: algorithms, languages and computer architectures;
(3) filtering; and
(4) astronomy.

Table 1 summarizes the various fields of activity city by city.

The following groups of applications illustrate the variety of image processing and pattern recognition researches currently being pursued in the Country. A recent volume edited by S. Levialdi ("Digital Image Analysis", Pitman, London, 1984) contains a representative set of contributions from Italian research groups.

<u>1. Decomposition of complex figures</u>. (Cordella and Sanniti di Baja, 1984). Shape decomposition of silhouettes is based on local thickness evaluation. The medial line of the figures, labelled according to the distance function from the background is appropriately partitioned into sets of pixels whose labels satisfy some given conditions. For the regions obtained by applying a reverse distance transformation to such sets a decision is taken about the attribution of overlapping parts of the regions. Figure components are obtained: labelled medial lines, LML's, are partitioned into subsets along which no significant label and/or direction changes are detectable. A correspondence is established between LML parts and simply shaped figure components. A labelled graph can be devised whose nodes are the LML components.

<u>2. Parameter encoding of video signals</u>. (Capo, Goglio and Zarone, 1984). Scope of the approach is to minimize the number of bits required to transmit pictures for a given level of distortion. Parameter encoding is used with the aim of extracting and transmitting only the basic features necessary for a specific application.

Importance is given to perceptual and psychophysical aspects of human vision in determining the basic features to be taken into account.

Table 1. Summary of the Research being Performed in Italy in Image Processing and Pattern Recognition

City	Research Themes			
	Analysis & description	Coding & filtering	System of computation	Applications (*astronomy)
Trieste				X*
Milan			X	X*
Pavia			X	X
Padua				*
Genoa		X		X
Savona		X		
Bologna				*
Pisa		X		X*
Florence				X*
Rome	X			X*
Naples	X	X		*
Bari	X		X	X*
Palermo	X			*
Catania				*

Some representative examples of image processing and pattern recognition in Italy.

Contour extraction and coding are performed for typical video-telephonic signals that have extremely high temporal redundancy. Both intraframe and interframe techniques are investigated.

3. Element for reconfigurable processing structure. (Marino, 1984) REST is a single-bit versatile module easily "concatenable" that allows implementation both of simple structures (arbitrary word-length processor) and of the most complex ones (arrays, multiprocessor, fault tolerant structures, dynamic architectures).

The REST module includes the memory, formed by single bit words (also the memory concatenates) and its most remarkable feature is to be itself both logically and physically reconfigurable.

Submodules of only three kinds are present on each slice:

(a) a controller;
(b) a memory processor; and
(c) a communication processor.

4. Recognition and mechanical parts. (Arbuschi, Cantoni and Musso, 1984). A generalization of the Hough transform is implemented on a standard minicomputer.

The recognition process requires the following steps:

(i) edge detection;
(ii) orientation of the edge segment for each edge pixel;
(iii) points are mapped and counted for each pixel in the parameter space through a table describing the shape being looked for (contours are incremented); and
(iv) a decision rule is used on counter values of the points at the parameter space.

5. Faint object discrimination in astronomy. (Malagnini, Pucillo and Santin, 1984). For the discrimination of faint astronomical objects such as stars and galaxies, a classification is based on the evaluation of suitable parameters extracted from the modified co-occurrence matrix. In the modular procedure employed, the modules are linked in a sequence of interactive and iterative subprocedures.

Arrays of 4000 x 4000 pixels were obtained from a scanned plate window of 4 cm x 4 cm that may contain about 2000 objects. By thresholding, subsets (regions) of 450 objects were produced: each object consisting of at least ten connected pixels within an array of 49 x 49 pixels. Generally, stars occur as point sources (compact), and galaxies as extended sources (diffuse).

Out of 450 regions, 399 were preselected by visual inspection (41 spurious images were found) of which 150 were used as training sets (50 representing background, 50 the galaxies and 70 the star images).

The gray level densities were compressed to 16 levels on 45 x 45 pixel subimages.

The approach is directed towards automatic selection to avoid noisy images.

The entropy distribution is studied for the training sets to derive useful classification parameters.

6. Review of Astronomical Image Processing in Italy. (Sedmak, 1984) Problems faced by astronomers today are analyzed along with the strategies being developed to guarantee efficient solutions.

At present there is a substantial integration between institutions and research projects in astronomy in Italy.

Astronomical image processing was carried out in a nearly incoherent environment until the definition of the ASTRONET Project in 1980.

The project was started in 1981 by the Italian Ministry of Education and the National Research Council. It marks a milestone for image processing in astronomy, and a network of standard hardware and software image processing system specialized for astronomical applications was established.

The scope and structure of ASTRONET is very similar to the British STARLINK network for astronomy and astrophysics.

ASTRONET nodes are presently located in the following cities: Bari, Bologna, Catania, Florence, Naples, Padua, Palermo, Rome and Trieste.

Greatest efforts were devoted to:

(a) spectra processing;
(b) two-dimensional field photometry;
(c) surface photometry;
(d) image discrimination and classification by statistical methods; and
(e) restoration of synthesis radiointerferograms.

7. A System for Interacting with Astronomical Images. (De Amicis and Di Biase, 1984). RIAIP (Rome Interactive Astronomical Image Processing) is a computer system developed at the University of Rome, Institute of Astronomy, for the analysis of images obtained from both ground based and orbiting observatories. The system, written in FORTRAN 77 for a VAX 11/780 computer, has friendly interactive interface for the astronomer/user. Also mixed aided and interactive or completely aided modes were implemented in a highly modular architecture.

The following processing options are included:

(1) loading and storing images of different sizes and types;
(2) different displays;
(3) computation of contours and profiles;
(4) convolution and filtering;
(5) rotation and scaling;
(6) production of hardcopies;
(7) arithmetic operations; and
(8) statistics on images.

Different images of 512 x 512 pixels can reside in the central memory at the same time for comparisons or multi-image operations.

8. A Pyramidal Architecture for Parallel Image Analysis. (Cantoni et al., 1984, 1985). PAPIA, a pyramidal architecture for parallel image analysis, is a multiprocessor system made of tapered layers of processors, each layer being a truly SIMD machine. Also, different layers can execute different instructions, thus becoming a multi-SIMD processing system, or alternatively, a given subset of layers can operate in the SIMD mode.

The single processor is horizontally 4-connected to its brothers on the same layer and vertically to a top father and to four bottom sons on its higher and lower layers, respectively.

The chips for this architecture, that have been built in Italy, are arranged so that 17 chips are on a single board to implement an elementary pyramid with four layers with a total of 257 boards. Also a high level language based on parallel Pascal has been provided for PAPIA.

9. An Image Processing Language with Icon Assisted Navigation. (Chang et al., 1985: collaboration U.S.A.-Sweden-Italy-Japan). IPL is a generic image processing language and also a programming environment that supports the language primitives for an image processing system.

The user navigates through the image data base and manipulates images by generalized icons. Logical, interactive and physical image processing sublanguages are integral parts of IPL.

10. Application of Image Processing to Geoscience Data. (Fabbri and Levialdi, 1984; Chang et al., 1984; collaboration Italy-Canada). In the earth sciences quantitative aspects are best appreciated visually in the form of maps and the ancillary statistical characterization.

Table 2. Summary Data from the Received Questionnaires

Group leader	City	Since year	Co-workers	Theme*	Res. activity**
Arcelli C.	Naples	1968	8	I	DIP
Barbagelata G.	Genoa	1972	16	A	OCRRMVDIPOTH
Cappellini V.	Florence	1976	6	I	BMDRESRMVDIP
Capria M.T.	Frascati	1982	6	I	RESASTGEOGRIPOTH
Costabile M.	Cosenza	1977	1	I	BMDEMVDIP
De Biase M.	Rome	1965	2	I	ASTDIP
De Floriani L.	Genoa	1981	2	I	GRA
Della Ventura A.	Milan	1972	1	IA	RESASTDIP
De Monte U.A.	Campof.	1983	5	A	RMVOTH
Di Gesù V.	Palermo	1974		IA	ASTGRA
Fabbri A.	Bologna	1978	3	IA	RESGEODIP
Fiorini R.A.	Milan	1974	6	TIA	BMDRMVGRPDIPOTH
Fonda S.	Modena	1978	3	A	BMDGRPDIP
Garibotto G.	Ferrania	1974	5	I	BMDDIP
Levialdi S.	Rome	1961	3	I	BMDDIP
Marino D.	Bari	1979	4	I	RESDIPOTH
Melli P.	Rome	1981	8	I	BMDRESASTDIP
Mussio P.	Milan	1974	4	IA	BMDASTGRADIP
Musso G.	Genoa	1981	4	A	OCRRMVIDIPOTH
Pareschi M.T.	Pisa	1983		A	RMV
Pamiggiani F.	Modena	1981	1	A	RMV
Santin P.	Trieste	1975	4	IA	RESASTGRPDIPOTH
Sechi G.	Milan	1983	8	A	ASTDIP
Sedmak G.	Trieste	1975	5	A	AST
Venturello G.	Orbass.	1979	20	A	RMV
Vernazza G.	Genoa	1976	4	I	BMDRESDIP
Vitulano S.	Salerno	1975	6	TA	BMDDIP

* T: Theoretical, I: Intermediate, A: Applied.
**BMD: Biomedical, RES: Remote Sensing, RMV: Robotics (machine vision), AST: Astronomical, GEO: Geosciences, GRA: Graphics, DIP: Digital Image Processing, OTH: Others.

In the light of the present development in statistical theory and computer techniques for spatial data analysis, systematic methods in thematic mapping for resource assessment are feasible. Also, texture analysis for relating morphology and physical characteristics in material sciences is analyzed.

The importance is stressed of methods of mathematical morphology and of new computer architectures now available for spatially distributed data.

A QUESTIONNAIRE DISTRIBUTED FOR CONSTRUCTING A COMPUTERIZED DATA BASE

During May-June 1985, a circular letter was distributed to all scientific and industrial environments in Italy, to capture most of the work done (Table 2).

An "update" version of the "state-of-the-art" of image processing in Italy will be produced to include a list of references of the most significant work done in the recent past.

A list of references, over four hundred, may be obtained by contacting the secretary of the Italian Group of Pattern Recognition (affiliated to the IAPR).

INDEX